Changing Teaching and Learning in the Primary School

Changing Teaching and Learning in the Primary School

edited by
Rosemary Webb

Open University Press

Open University Press
McGraw-Hill Education
McGraw-Hill House
Shoppenhangers Road
Maidenhead
Berkshire
England
SL6 2QL

email: enquiries@openup.co.uk
world wide web: www.openup.co.uk

and Two Penn Plaza, New York, NY 10121–2289, USA

First published 2006
Copyright The Editors and Contributors © — 2006

A catalogue record of this book is available from the British Library

ISBN 10: 0335 219500 (PB) 0335 219519 (HB)
ISBN 13: 978 0 335 219506 (PB) 9780 335 219 513 (HB)

Library of Congress Cataloging-in-Publication Data
CIP data applied for

Typeset by YHT Ltd, London
Printed in Poland by OZ Graf. S.A.
www.polskabook.pl

Contents

Notes on Contributors   *vii*

Preface   *xi*
Andrew Pollard

Introduction   **1**
Rosemary Webb

1   Education Policy under New Labour   9
Graham Vulliamy and Rosemary Webb

2   National Policy on Primary Education: Inconsistency and Uncertainty
over the Whole Curriculum   18
Jim Campbell

3   Teachers' Perspectives on Teaching and Learning in a Performativity
Culture   33
Rosemary Webb

4   From 'TA' to Assessment for Learning: The Impact of Assessment
Policy on Teachers' Assessment Practice   47
Caroline Gipps, Bet McCallum, Eleanore Hargreaves and Alison Pickering

5   Pupils' Views of the School Experience   60
Cedric Cullingford

6   Learning to Love Learning? – What the Pupils Think   71
Yolande Muschamp and Kate Bullock

7   New Technologies and 'New Teaching': a Process of Evolution?   81
Gary Beauchamp

8   Pedagogy at Key Stage Two: Teaching through Pupil-Teacher
Partnership   92
Peter Silcock and Mark Brundrett

9 Promoting Inclusive Education: from 'Expertism' to Sustainable
Inclusive Practices 103
Elias Avramidis

10 Teaching Strategies for Pupils with SEN: Specialist or Inclusive
Pedagogy? 115
Ruth Kershner and Lani Florian

11 Widening the Inclusion Agenda: Policy, Practice and Language
Diversity in the Primary Curriculum 128
Jean Conteh

12 The Butterfly Effect: Teaching Assistants and Workforce Reform
in Primary Schools 139
Hilary Burgess

13 What a Performance! The Impact of Performance Management and
Threshold Assessment on the Work and Lives of Primary Teachers 149
Ian Menter, Pat Mahony and Ian Hextall

14 Leading and Managing Teaching and Learning 161
Linda Hammersley-Fletcher and Rosemary Webb

15 Primary Teacher Professionalism 173
Graham Vulliamy

References 185
Index 215

Notes on Contributors

Elias Avramidis is a Lecturer in Education at the University of York. His research interests are in the areas of special needs and inclusive education, educational psychology and quantitative methodology.

Gary Beauchamp taught in primary schools for many years before becoming a Lecturer at Swansea University. His research interests are diverse but currently focus on the role of information and communications technology in teaching and learning, particularly in the primary school.

Mark Brundrett is Senior Research Consultant in the Centre for Educational Leadership at the University of Manchester, before which he was a Professor of Educational Leadership at the University of Hull. He has taught in all phases of the education system and was a primary school headteacher for 5 years. He has published extensively on primary education and in the area of educational leadership.

Kate Bullock is a Senior Lecturer at the University of Bath. Her recent research has explored the interface between student learning, educational relationships and school organization.

Hilary Burgess is Director for Postgraduate Studies in the Centre for Research in Education and Educational Technology (CREET) at the Open University. Her research interests are in the areas of primary teaching and mentoring in primary and secondary schools.

Jim Campbell is Professor of Education at the University of Warwick and Director of Research at The National Academy for Gifted and Talented Youth. He has published widely in the fields of primary education, education policy, teacher effectiveness and gifted education.

Jean Conteh is a Senior Lecturer in primary education at the University of Manchester. She has many years' experience of primary teaching and teacher training in multilingual contexts in Africa, South Asia and the UK. Her research interests are the professional roles and identities of bilingual teachers in primary schools.

Cedric Cullingford is Professor of Education at the University of Huddersfield. He is particularly interested in the personal experiences of those who are learning from a variety of sources, especially the very young, and the effects of early years on subsequent behaviour.

Lani Florian is a Senior Lecturer in Special and Inclusive Education at the University of Cambridge. Her research interests focus on models of provision and teaching strategies for meeting special educational needs in inclusive schools.

Caroline Gipps is Vice-Chancellor of the University of Wolverhampton. Previously she was Deputy Vice-Chancellor at Kingston University, and Professor of Education and Dean of Research at the University of London Institute of Education. She trained as a psychologist and worked as a primary school teacher before moving into a career in research. She has published widely on policy and practice in assessment, and was President of the British Educational Research Association (BERA) in 1993.

Linda Hammersley-Fletcher is a Senior Lecturer within the Institute for Education Policy Research at Staffordshire University. Her research specialism covers all aspects of primary school leadership and management.

Eleanore Hargreaves is a Lecturer in Assessment for Learning at the London Institute of Education. Her current research focuses on the formative use of self-assessment, peer assessment and feedback.

Ian Hextall is a Senior Research Fellow at Roehampton University. He has worked with Pat Mahony on a number of research projects funded by the Economic and Social Research Council.

Ruth Kershner is a Lecturer in Education at the University of Cambridge. Her current research interests are in the fields of teaching pupils with learning difficulties and the uses of ICT in the primary classroom environment.

Bet McCallum is a Research Officer at the London Institute of Education. Her current research interests are in formative assessment in primary schools, young children's self-evaluative strategies and the curriculum and assessment in pre-schools.

Pat Mahony is Professor of Education at Roehampton University. She has researched extensively on education policy, teachers' work, and gender.

Ian Menter is a former primary teacher who is now Professor of Teacher Education at the University of Glasgow. His research interests are in teacher education, teacher supply and retention, and primary school teachers' work.

Yolande Muschamp is a Senior Lecturer at the University of Bath where she is currently Head of the Department of Education. Her research focuses on the impact of national policies for primary and middle years education through qualitative studies of schools and classrooms.

Alison Pickering is a Lecturer at Kingston University, London. She has been involved in research with Caroline Gipps on the assessment, teaching and feedback strategies of primary teachers.

Peter Silcock is Visiting Professor of Education at the University of Hertfordshire. He was Chair of the Association for the Study of Primary Education (ASPE) in 2000/3. His main research interests are in primary school teaching and learning.

Graham Vulliamy is Emeritus Professor of Education at the University of York. He was President of the British Association for International and Comparative Education (BAICE) in 2002/3 and has published widely on comparative education, sociology of education and, in collaboration with Rosemary Webb, primary school teachers' work.

Rosemary Webb is a Reader in Education at the University of York. She has had a varied career in primary education including as a teacher, a professional officer at the National Curriculum Council, a lecturer and researcher. She was Chair of the Association for the Study of Primary Education (ASPE from 1994 to 1997) and is currently the convenor of the BERA/ASPE Special Interest Group on 'Primary Teachers' Work'.

Preface

For practitioners and policy makers with an interest in *evidence*, this book is a sort of 'gift'. Within its covers, nice and tidy, are many insightful analyses about recent policy and practice in primary education. Of even more significance are the challenges it poses for the future.

There are many specific messages about 'what is' and 'what might be' in relation to topics such as pupil perspectives, classroom relationships, new technologies and pedagogies, assessment, inclusion, language diversity, workforce reform, leadership and professionalism. Beyond these, however, I believe there is a more fundamental and enduring message.

The major underlying implication of this collection is that policy and practice in primary education should be based on *evidence-informed principles* concerning the learning of young children. Provision for curriculum, pedagogy, assessment and institutional arrangements should be consistent with such principles.

Sadly, as the chapters by Vulliamy and Webb and by Campbell demonstrate, New Labour has, to date, been little more successful at this than were the Conservative governments that preceded them. Commitments to high standards *and* inclusion may be commendable but practical implementation has been characterized by pressure for narrow performance and by competition between schools, which itself is differentiating. In the face of such structural imperatives, occasional attempts to 'enrich' the curriculum, affirm the importance of pupil motivation and 'enjoyment' or encourage new 'networked learning communities' are undermined. The contradictions are too stark. Indeed, the irony is that the very pressure to enhance standards seems at risk of undermining children's motivation and engagement with learning *per se*. The long-term ambition of a nation of lifelong learners is made harder by educationally naïve pressure for short-term performance.

And yet, as I write this preface, a newspaper headline reads: 'Exams cut by third as stress on pupils soars' (*Observer*, 26 March 2006) and the Chief Executive of the Qualifications and Curriculum Authority is reported as being determined to reduce the overall burden on pupils. Earlier in the week, it was announced that the Secretary of State for Education was to commission a review of the principles on which teaching and learning should be based to 2020 – and, of course, 'personalized learning' is now foregrounded in almost all policy initiatives.

We do not know what the future holds. Perhaps, indeed, there will always be contradictions in the education policies of governments as policy makers seek to match what is known about education and learning with social expectations and political expediency. In our contemporary democracies, researchers charged with assembling evidence operate, alongside practitioners, in the spaces that result from such tensions.

After almost a decade of New Labour it is therefore very appropriate that researchers should take stock of the strengths, weaknesses and consequences of recent education policies in respect of primary education, and we are fortunate that Rosemary Webb and her colleagues from the British Educational Research Association (BERA) and the Association for the Study of Primary Education (ASPE) have stepped up to tackle this task. A similar role was fulfilled in 1992 when a previous BERA/ASPE task group offered a research-based critique of the Conservative government's policies on curriculum and assessment. It was one of many voices and interest groups expressing concerns – and the curriculum was reviewed soon after.

Today, there is a strong commitment by governments in all parts of the UK to consider evidence carefully. There are also now major reviews going on in all four countries. With care, and in partnership with others, it may yet be possible to overcome contemporary dilemmas and to provide the high quality, rounded and fulfilling education for all to which so many aspire.

This book helps considerably in understanding contemporary problems and challenges in primary education – it is important, timely and deserves to be widely read.

Professor Andrew Pollard
Institute of Education,
University of London.
Director of ESRC's Teaching and Learning Research Programme (TLRP)

Introduction

Rosemary Webb

This book offers a research-based critique of New Labour education policy from 1997 to 2006 and the impact of that policy on primary classroom practice, pupils' experiences and primary teachers' work and professionalism. Its predominant focus is on teaching and learning at key stage two (KS2) because the junior years do not enjoy the range and depth of support and guidance provided by early years and preschool research groups and organizations. The chapters are derived from the work of a special interest group (SIG) on primary teachers' work consisting of researchers who are members of the British Educational Research Association (BERA) and/or the Association for the Study of Primary Education (ASPE) – the latter is a major UK charitable organization (with no political affiliation) that is committed to the study of primary education. Between 2003 and 2005 the SIG met to review published research on primary school policy and practice and to share the findings of the ongoing work of SIG members. An important starting point for the SIG's work was a collection of papers produced in 1992/3 by a similarly constituted BERA/ASPE task group – Andrew Pollard (ed.) (1994) *Look Before You Leap: Research Evidence for the Curriculum at Key Stage Two.*

Look Before You Leap focused on the fundamental issues arising from the implementation of the National Curriculum and its associated assessment procedures at KS2 in order to assist those engaging in national policy review and formulation. At the time the task group did not anticipate the speed with which the government would respond to the increasing revelation of the difficulties caused by the overloaded National Curriculum and its un-manageable assessment. Consequently, as task group members were putting together the first drafts of their papers, the newly constituted School Curriculum and Assessment Authority (SCAA) – the predecessor of the Qualifications and Curriculum Authority (QCA) – chaired by Sir Ron Dearing was asked to conduct a review of the National Curriculum and its assessment (Dearing 1993). The papers, which were sent to inform the SCAA review, raised many points of both principle and implementation that have subsequently been debated, addressed or supplanted by new concerns. It is interesting with hindsight to revisit the two overarching recommendations that the task group made: 'the need for a flexible and enabling curriculum framework' and 'the development of greater trust, respect and partnership between the government and teachers' (Pollard 1994: 8).

Over the intervening period between the meetings of the original task group and those of the SIG, the demands of New Labour's standards agenda have resulted in an increasingly narrow curriculum emphasizing the basic skills of literacy and numeracy to the severe detriment of the foundation subjects. Irresolvable tensions have been created because the government, while coercing schools to devote maximum time and effort to raising pupil attainment in high-stakes literacy and numeracy tests in order to meet national targets, also recognizes the desirability of a broader and richer curriculum. This has led to internal contradictions in government policy, such as announcing in June 2005 that there would be additional earmarked funding for the music services to support the 'wider opportunities programme' that, among other initiatives, was going to provide instrumental tuition at KS2 and then in December 2005 reneging on this commitment by putting the monies directly into schools and enabling headteachers to spend them on other priorities. Also, primary schools are exhorted to 'bolt on' to the curriculum additional knowledge and skills, such as citizenship and the European dimension, and from September 2009 at KS2 they will be expected to teach a modern foreign language.

The problems of rescuing the current curriculum from these contradictory reductionist/expansionist pressures and the realization that a very different curriculum from the past might be needed to prepare children for the future have led some to urge a return to first principles (Richards 1998). Given the massive personal and professional investment that teachers have made to implement government curriculum reform, and given what has been learned from this process and its potential to be built upon, this does not seem to be a practical option. However, the introduction of the Primary National Strategy and the ways in which teachers have chosen to interpret it heralds a more flexible approach to the National Curriculum enabling schools to adapt it to meet the needs of their pupils and local circumstances. This could be the short-term solution from which longer term more fundamental questions could be generated and addressed. However, if creativity, experimentation and innovation by teachers are to be encouraged there will need to be a fundamental change in the educational climate. For this to occur the government needs to reduce the stranglehold of accountability and dispense with the testing regime responsible for the current all-pervasive and stifling culture of performativity.

The domination of the performativity culture in teaching and learning and its negative effects on teachers and pupils is emphasized by research into diverse aspects of primary schooling and therefore necessarily emerges as a major theme in this book. When New Labour came to power in 1997 there were high expectations of a new positive relationship being forged between the government and teachers. However, these expectations were short-lived, as the White Paper *Excellence in Schools* (DfEE 1997b) issued just after the new government took office revealed the highly centralist intentions of its education policy. Teachers gained the impression that the government regarded them as part of the problem rather than the solution, a perception that intensified with the introduction of each new accountability measure. Lack of trust, or even it seemed interest, in their professional judgement endangered morale and threatened teacher recruitment and retention.

Although this book reflects the climate of negativity engendered by government reforms, through teachers' voices we also identify some benefits for classroom practice. For example, the introduction of the Literacy and Numeracy Strategies brought widely acknowledged improvements in teaching methods and classroom organization, illustrating that in this respect teachers' perspectives are strongly at variance with the critiques by academics of the government's centralized prescription of teaching methods. Also, the teacher assessment component of national assessment prepared teachers for Assessment for Learning and the emphasis on personalized learning – both initiatives in the Primary National Strategy that receive general support. The investment by the government in resources, especially in information and communication technology (ICT), has also been welcomed by schools. It is a testament to teachers' commitment to strive for improvements in teaching and learning and higher standards for their pupils that through the implementation of the strategies they changed not only their policies and practices but also in many instances their attitudes and values.

Teacher voices are central to the chapters in this book and so are those of pupils. John Holt's (1982) *How Children Fail* revealed the adverse effects on pupil motivation and learning of what he perceived as the routinized and boring nature of much of their school experience. Since his seminal work there has been a slow but steady growth in research into pupils' views on all aspects of education. In relation to our understanding of children and their primary schools, the research of Pollard and his colleagues has made a major contribution, which includes portraying pupils' perspectives on the formal and hidden curriculum (Pollard *et al.* 1997), pupil 'life-stories' through primary schooling (Pollard and Filer 1999) and the impact of recent education policy on pupils' perceptions of teachers, teaching and learning (Pollard *et al.* 2000). This body of research demonstrates unequivocally the importance and value of listening to pupils' views and the moral and practical imperatives for taking these into account in policy making at all levels and in planning classroom practice.

Research in this book by Cullingford alerts us to the continuity of pupils' experiences with those exposed by Holt, irrespective of the party in government and the particular curriculum specifications being implemented. The findings by Muschamp and Bullock suggest that the current imposition of curriculum content on pupils irrespective of their interests and preferred approaches to learning is resulting in reduced pupil motivation and opportunities to become independent learners. It is ironic that in such a market-driven educational system, and one that claims to be evidence based, pupils as the consumers have no say in the nature of the National Curriculum and little choice at school level in what or how they study.

In their chapters SIG members have reviewed and synthesized some key findings and analyses of recent and ongoing research. In doing so they present evidence that is very critical of some aspects of New Labour's reforms and evidence supportive of other aspects. The aim is above all to be informative but also to be constructive, as is detailed in the brief descriptions below of the chapter contents. Hence, for example: Silcock and Brundrett develop the concept of partnership teaching whereby pupils could have much greater input into the content of, and approaches to, teaching the curriculum; Kershner and Florian find a wealth of knowledge about pupils with special educational needs that could usefully be more widely drawn upon to support and personalize the learning of all pupils; and Beauchamp explores the potential contribution of ICT to the further development of primary pedagogy.

The primary readership for this book is envisaged as threefold. First, teachers and students in initial teacher training who require a substantial overview of where we are in primary education as regards teaching and learning, why we are there, and where we will go next. Second, members of the educational research community who are seeking information on, and ideas for, research projects on teaching and learning, whether they are carrying out research in institutions of higher education or are teacher researchers in primary schools. Third, policy makers at all levels who seek evidence on any of the areas addressed by the book in order to make informed judgements on ways forward.

What does each chapter tell us about changing teaching and learning in the primary school?

To set the context for the chapters that follow, our collection opens with a review of 'Education policy under New Labour' focusing particularly on those reforms that have directly affected teaching and learning at KS2. Vulliamy and Webb show that, although there are continuities between New Labour policy and that of the last Conservative government, the different rationale underpining the former is one of social justice and social inclusion. However, the contradictions between the rhetoric and the reality of these policies as experienced by teachers and pupils and the limitations and benefits for schools of their implementation are portrayed in the chapters that follow.

In 'National policy on primary education: inconsistency and uncertainty over the whole curriculum' Campbell goes back to the findings of the HMI survey *Primary Education in England* (DES 1978). Through taking a historical perspective, he demonstrates that the period between the Great Debate, started by Prime Minister James Callaghan's speech at Ruskin College in 1976, to the present has one defining characteristic: the 'colonization' by the government of the primary school curriculum. He argues that this 'colonization' process can be viewed as falling into three overlapping phases. The first phase from 1976 to about 1986 was characterized by *gentle professional persuasion* from HMI. The second phase from 1987 to 1997 was a period in which central government sought to impose *standards and accountability by statute*. A third phase starting around 1992/3 and probably incomplete is characterized by the imposition of a *performance culture* on primary schools. Campbell's analysis of government policy throughout these phases reveals that curriculum policy has been inconsistent, contradictory, overcentralized, and focused on short-term change at the expense of sustainable improvement. This, he argues, might have been avoided if New Labour policy makers had gone back to the 1978 primary survey for evidence-based principles on which to develop the whole curriculum.

'Teachers' perspectives on teaching and learning in a performativity culture' takes us from the policy-making arena into primary schools to hear teachers' voices on the impact of the government's standards agenda on them, their pupils, and the curriculum. Webb draws on the database of an ongoing qualitative research project in 50 schools to report on teachers' experiences of the implementation of the National Literacy and Numeracy Strategies and their responses to the Primary National Strategy. She finds that teachers were generally very positive about changes in teaching methods directly resulting from the strategies, such as the increase in whole-class teaching and making learning objectives explicit, particularly because of the perceived benefits of these for pupil learning. However, the chapter also documents the continued escalation in the negative effects of targets, tests and league tables on teaching and learning. This leads her to conclude that, for teachers to have the confidence to experiment and so take forward further developments in teaching methods, they need to be freed from the shackles of performance measures.

Moving from the adverse effects of the government's regime of national testing to positive aspects of its legacy, Gipps and her colleagues focus on key trends and issues in the development of teacher assessment (TA) in primary schools. 'From "TA" to "assessment for learning"' reviews the growing body of evidence on teachers' classroom assessment practices from the introduction of National Curriculum assessment to the more recent Assessment for Learning initiative. In so doing it identifies how teacher perspectives on assessment practices and how the nature of these practices have changed over time, particularly in relation to the role of strategies for providing feedback for pupils, which are fundamental to Assessment for Learning. While Gipps *et al.* fear that government support for the latter could give rise to yet more central prescription and provoke teacher resistance, they are confident that given proper support and respect teachers will adopt Assessment for Learning practice.

In 'Pupils' views of the school experience' Cullingford exposes the real meaning of school for many children and identifies the centrality of interactions and relationships with teachers and peers in defining the nature of school experiences. Pupils' views of the curriculum and the difference between what they are taught and what they would like to study are explored, and their assessment of what they think they really learn examined. He concludes by considering what teaching and learning in schools and classrooms would be like if policy makers and teachers listened to pupils.

Muschamp and Bullock in 'Learning to love learning?' draw on an interview-based study of year 6 pupils, as they complete KS2 and move through to year 7, to provide an analysis of what children understand about the learning process and how they conceptualize it. Their findings echo Cullingford's discussion in the previous chapter in relation to children's perceptions of the dominance of teacher control and expectations. They point out that current initiatives in teaching and learning challenge teachers to reflect on their practice and devise more creative ways to engage children in the learning process. However, their research reveals a stark contrast between the rhetoric of such initiatives and pupils' perceptions of the responsibility and ownership that they have for their learning.

Information and communication technology has the potential to motivate children and enable them to take control of their own learning. However, as argued in 'New technologies and "new teaching"', before ICT can bring about a transformation in teaching and learning teachers need to incorporate it into their pedagogy. Beauchamp considers the ways in which features of ICT, such as interactive whiteboards, could effect radical changes in teachers' practice leading to a 'new pedagogy'. He compares these possibilities with research evidence on the reality of the impact of ICT on the teaching of primary teachers and finds that they are using the new technologies both within the framework of their existing pedagogy and in the development of new teaching strategies according to subject demands and pupil needs. He concludes that this could lead to a diversity of 'new pedagogies' across the curriculum.

Silcock and Brundrett also explore the possibility of primary teachers developing a new pedagogy. They draw on research evidence to explain, justify and exemplify co-constructive pedagogy whereby pupils and teachers co-determine classroom practice through negotiation and interaction. They view such partnership teaching as a particularly appropriate means of realizing the dual and, as illustrated in the preceding chapters, often conflicting aims for KS2 pupils that they should be prepared well for formally set tasks and tests and yet find their lessons enjoyable and personally rewarding. This chapter concludes by providing illustrations as to how schools might put the principles of partnership teaching into practice.

Avramidis addresses the issue of 'Promoting inclusive education' and argues that, despite the government's explicit commitment to providing a more equitable education system, the progress towards inclusion is slower than many would wish and is fraught with difficulties. He analyses the effects of the two main barriers to promoting inclusion most commonly represented in the literature – the competitive performativity culture and teachers' inadequate preparation for working with pupils with special educational needs. He concludes that inclusion is a socially complex process requiring a reformulation of national policy and changes to initial teacher training. He also advocates continuing professional development within schools that are working together as 'communities of knowledge' to enable teachers to meet the needs of all learners within inclusive frameworks.

Developing an inclusive pedagogy applying to all learners is also a priority for Kershner and Florian who, in 'Teaching strategies for pupils with SEN', explore what such a pedagogy might look like. They demonstrate that research on SEN has provided a wealth of knowledge about teaching pupils with learning difficulties on which teachers can draw to help all children to engage in active learning and to make progress in relation to the curriculum. The Primary National Strategy and initiatives such as those related to personalized learning, are viewed as supportive for their contribution to ways of understanding and knowing pupils. However, most importantly, and echoing a key message of this book, we are advised to seek and act upon pupils' perspectives and preferences on how they can be helped with their learning.

In 'Widening the inclusion agenda' Conteh explores issues of inclusion for a diverse group of learners who are not always recognized within definitions of the term – those with English as an additional language (EAL). She revisits the controversies that have affected the achievement of these learners and explores ways in which research is offering insights into significant ways forward that genuinely play to their strengths and enhance their opportunities for success. Two developments that she finds particularly helpful are the 'funds of knowledge' approach to characterizing and shaping home-school links and the 'many pathways' model, which helps to widen our understanding about literacy learning.

As a result of the government's workforce remodelling agenda, teaching assistants are playing an increasingly central role in supporting teaching and learning. In 'The butterfly effect' Burgess raises some key questions posed by this agenda relating to the potential effect of the deployment of teaching assistants on educational standards, teachers' workload and pupil learning. She finds that research provides insights into how pupils perceive teaching assistants and the advantages and disadvantages of their enhanced role for teachers. The greater use of teaching assistants clearly has the potential to assist curriculum enrichment and provide additional opportunities for pupil learning but in order for this to happen Burgess suggests that there are considerable constraints to be overcome.

'What a performance!' presents some findings from an ESRC-funded study that analysed the impact of a particular element of the performance management regime – namely threshold assessment. The primary school project data revealed widespread cynicism about the overall approach to the threshold and few teachers believed that it had resulted in a positive impact on their own teaching. In addition, there were some very negative emotional impacts on individuals and groups of teachers. Feelings about the process were largely determined by how it was dealt with by headteachers who appeared influenced by management priorities and whole school responsibilities rather than by the 'objective' assessment of individual performance. Menter, Mahony and Hextall acknowledge that aspects of the standards agenda have brought gains but at great cost to primary teachers' professional identity and personal investment in their work.

In 'Leading and managing teaching and learning' Hammersley-Fletcher and Webb examine the rhetoric and the reality of 'distributed leadership' and the realization of primary schools as 'professional learning communities'. They find that the established hierarchical management and leadership structures, combined with the dominance of instructional leadership by headteachers as a result of the performativity culture, render distributed leadership unrealistic in many schools and promote a narrow standards-driven view of professional learning. However, research shows that, despite these constraints, heads who prioritize the transformatory possibilities of their role can develop their schools as professional learning communities that foster both innovation and critical reflection on government policy.

'Primary teacher professionalism' concludes the book by bringing the teacher's voice into the debate about the impact of New Labour's reforms on primary teacher professionalism. Vulliamy argues that an analysis of primary teacher perspectives on this issue, as revealed in a number of recent research projects, does not unequivocally support either the government's conception of the 'new professionalism' or the widespread critique of it by academics. He explores why, on the one hand, the changes brought about by the National Literacy and Numeracy Strategies were viewed as enhancing teachers' professionalism whereas, on the other hand, the government's standards agenda and its associated regime of testing and target setting, performance management and inspection was viewed as diminishing their professionalism. He concludes that, in response to government intervention, notions of primary teacher professionalism are undergoing review and reconstruction by primary teachers. Such notions are influenced by past and present ideology, policy and practice, and display multiple and situational dimensions.

1 Education Policy under New Labour

Graham Vulliamy and Rosemary Webb

The New Labour government came to power in Britain with its Prime Minister, Tony Blair, famously touting the slogan 'education, education, education'. For some, including progressive educationalists and Old Labour supporters whose primary concern was an amelioration of the traditional inequalities in access to education for the disadvantaged, such a policy commitment to education heralded the possibility of a clean break from the prior emphases of a Conservative government that had attempted to change the face of education with its 1988 Education Reform Act (ERA). They were to be disappointed. Instead, the New Labour government, as we shall see, continued and even intensified the policy directions of its predecessor with its further slogan 'standards, not structures' eschewing the need for any reform of the market-oriented system of schooling created by the ERA policies of open enrolment and local management of schools. However, what *did* change was the rationale for education policy development under New Labour and this was accompanied by significantly increased government investment devoted to state education.

In this chapter we outline some of the main education policy developments introduced by New Labour in order to provide a context for the discussion/reporting of research findings to be found in subsequent chapters. The focus here is on England with a reminder, firstly, that Scotland and Northern Ireland have historically always had very different policies and, secondly, that English and Welsh policy – initially framed together with the ERA – have increasingly diverged following moves to Welsh devolution in 1997.

The New Labour vision for education

New Labour's approach to change is encapsulated in the 'high challenge, high support' vision described by Michael Barber (Barber 2001: 19l), who directed the DfES's Standards and Effectiveness Unit before moving on to be head of the Prime Minister's Delivery Unit. This vision is fuelled by a belief that public services need to be reformed radically in the context of the new low-tax economies associated with global economic pressures. The government believes that, without such reforms, the continued use of such services by the public will be threatened and a consequent flight to private education will result in a further intensification of social and economic inequalities in access to schooling. The starting point for these reforms was a belief that 'the education system will never be world class unless virtually all children learn to read, write and calculate to high standards before they leave primary school' and that 'at the time of the 1997 election the national data showed how far we were from achieving this goal' (Barber 2001: 23).

The 'high challenge' component of the 'high challenge, high support' vision was used to justify high levels of government prescription in areas that had previously been viewed as lying at the heart of teachers' professional autonomy. Thus, for example, prior to the 1988 Education Reform Act, schools and teachers had not been subject to any prescription concerning curricula or pedagogy, and teaching methods, in particular, were viewed as the product of professional judgement (McCulloch *et al.* 2000). The Education Reform Act introduced, for the first time in English schools, government prescription over curriculum content, but it was made explicit that: 'The Education Reform Act does not prescribe how pupils should be taught. It is the birthright of the teaching profession, and must always remain so, to decide on the best and most appropriate means of imparting education to pupils' (NCC 1990: 7). This position changed markedly with the New Labour government's implementation of the National Literacy and Numeracy Strategies in 1998 and 1999 respectively. The strategies introduced daily literacy and numeracy hours into primary schools and, crucially, specified class organization and teaching methods. The justification for this was that 'the time has long gone when isolated unaccountable professionals made curriculum and pedagogical decisions alone without reference to the outside world' (DfEE 1998c: 14). Implementing the strategies, which Earl *et al.* (2003: 11) have described as the 'most ambitious large-scale educational reform initiative in the world', involved a new approach to educational change in which the more traditional concerns of policy makers to attempt to keep teachers on board during the process of change were shelved:

> Winning hearts and minds is not the best first step in any process of urgent change ... Sometimes it is necessary to mandate the change, implement it well, consciously challenge the prevailing culture and have the courage to sustain it until beliefs shift. The driving force at this critical juncture is leadership ... it is the vocation of leaders to take people where they have never been before and to show them a new world from which they do not want to return.
>
> (Quoted in Mahony *et al.* 2004c: 452)

The 'high challenge' ethos can also be seen in the manner in which the New Labour government, just two weeks after gaining office in May 1997, set ambitious literacy and numeracy targets to be achieved by 2002. These targets set the tone for an intensification of the performativity culture underlying the standards agenda discussed in the next section.

The 'high-support' component of the 'high challenge, high support' vision is illustrated by the increase in UK education spending from 4.7 per cent of GDP in 1997 to 5.3 per cent by 2003/4 with an expectation of 5.6 per cent by 2007/8 (Stewart 2005). Extra resources were targeted at buildings and equipment (£10 billion in the 3 years between 2001/2 and 2003/4) and teachers' salaries in an explicit attempt to remedy the prior Conservative government's underresourcing of education (Mansell *et al.* 2005). In addition to a general raising of resource levels for education, two characteristically New Labour emphases emerged in funding. The first was a policy commitment to reduce child poverty and to prioritize resources for disadvantaged areas to combat social exclusion, with initiatives such as *Excellence in Cities, Education Action Zones* and *Sure Start* (Chitty 2004). The second was a massive investment in ICT for schools to help reinforce both the government's economic policy of creating a high technology and high wage economy that can compete in global markets and the anticipated need for more flexible lifelong learning opportunities in a rapidly changing globalized world. Thus, for example, in 1998 the government launched the National Grid for Learning (NGfL), which provided a network of information and learning materials and funding for schools through the Standards Fund and its associated Virtual Teachers Centre (Selwyn and Fitz 2001).

In the remainder of this chapter, given the focus of the book, we will concentrate on those New Labour policy initiatives that have had the most impact on teaching and learning at key stage two (KS2) and these will be discussed under three broad themes: the standards agenda, the inclusion agenda, and workforce remodelling. It should be noted that this excludes both some primary school initiatives such as the commitment to reduce class sizes in key stage one (KS1) (Blatchford 2003), which have had minimal impact on KS2, and some of New Labour's most controversial educational policies such as the extension of market forces, choice and private investment within the secondary school sector with, for example, specialist schools and city academies (Harris and Ranson 2005).

The standards agenda

New Labour's standards agenda is the policy focus that best illustrates the continuities with the previous Conservative government's policy on education. The latter, as argued by Ball (1990), had its ideological underpinnings in different and sometimes conflicting aspects of 'new right' ideology. On the one hand, moves towards the local management of schools and open enrolment reflected a neoliberal ideology and, on the other, the implementation of a national curriculum and associated assessment tests reflected a neoconservative ideology. The transition to New Labour maintained the basic thrust of these changes (Whitty 2002), whilst intensifying the emphasis on raising standards, fuelled by worries that English primary school pupils were falling behind in the global competition for basic skills (Reynolds and Farrell 1996).

The neoliberal component of the strategy to raise standards was based on a belief that the encouragement of market forces and competition, together with the provision of information to parents on the relative performance of schools, would ensure that pressure from parental choice would drive up standards. Those schools that did not provide what parents wanted would – like failing businesses in the competitive world of industry – need to be closed. This requires a strong emphasis upon the measurement of school performance and the widespread publicizing of such measurement – an intensification of a culture of 'performativity', defined by Ball (2003: 216) as 'a technology, a culture and a mode of regulation that employs judgements, comparisons and displays as means of incentive, control, attrition and change – based on rewards and sanctions (both material and symbolic)'. In terms of specific policies since 1997, this has meant the continuation of national SATs testing at KS1 and KS2 and a more pronounced emphasis upon league table comparisons of schools' results. This, in turn, has led to the intensification both within LEAs and schools of a target-setting culture whereby expectations of raised performance levels in individual pupils' test scores are built into the planning process with managerial initiatives directed specifically at achieving these.

If league table results are one means by which parents can compare schools, another is the publication of the results of Ofsted inspections. The latter have been viewed by New Labour as a key component of its standards agenda in two ways: firstly, by focusing inspections specifically on the extent to which schools are achieving acceptable levels of test performance results for their children and, secondly, through a policy of 'naming and shaming' schools whose pupils badly underform in such tests and developing action plans for such schools to promote improvement. Underlying both the Ofsted inspection strategy and the wider performativity discourse is an assumption that school 'failure' is a problem that is internal to the school – caused by poor teaching or poor management – and that can therefore be solved by internal school improvements; in extreme cases this could mean forcibly closing a school and reopening it with new staff, including so-called superheads, under the New Labour government's fresh-start programme. Justification for such an approach was taken from school effectiveness research findings, which were taken to highlight the existence of different performance levels in schools of apparently similar levels of disadvantage. However, as argued elsewhere (Vulliamy 2000), the school effectiveness research tradition not only fails adequately to address the questions of 'effectiveness for whom?' and 'effectiveness at what?' but also exaggerates the extent to which individual schools can challenge deep-seated structural economic and social inequalities.

A continuation of the previous government's neoconservative ideology can be seen in New Labour's maintenance of centralized government prescription of curriculum and assessment and its extension to central prescription of teaching methods in the literacy and numeracy strategies, accompanied by reforms in teacher training designed to promote the new teaching styles associated with the strategies. However, whilst both the government and Ofsted claimed that the strategies had significantly improved standards in literacy and numeracy – claims that were subject to widespread criticism from researchers (Tymms 2004; Richards 2005) – there was increasing evidence from research that the performativity agenda was privileging the 'effective' at the expense of the 'affective' (McNess *et al.* 2003). A survey by Galton *et al.* (2002) for the NUT demonstrated the manner in which literacy and numeracy were squeezing other subjects and activities out of the curriculum, especially in relation to art, music and drama.

Brehony (2005) traces the manner in which such policy concerns at distortion in the primary curriculum, together with a perceived need to restore some initiative to primary teachers whose confidence had been severely dented by the imposition of the strategies, culminated in the development of a new Primary National Strategy (PNS) with the government's publication of *Excellence and Enjoyment: a Strategy for Primary Schools* (DfES 2003b). He suggests that pressure for a new policy direction was coming from a broad coalition that were against the emphasis on testing and qualifications, which was perceived as detrimental to the development of the creativity and innovation required of a globalized knowledge-based economy. Hence the PNS calls for schools 'to take control of their curriculum, and to be innovative' (DfES 2003b: 16). Such a knowledge-based economy was also viewed by those with influence on government policy, such as the Specialist Schools Trust, as requiring individualized learning linked to ICT and assessment (see Clarke 2003). The PNS thus declares that 'learning must be focused on individual pupils' needs and abilities' and that 'assessment for learning is a powerful tool for making sure that learning fits individual needs' (DfES 2003b: 39). Teachers' improved use of assessment is to be achieved through the provision of data including the information provided through the 'autumn package' (now updated by the Pupil Achievement Tracker) sent to schools. As Harris and Ranson (2005) argue, such an approach to 'personalized learning' – fitting particular teaching and learning strategies to individual pupils' diagnosed needs – subsequently became a key plank in the government's *Five Year Strategy for Children and Learners* (DfES 2004a) and its vision for customization and corporatization of secondary schooling.

The promotion of innovation and creativity in *Excellence and Enjoyment* sits uneasily with the reiteration within it of the familiar messages of the standards agenda: 'testing, targets and tables are here to stay' (DfES 2003b: 20). In the foreword Charles Clarke, the then Secretary of State for Education, claims that 'enjoyment' derived from 'excellent teaching' is 'the birthright of every child'. However, for him 'excellent teaching' means the achievement of high standards in literacy and numeracy that 'gives children the life chances they deserve'. Thus the intention of the PNS is to enrich the curriculum but not at the expense of the standards agenda. The focus on literacy and numeracy should remain and gains should be built on by 'developing the Strategies still further, and not losing sight of important fundamentals like the value of discrete literacy and mathematics teaching through the literacy hour and daily mathematics lesson' (DfES 2003b: 27).

The inclusion agenda

Where the New Labour government's standards agenda can be seen as a continuation of the previous Conservative government's policy, a sharp break with the latter can be seen in New Labour's policy commitment to social justice and inclusion. On coming to power in 1997 it set up a Social Exclusion Unit (SEU 1997) with a broad remit to tackle the high levels of poverty and deprivation inherited from the previous government and to implement policies in schools to counter truancy and exclusions (SEU 1998). Tackling social exclusion became a major policy goal of the government and in this context pupil exclusions from school – which had risen alarmingly in the first half of the 1990s – were viewed as a problem because of their perceived link with a section of society alienated from the mainstream by poverty, unemployment and criminality (Vulliamy and Webb 2000). Resources were targeted at disadvantaged areas, often in the form of short-term projects, and there was an emphasis upon 'joined-up' solutions to such problems involving cooperation between relevant agencies, such as education, social services, health and the police (Webb and Vulliamy 2001). Such an approach was to lead later to the concept of 'extended schools' and the *Every Child Matters* agenda, whereby schools could act as the focal point for interagency work, including the provision on site of childcare facilities and other community-based initiatives (DfES 2004b).

As Gewirtz *et al.* (2005) argue, one of the main assumptions underlying the targeting of extra educational resources into disadvantaged areas was that educational attainment could be improved by greater parental and community involvement in schools. Their research on the *Education Action Zone* (EAZ) programme illustrates the manner in which such zones – usually encompassing two or three secondary schools together with their feeder primary schools – were encouraged to innovate with schemes such as family learning classes, home-school liaison workers and training for parents to work in schools as classroom assistants. Such initiatives have since become widespread in primary schools in inner-city and disadvantaged areas.

If combating exclusion is one aspect of the government's inclusion agenda, another is an increasing commitment to the education of children with special educational needs in mainstream schools. Declaring a 'tough-minded determination to show that children with SEN are capable of excellence' (DfEE 1997a: foreword), some special schools have been closed and extra resources have been provided to support the integration of SEN pupils in mainstream schools both in terms of infrastructure, such as the provision of ramps for wheelchairs, and the provision of support personnel for individual pupils. However, as argued elsewhere (Vulliamy and Webb 2000), there is a fundamental conflict between this aspect of the government's inclusion agenda and the government's standards agenda. If a school's 'success' is measured only by SATs results, then there is a disincentive for schools to accept SEN pupils and an incentive for more privileged parents to choose schools with few 'problem' children in them. More generally, the New Labour government's attempts to promote social justice and to reduce the gap in achievement levels between the advantaged and the disadvantaged are vitiated by a continuing emphasis on a performativity discourse with its 'twin pillars of accountability (inspection, test scores, league tables) and standards (target setting, monitoring, raising achievement plans)' (Harris and Ranson 2005: 573).

Workforce remodelling

Tony Blair, addressing a teacher union conference in 1999 declared that the government's objective was to 'restore teaching to its rightful place as one of Britain's foremost professions . . . recognising the need for a stepchange in the reputation, rewards and image of teaching, raising it to the status of other professions such as medicine and law' (Blair 1999). The mechanism for doing this was laid out in the policy document *Teachers Meeting the Challenge of Change* (DfEE 1998c) and a subsequent paper, *Professionalism and Trust: the Future of Teachers and Teaching* (DfES 2001b) with proposals to 'modernize' the profession and embrace a 'new professionalism'. The context for this modernization process was that by the late 1990s there were increasing government concerns about teacher retention and recruitment and that the current pay scales meant that teachers could only earn higher salaries by promotion away from classroom teaching to managerial posts within schools. Consequently the government wanted to move away from the traditional pay structure whereby extra payment was given to teachers for taking on extra responsibilities towards a pay structure in which teachers who were regarded as especially competent could be awarded a higher salary. This led in 1998 to the establishment of the new post of advanced skills teacher for teachers who were thought to be particularly good at their job and who were willing to advise and support other teachers in the same or a different school (Wragg *et al.* 2004). More recently, all schools were required to review and rethink their staffing structures by the end of 2005 in order to replace existing management allowances with teaching and learning responsibility (TLR) payments to be implemented by the end of 2008. Furthermore, in September 2006 the government will also introduce the 'excellent teacher' scheme for classteachers, the job description for which has yet to be written.

In 2003 there was a National Agreement on *Raising Standards and Tackling Workload* signed by most public sector unions, employers and the government. This agreement can be viewed as another element in the government's wider 'school workforce remodelling' agenda, which was intended to initiate a fundamental reorganization of the management of schools and the remuneration of teachers in England. The agenda contained proposals for a major expansion of classroom support assistants, the allocation of 10 per cent of teachers' time for preparation, planning and pupil assessment (PPA time), redesigned patterns of progression through the career structure and the introduction of a 'fast-track' to allow speedy progress through the restructured levels of the teaching force (Menter *et al.* 2004).

Key elements of this modernizing agenda were the adoption of a new performance management system within schools and the introduction of performance-related pay. As noted by Mahony and Hextall (2000), the importation of such principles from the private sector of industry and business formed part of a 'new public management' strategy, which has been widely adopted internationally as a response to global pressures that reinforce competition and the need for low-tax economies. The first stage of the government's new incentive pay scheme – called *threshold assessment* – was that experienced teachers had to apply formally and in writing if they wanted to progress beyond the normal salary scale and proceed through this threshold to an upper pay spine, earning an additional £2000 per annum. The second stage was the introduction of a performance management system within schools whereby individual teachers were assessed annually and targets set for improvement. Decisions had to be made concerning which teachers should progress even further up the higher pay scale. Wragg *et al.* (2004: vii) point out that 'this was the first time such a widespread incentive pay scheme had been initiated in UK schools, so it was both controversial and contested'.

Conclusion

The New Labour government's reforms discussed in this chapter are symptomatic of wider educational reforms being promoted by international agencies such as the World Bank, the IMF and the OECD as the most appropriate response to the pressures of economic globalization. As Ball (2003: 215–16) puts it, such reforms are 'embedded in three interrelated *policy technologies*; the market, managerialism and performativity', which when employed together 'offer a politically attractive alternative to the state-centred, public welfare tradition of educational provision' by 'aligning public sector organizations with the methods, culture and ethical system of the private sector'. However, whereas globalization provides the backdrop to such reforms, a process of glocalization (Robertson 1995) results in such reforms being mediated and adapted in different ways in different national cultures. This can be seen in comparative studies of such primary school reforms in England with those in other countries such as Finland (Webb *et al.* forthcoming), Scotland (Menter *et al.* 2004) and New Zealand (Vulliamy *et al.* 2004).

The New Labour government has, following Giddens (1998), characterized its approach as 'The Third Way' alternative to the prior Conservative government's 'New Right' approach. However, Power and Whitty's (1999: 541) early assessment of New Labour reforms characterizes their 'middle way' as being 'skewed heavily to the new right'. Such a viewpoint is shared by most academics who have subsequently commented on the reforms. Thus, although the increased investment accorded to education has been generally welcomed, as Thrupp and Tomlinson (2005: 551) put it: 'The contradictions between a rhetoric of social justice and social inclusion, and the realities of divisiveness and injustice within a society pursuing market policies sustained by competition and "choice" reserved for privileged choosers, have become increasingly obvious.'

The New Labour government's modernizing agenda has been widely criticized for its overprescription in terms of curriculum and pedagogy (for example, Davies and Edwards 2001), for the deleterious consequences of its emphasis on performativity (for example, Fielding 2001) and for the manner in which its prescriptive accountability measures accompanying a new discourse of 'professionalism' undermine the autonomy and confidence of teachers (for example, Mahony and Hextall 2000). For those commenting specifically on the primary phase of schooling (Woods *et al.* 2001; Brehony 2005), such reforms are generally viewed as undermining the child-centred ethos that has been seen as central to the culture of English primary schooling since the publication of the Plowden Report (Central Advisory Council for Education 1967).

2 National Policy on Primary Education: Inconsistency and Uncertainty over the Whole Curriculum

Jim Campbell

Introduction: the problematic nature of policy analysis

Analysing education policy is not straightforward. Education policy can be thought of, following Furlong and White's classification (cited in Edwards 2003), as having three interrelated aspects, namely, policy *formation*, policy *implementation* and policy *evaluation*. Irrespective of its relation to research, education policy is a problematic concept in all three respects. Policy formation is often developed behind closed doors of the civil service, with compromise and personal ambition sometimes combining with luck so that policy intentions are often opaque. Some harsh judgements, dismissing the rational decision-making character of policy formation exist. Shipman (1984) argued that horse trading was the appropriate metaphor for policy formation and Briault (cited in Kogan 1975) talked of a triangle of tension between the national, local, and individual school, levels. Ponting (1986), in an insider's account of policy making in the civil service, claimed that policy making had to be constructed as emerging *ad hoc* through a series of compromises between departments headed by powerful ministers with their own ambitions. For outsiders to these processes, understanding the nature and purpose of a policy becomes much more difficult than is sometimes recognized.

Moreover policy implementation is often driven by a political timetable, usually shorter than the time needed for robust trial and evaluation. What passes for policy implementation thereby becomes a *de facto* pilot for future policy formation by experience. For example, the policy established in the Education Reform Act 1988 that there was to be a common curriculum in 10 subjects up to the age of 16 for all pupils, was amended some 12 years later to allow students to opt out of some subjects, such as modern foreign languages, and to add statutory provision for citizenship education for all students. What the drivers for these changes were remains unclear, but they might be thought to include the shortage of modern language teachers and the experienced difficulty of forcing students with little ability and interest in languages to study them beyond the age of fourteen. The introduction of citizenship might be interpreted as driven largely by concerns in the Home Office, about lack of civic awareness, including alienation from politics, and excess of anti-social behaviour in public spaces, amongst young people. It becomes difficult to discern when what was thought of as policy implementation has ended its trial period and has become established.

If formation and implementation are so uncertain, evaluation runs the risk of becoming either misdirected or at best fuzzy in focus. Thus any analysis of policy has to be constructed fairly tentatively. However, despite the uncertainty, the task is necessary if researchers and policy makers are to learn from experience. Perhaps the Freedom of Information Act will deliver greater transparency in the future and thus make life easier for policy analysts, but we should not hold our breath.

The colonization of the curriculum

My intention in this review is to go further back beyond 1994 and the *Look Before You Leap* collection of papers (Pollard 1994), because I think that the period has to be understood from a longer perspective, and especially in relation to the empirical and normative aspects of the survey by HM Inspectorate (DES 1978); *Primary Education in England*. Nonetheless I shall also attempt to bring a sharp focus on the policy formation and implementation particularly in respect of the last decade.

Although most historical 'periods' are largely artificial constructs, the time between the Great Debate, started by Prime Minister James Callaghan's speech at Ruskin College in 1976, and the publication of national tests results for 11-year-olds in 2004 has one defining characteristic: the colonization by the government of the primary school curriculum, its aims, nature, assessment and modes of delivery. By colonization, I mean, metaphorically, the 'settlement in a hostile or newly conquered country' (*Shorter Oxford English Dictionary*) so as to control and administer it according to purposes set by the colonizing authority. The purposes of non-metaphorical colonization tend to be criticized as exploitative of the colonized, but colonization of the primary school curriculum may be justified on the moral grounds of increasing accountability to parents and raising standards of pupil attainment.

In 1976, the metaphor of the curriculum as a secret garden, although already being over-used, had some resonance with reality. In 1983, it was still possible to produce case studies of primary classrooms where teachers innovated in their curriculum simply because it took their fancy or it followed a recently acquired interest (Campbell 1985: 13–14). But, by 1998, the DfEE confirmed that no primary school had been allowed to experiment with its curriculum since 1989 (Campbell 1998: 99).

It is easy to exaggerate the extent of real change. In the 1970s, curricular autonomy was not much in evidence in primary mathematics, where a national survey by HMI found overdependency on commercial schemes and low levels of innovation in primary science (DES 1978). The impact of government intervention might likewise be overstated. Pollard *et al.* (1994) found a range of responses to government reforms among their sample of primary schoolteachers, including 'compliance,' but they also reported, as the majority response, 'incorporation' – appearing to change, but incorporating changes into existing practices and thereby lessening the impact. Amongst a minority, they reported 'resistance' – simply not implementing the reforms. More recently, Richards found small primary schools 'domesticating' the highly prescriptive national curriculum (Richards 1999: 91).

Thus, understanding the post-1976 period has not been helped by the tendency to romanticize the value of primary teachers' autonomy or to demonize state intervention. It is however, possible to construct the colonization process as falling into three phases, although there are overlaps, not clean breaks, between them.

Three phases

The first phase was from 1976 to about 1986, during which time Her Majesty's Inspectorate (HMI) built a professional acknowledgement about problems in primary education, and a consensus about the need for a national curriculum framework that could provide for commonality of curricular experience but left decision making about content, pedagogy and curriculum organization at the school level. It was a phase characterized by *gentle professional persuasion* from HMI, which successfully moved the system toward common priorities and broad frameworks. (See Campbell 1989 for a fuller discussion of the role of HMI in this period.)

The second phase was from 1987 to 1997, during which time detailed statutory prescription of the curriculum was imposed on every school from the central government, which established a discrete set of mechanisms regulating curriculum content and published measures of school performance for parents and other consumers in order to lever up standards. It appeared to undermine teacher judgement about the detail of the curriculum and was strongly contested. (See Tomlinson 1993 for a fuller analysis of the process.) It was a phase characterized by the attempt to impose *standards and accountability by statute*. Although the accountability measures were effectively secured, improvement in standards proved elusive.

The third phase started about 1992/3 but came into full force after the election of the New Labour government in 1997, when an assault on the professional culture and orthodoxies in primary education was launched in the face of continuing evidence that the national curriculum, testing and inspection were failing to raise standards. The phase, probably as yet incomplete, is characterized by the imposition of a *performance culture* on primary schools, a concentration on raising standards in literacy and numeracy through an officially sponsored pedagogy. The early part of this phase was driven by the domination of HMCI Chris Woodhead in matters of primary curriculum policy.

1976–1986: gentle persuasion

At the time of the Great Debate, Bennett's ground-breaking and controversial study of teaching styles (Bennett 1976) triggered a moral panic about primary pedagogy. Bennett's findings – teaching styles that he called 'informal' were less effective than others at enabling children to learn the basics – mirrored the widely publicized concerns of the Black Papers that preceded Bennett's study. In retrospect, however, a more pervasive, less melodramatically received influence was embodied in an empirical survey of classroom practice, *Primary Education in England*, conducted by HMI (DES 1978). There has been no dispute that the 1172 classrooms of 7-, 9-, and 11-year-olds constituted a representative sample nationally. Some of the findings were potentially dynamite. In a series of tables presented as annexes, HMI reported that more able pupils were consistently, across all ages and all subjects, set work poorly matched to their abilities and that there were low expectations of pupil performance by teachers, especially in inner cities. The curriculum was not generally planned to incorporate progression, and was narrowly focused on the basics of mathematics and English, with poor or patchy provision in most other subjects.

The findings of *Primary Education in England* could have been used publicly to attack primary teachers for incompetence and the failure to provide an entitlement curriculum. That this did not happen may lie in the fact that HMI had incorporated a normative reform agenda into the survey's empirical base and set about implementing it by gently persuading the profession, the civil service and ministers that there were real problems in primary education that needed to be addressed. This agenda included: the need to broaden the primary curriculum from its concentration on English and Mathematics, to raise standards of cognitive attainment, especially for the able pupils, to match work set to pupils' different capacities, and to create more continuity and progression in the curriculum. The seeds of the national curriculum, with its four linked concepts of 'standards', 'breadth and balance', 'differentiation' and the 'entitlement curriculum' were sown in the survey, and came to fruit in a series of HMI-influenced policy documents, between 1978 to 1986, most notably the DES national framework proposal, *The School Curriculum* (DES 1981), the HMI series, *The School Curriculum 5–16* (DES 1985c) and the Third Report of the Education Select Committee (House of Commons 1986). The latter report proposed a national framework for the primary school curriculum, giving as a principal justification the notion that children were entitled to a specified curriculum. Through these documents, not all of them formally written by HMI, gentle persuasion delivered a professional consensus about the broad objectives for the curriculum.

The official government position on primary education came in the forcefully articulated 1985 White Paper, *Better Schools* (DES 1985a), where the arguments advanced by Sir Keith Joseph to the 1984 North of England Conference for the establishment of a 'broad agreement about the objectives and the content of the school curriculum' were codified. In paragraph 31, the White Paper linked curriculum reform to accountability quite directly. Clarity about curricular objectives would enable schools' performance to be 'more fairly judged against agreed expectations', and was, 'a prerequisite for monitoring progress over time in the achievement of higher standards of performance.'

On primary practice, the White Paper was critical:

> There are rarely effective mechanisms for ensuring that declared curricular policies are reflected in the day-to-day work of most teachers and pupils.
>
> Many teachers' judgements of pupils' potential and of their learning needs tend to reflect preconceptions about the different categories of pupils ... As a result, expectations of pupils are insufficiently demanding at all levels of ability ... [paras 17–21]
>
> ... the Government believes that, not least in the light of what is being achieved in other countries, the standards now generally attained by our pupils are neither as good as they can be, nor as good as they need to be if young people are to be equipped for the world of the twenty-first century. [para 9]

Nonetheless, *Better Schools* did not advocate a prescriptive national curriculum; it proposed agreement about a broad framework only and ruled out anything more detailed.

> It would not be appropriate for either the Secretaries of State or the LEA to determine the detailed organisation and content of the programme of the pupils of any particular school ... It would not in the view of the Government be right for the Secretaries of State's policy for the range and pattern of the 5–16 curriculum to amount to the determination of national syllabuses for that period. (paras 35–36)

The political recognition of substantial problems in the curriculum was supported by two major research studies into primary practice. Most directly, the ORACLE project (Galton and Simon 1980; Galton *et al.* 1980) had demonstrated that a 'class enquiry' pedagogy, practised by a minority of teachers, with greater proportions of time spent engaging pupils in whole-class interaction with the teacher, was associated with higher cognitive performance by pupils. Bennett *et al.* (1984) had shown that even the most highly regarded teachers had difficulty in differentiating effectively in primary classrooms.

The period ended with the publication of the Second International Mathematics Study (SIMS), reporting international comparative performance in school mathematics. This study's findings were interpreted as showing the performance of English 13-year-olds to be mediocre compared with our economic competitors, some 1 to 2 years behind on average, and, most unnervingly, to have declined relative to other countries since the First International Mathematics Study, (FIMS) some 20 years previously. The detailed analyses of these data are explored in Travers and Westbury (1989) and reviewed by Reynolds and Farrell (1996, see especially pp. 24–7) but it is the policy consequences that are most relevant here. The SIMS results appeared to confirm, in respect of mathematics, all the messages about poor standards coming, however gently, from HMI since 1978. As Brown (1996: 211) put it: 'The SIMS league tables undoubtedly hastened the political imposition of the English national curriculum.'

1987–1996: standards and accountability by statute

The Education Reform Act of 1988, preceded by a consultation paper in 1987, introduced a statutory and highly detailed curriculum comprising 10 subjects, statutory assessment and testing at age 7 and 11, and the publication of results. The Acts that followed provided for statutory inspection of schools and publication of the inspection report, with the responsibility for the conduct of inspections being given to a unique non-ministerial government department, the Office for Standards in Education (Ofsted). There were, however, important inhibitors, of special salience for primary schools, built into the 1988 Act, designed to restrict the extent of government penetration into classroom practice. The state was prohibited from prescribing textbooks, teaching methods and time allocations for particular subjects. These were all left to individual schools.

There are many narratives, including from some of those closely involved in implementing policy (Baker 1993; Black 1993; Graham and Tytler 1993) attempting to explain how education policy moved as sharply away from the 1985 White Paper position on the curriculum to the detailed prescription that followed. Although there have been substantial academic analyses of the consequences of the reforms, the origins of the dramatic policy *volte face* are less clearly established. (Ball's 1990 work involving first-hand accounts from policy makers is a rare exception to this syndrome of uncertainty.) There are anecdotes of Mrs Thatcher's hairdresser inventing the curriculum whilst giving her a perm; there is the public record of Sir Keith Joseph's opposition in the House of Lords to the excessive detail proposed, on neoliberal and pragmatic grounds. There is the claim that Kenneth Baker saw a way of leaving a lasting mark on political history by bringing in massive and far reaching reforms, which he linked historically in importance to the Balfour and Butler Acts.

Against these explanations, which rely on personal beliefs and ambitions of senior politicians, there was, according to Graham, the fact that the civil service seized the opportunity to intervene directly:

> There was also a marked change in the attitudes of civil servants after the introduction of the 1988 Education Reform Act, which they rightly saw as their first chance of having real power over state education. There was a volatile mixture of palpable fear of failing to deliver what was expected of them and a determination to run the whole programme. This was the first time ever that the DES had control of the curriculum and it was the beginning of the demise of HMI, although that was barely appreciated at the time.
>
> (Graham and Tytler 1993: 13)

Although Graham can not be thought of as disinterested, he makes a convincing case that a big part of the bureaucratization of the curriculum arose from the obsessive wish in the civil service to control it and ensure its effective delivery at the school level. The explanations from personal ambition and civil service opportunism are not contradictory but mutually reinforcing, if it is assumed that Baker's ambition could be realized most effectively by harnessing the service to it.

Despite this, the attempt to raise standards in primary schools by statute was characterized by a profound misunderstanding of everyday practice in state primary schools. The policy failure arose from an unwillingness at the centre of government to establish curricular priorities on the one hand or give attention to pragmatic implementation details on the other. The best illustration of these twin failures concerned policy on the teaching of English, including literacy. At the level of priorities, even teachers in the most disadvantaged areas, who wanted to concentrate almost exclusively on teaching literacy and numeracy, were required to implement a 10-subject curriculum, which forced them to reduce the time they had previously spent teaching children to read (see Campbell and Neill 1994a). At the pragmatic level, there was palpable ignorance about, or neglect of, research on time allocations for different areas of the curriculum. Guidance to the working parties writing the syllabuses proposed that about 20 per cent of curriculum time should be spent on English. This is about 10 per cent less than teachers anywhere in the world give to teaching the national language (see Meyer *et al.* 1992), and 10 per cent less than teachers in this country typically gave to English, according to every relevant study in the postwar period, including some conducted for the DES, had shown (see Campbell and Neill 1994a). The 'reform' of the primary curriculum, designed to raise standards of pupil attainment, was pressurizing infant teachers to spend less, not more, time on teaching literacy, and the curriculum model underlying the reforms was reinforcing that pressure. The consequence was immense stress amongst teachers trying conscientiously to make the reforms work and, 4 years after the reformed primary curriculum was introduced, official sources acknowledged that it had led to superficiality in pupil learning and was undeliverable even by the most able teachers (NCC 1993; Ofsted 1993a). A review designed to slim down the statutory curriculum (Dearing 1993) proposed 'discretionary time' equivalent to a day a week, free of national prescription, but was able to do so only by introducing an unconvincing set of 'curricular arithmetic', pretending that English and mathematics could take less time than they needed.

All the research showed that primary teachers had welcomed the idea of the national curriculum, found the idea of a 'broad and balanced' curriculum attractive, and responded positively to the idea of having an agreed syllabus to guide their planning. Primary teachers devoted increasingly long hours attempting to make it work and finding that in the end they were unable to do so. A metaphor of a 'running commentary' captured the sense of frustration and dissatisfaction of most primary teachers at the time:

> Well what is frightening now is that we are being blinkered now into the national curriculum . . . I am noticing it far more now that I never complete what I hope to achieve. There is always, like, a carry-forward so that you never get the feeling at the end of a session or day, 'Great, I've done this that I hoped that we would do' . . . there is this running commentary, really, in the background saying that 'You haven't done this, or You haven't done that' which I find very annoying considering that you work so hard.
>
> (Infant teacher quoted in Campbell and Neill 1994b: 67)

By 1996 the results of the Third International Mathematics and Science Study (TIMSS) were showing continued relative decline in Mathematics performance by English pupils, and some researchers (Campbell 1996; Brooks 1998; Foxman 1998) were showing that the national curriculum had failed to raise standards in primary schools some 7 years after its introduction.

There is a slightly different perspective, less focused on the detail of the curriculum and more on accountability to consumers. It reflects much of the neoliberal thinking provided to the government as the national curriculum proposals were out for consultation and is best embodied in an address by the Permanent Secretary in the DfEE (Bichard 1999). Bichard argued that the Education Reform Acts of the late 1980s and early 1990s were good examples of the need 'to confront vested interests' – that is, that they were fundamentally about breaking the producer dominance in the education service in order to render it more consumer-led. On Bichard's criterion, by 1996, the post-1987 policies, far from being failures, should be judged to have been outstandingly successful. Curriculum reform was less important an objective, despite the rhetoric attached to it, than levering in mechanisms for accountability.

1996 to the present day: imposing the performance culture on primary schools

There has been a long line of critical analysis focusing on the influence of the professional culture in primary schools into which any reformed curriculum has to embed itself. It is 'cosy, insulated . . . quite cut off from the complexities of politics' (White 1982); generalist rather than specialist (Alexander 1984); nurturant, caring and self-sacrificing (Steedman, undated); it values the affective relationships with pupils (Nias 1989). It is collaborative and collegial, not competitive, and there is a commitment to differentiated learning, with individualized and small-group pedagogy (Webb and Vulliamy 1996). There is little in any of these analyses to suggest that the professional culture values high cognitive performance and there has been a long trend in the research evidence that it too unquestioningly embodies low expectations (DES 1978). The cultural critique has a long history, but it was reinvigorated with the discussion paper *Curriculum Organisation and Classroom Practice in Primary Schools* (Alexander *et al.* 1992) often referred to, mistakenly, as the 'Three Wise Men' report. Presented explicitly as a paper for discussion, the authors nevertheless developed an attack on the culture of primary education, concentrating on the ineffectivenesss of the pedagogical practices it supported.

The discussion paper generated controversy amongst academics in primary education, mostly because of its apparent authority. Of the three authors, two – Alexander and Rose, respectively a professor specialising in primary education and the most senior primary specialist HMI – were leading experts in the field and the paper had been based on a trawl of most of the relevant research. For this reason, the attack on primary culture was deeply resented in the profession (see Richards 1999: 105–8). Much critical comment (for example, Dadds 1992; Carr 1994) was focused on Alexander, the one independent academic among the wise men, who has since provided a self-justificatory insider's account of the writing of the paper (Alexander 1997).

The academic controversy was unfortunate in that the concentration on one paper diverted attention away from the more sustained cultural attack, which was to intensify from 1996 onwards. The attack was based on three assumptions about primary education:

- it was continuing to under-perform in literacy and numeracy;
- too much time was spent by pupils on creative activities lacking intellectual challenge; and
- the problem was culturally systemic, and embodied in teaching methods insufficiently focused on direct instruction.

These assumptions could be justified by referring to some of the basic texts on primary education (for example, Alexander 1997) but they became associated with Chris Woodhead, the third wise man, now HMCI, who had recognized that the weakness of the statute-based reforms was that they had been merely technical – changing components of the curriculum, altering the nature of tests – but had treated the professional culture as unproblematic. By 1998, he made explicit his view that the problem lay holistically in the professional culture.

> The lesson of the last ten years is as bleak as it is clear. The government of the day can reform each and every element in the educational enterprise, but if these reforms do not challenge the orthodoxies which have dominated classroom life in too many schools for the past forty years, then they will do nothing to raise standards.
>
> (Woodhead 1998: 1)

The status of the attack on primary education was raised in 1996 through a series of public statements about the poor performance of primary schools from a powerful Trinity – HMCI Woodhead, soon-to-be Prime Minister Blair, and Prince Charles. Prince Charles, on the day his divorce settlement was made public, when he might reasonably be expected to have other things on his mind, announced that there was, 'dishearteningly widespread evidence of underperformance in schools, particularly in the primary sector' (*Guardian*, 12 July 1996). And Blair, as Labour leader, at what one might once have thought of as the other end of the social spectrum from royalty, promised 'a radical improvement in primary school standards. We do not share the view that primary school standards are adequate. They aren't. Fifty percent of children are failing to reach appropriate levels in numeracy and literacy tests at age eleven. That is unacceptable' (Labour Party 1996: 1). HMCI Woodhead's Annual Report (Ofsted 1996: 8) noted '. . . overall standards need to be raised in about half of primary schools'. Which was the Father and which the Son in this Trinity was unclear, but Woodhead, who the previous year had claimed that 15,000 teachers were incompetent, was the moving, though probably not the Holy, Spirit in it.

The election of the Labour government brought in a continuation, and an intensification, of the focus on literacy and numeracy, established under the Conservatives in 1996. Early in 1998, Secretary of State David Blunkett relaxed the statutory requirement to cover all the non-core foundation subjects in full, extended the National Literacy and Numeracy projects into 'strategies' for daily literacy and numeracy hours in all schools, and required schools to set targets for improvement in the percentage of 11-year-old pupils reaching Level Four in national tests in English and Mathematics by 2002. The significant point about these strategies was that they specified teaching methods and time allocations; they were accompanied by weekly and termly plans for the topics to be covered, and associated teaching methods, including the amounts of time to be devoted to whole-class interactions, individual or group work and a final plenary session. Since governing bodies of primary schools were expected, but not required, to introduce these lessons, the prohibition on prescribing teaching methods or time allocations in the 1988 Act was not actually broken in the letter but was clearly against the spirit, of the law. The overriding purpose had been made clear by Barber (1996: 33), anticipating, or influencing, Woodhead:

> Let us imagine that an incoming government chooses to give top priority to raising standards of literacy ... What in practice does it mean to give something priority? *Statute would have little or nothing to do with it. The central challenge would be to change teachers' behaviour in classrooms.* [my emphasis]

The speed of implementation was very fast, and largely uncontested. The literacy and numeracy hours, in any case, were widely welcomed by most primary teachers (Ofsted 1999b) – see also Chapters 3 and 15. In three short years the professional culture appeared to have been transformed: significant increases in the amount of direct instruction in lessons planned with clearly delimited and achievable objectives defined nationally; reduced amounts of time on creative activities; almost uniform teaching methods, and the acceptance of performance targets for literacy and numeracy that would have been thought unrealizable 10 years previously. The target setting in particular challenged complacency in middle-class schools and social determinism in the inner cities, because targets for improvement and the percentages of pupils expected to reach Level Four, were benchmarked, admittedly crudely, against the performance in schools with similar intakes.

Criticism of the apparent destruction of the 'broad-and-balanced' curriculum was scathingly dismissed by Woodhead (1998), and the Secretary of State made it clear that whatever the outcomes of the review by QCA, the emphasis on mathematics and English would remain in place in primary schools beyond 2000. He could find support in HMCI's Annual Report for 1998 (Ofsted 1999a), in which significant improvements in the quality of teaching and in standards of pupil attainment were drawn to his attention. When the Green Paper, *Teachers: Meeting the Challenge of Change* (DfEE 1998c), was published, laying out provision for performance-related pay, fast tracking, and holding back salary increments for the poor performers, a system for reinforcing the performance culture in primary schools became available (see Chapter 13). By September 1999, the state was effectively controlling, by defining, four previously contested areas; curriculum priorities, teaching methods, curriculum time allocation, and national targets for pupil performance.

Discussion

I have constructed the period under review as a three-phased policy development on the primary curriculum. It is doubtful whether policy makers have such rational long-term planning periods but in retrospect that is what seems to have happened. It is early to be sure about the outcomes of the third phase but the transformation of the professional culture embodied in the literacy hour suggests that successful colonization of the curriculum is taking place. If it succeeds in raising teacher expectations and pupils' attainment in literacy and numeracy permanently it will have been justified.

The policy frame also seemed to be changing yet again in 2003/4, probably in response to the perception that the resistance in the professional culture had been effectively undermined. The new relationship with schools (NRS) and the new Primary Strategy promised greater autonomy to the schools and to some extent the possibility of tailoring their curriculum more distinctively to reflect the needs and character of their pupils. There has been a powerful, if somewhat intemperately expressed, criticism of lack of pedagogical principle in the Primary Strategy by one of the erstwhile three wise men (Alexander 2004), but that may be to misunderstand the policy driver, which seems to be more about creating a *sense* of reduced bureaucracy and government control at the school level amongst schools judged to be effective in the curriculum than it is about fundamental principles. A particular irony in the Strategy is the rediscovery of the needs of gifted and talented pupils, given their identification in 1978 referred to earlier and the expectation that the curriculum will need to become even more clearly differentiated (so as to embody 'personalized' learning) for this group in particular.

From the perspective of the whole curriculum, however, the Primary Strategy is simply another change of direction, with renewed emphasis being placed on those aspects of it neglected in the Blunkett-led drive to concentrate on literacy and numeracy, namely, creativity, the arts, history and geography and physical education, the latter also influenced by moral panic about obesity. This emphasis fairly reflects the evidence from the Toronto-based evaluation of the national literacy and numeracy strategies (Earl *et al.* 2003) in which it was concluded that rises in literacy and numeracy standards were probably robust but had been bought at the expense of delivering the broad and balanced curriculum. Another casualty of the raised standards according to Earl and her colleagues was a loss of a sense of ownership of curriculum change amongst the teachers and this might lead to lack of sustainability of effect and loss of capacity in the profession. This was because a policy imperative leading to high dependency and another stressing the need for increased capacity building were pulling in mutually contradictory directions.

It is fair to assume that this evidence from Earl *et al.* (2003) could also be adduced in support of the NRS and increased school-level autonomy in some areas of curriculum. As with gifted and talented pupils, we have been there before, in the 1978 *Primary Education in England* (DES 1978) where it was argued that higher standards in literacy and numeracy were associated with a broad curriculum rather than a narrow concentration on teaching literacy and numeracy (the implication was that the higher standards were caused by the broad curriculum). The 1978 survey had at least the force of a representative group, whereas its modern version, the Ofsted report on *The Curriculum in Successful Primary Schools* (Ofsted 2002a) made the same claim, that high standards in the basics of literacy and numeracy could be achieved without losing the broad and balanced curriculum, but backed it up by only 10 case-study schools, which must have been unrepresentative if Earl and her colleagues were right.

There remain four substantial uncertainties, however. First, the measures of improved standards in primary schools are almost entirely controlled by the government and exclusively concentrated on the core subjects. There is no independent agency systematically evaluating the impact of the new curriculum as a whole. As Richards (1998: 141) pointed out, the assertion in the 1997 White Paper that we have, 'sound, consistent national measures of pupil achievement' is debatable. Most of the measures depend on the reliability of national testing and Ofsted inspection data, which has been contested. A more independent agency for the monitoring of standards over time is called for if confidence in apparent improvement is to be secured. Moreover, although test reliability has been improved since standardization in 1996, test validity has yet to be demonstrated. We do not know whether raised performance in the national curriculum tests will actually deliver raised literacy and numeracy performance in real life or in international comparisons.

Second, the extent of curriculum colonization remains problematic, especially given the frequent changes of strategic and tactical approaches to the issue of how much of the curriculum should be laid down in statute. Richards (1999) argued that a 'neoelementary' curriculum, with a core of English, mathematics, religious education, science (supported by ICT) squeezing out other subjects, might be the outcome of the Labour reforms. Although the QCA review (QCA/DfEE 1999) argued for most of the curriculum to be specified nationally, the QCA has been marginalized in the post-1996 developments so far. An equally convincing trajectory is that the neoelementary core should become the limit of state control, with autonomy for primary schools in the rest of the curriculum. On this assumption, even if the expected time allocations of the literacy and numeracy hours remain in force, the state-prescribed core would account for roughly 14 hours out of approximately 24, freeing up the equivalent of two days a week for school-based decisions. Such a development would, at a stroke, be in line with neoliberal ideology (for example, Letwin 1988), with the 1997 White Paper's slogan 'intervention in inverse proportion to success', and with the priorities espoused by both Woodhead and the Primary Strategy (unlikely bed fellows though they appear to be). It would also hand back a restricted but significant amount of discretion to practitioners. As happens in real colonies, curriculum colonization would have brought some freedoms as well as dependency.

Third, since 1997 policy for raising standards has focused powerfully on pedagogical change or, more precisely, taking Alexander's (2004) critique into account, on teaching methods; on training primary teachers to alter their teaching methods towards more whole-class interaction. At the level of the individual classroom such a change may significantly affect pupil *progress*, but the international studies of school effectiveness show, at the national level, relatively small contributions from teaching methods to variance in pupil *attainment*, which tends to be largely influenced by factors outside the control of the school. Reynolds and Farrell's (1996) review puts the school contribution between 8 per cent and 14 per cent, depending on the systemic variation between schools. We are operating with an inexact science and should not dismiss any potential basis for raising standards, and certainly not dismiss methods of improving pupil progress, but on the basis of the evidence available, the almost exclusive focus on teaching methods, however commonsensical, may not deliver the extent of change in pupil attainment required nationally. Most interestingly, the followup study to the ORACLE project by Galton *et al.* (1999), showed that although there had been increases in amounts of whole-class teaching in 1996 compared to 1976, there had been associated increases in 'easy riding' (that is, slowing down of work rate) by pupils, reminding us that curriculum reform always has unintended consequences. (Easy riders tend to be high achievers.) We need an explanation for the plateau effect in literacy and numeracy standards across the last 2 years at age 11, and it may be that part of the explanation lies in the concentration on improving teaching methods at the expense of more broadly based school self-evaluation (MacBeath 1999). The former can deliver short-term change but not build the capacity for sustainable improvement claimed for the latter.

Finally, any ambitions for the whole curriculum, whether held at the school, local authority or national level, can only be realized if there is a clarity and consensus over policy over a sustained period. The post-1988 period has been driven by unusually strong directional swerves – from the broad and balanced curriculum of the 1988 Act, through Dearing's (1993) review, through the Blunkett relaxations of statutory force on the foundation subjects in 1998 and the national initiatives in literacy and numeracy, to the new Curriculum of 2000 (with its mysterious association with a Values Forum), to the 2003 Primary Strategy, with its rediscovery of creativity, school distinctiveness and gifted pupils. Even allowing for the uncertainties involved in policy analysis, alluded to at the beginning of this chapter, you have to say of whole curriculum policy over this decade: 'Policy? What policy?'

The irony is that there might have been such consistency over a sustained period if current policy makers had gone back to 1978 for the establishment of some evidence-based principles for the whole curriculum.

3 Teachers' Perspectives on Teaching and Learning in a Performativity Culture

Rosemary Webb

Introduction

Chapter 1 documented the key components of New Labour's education policy, and explained the nature of, and the rationale for, the standards agenda and how that has reinforced a culture of performativity. This chapter reports teachers' views on the impact of this agenda on teaching and learning with a specific focus on the effect of the regime of targets, tests and league tables, the National Literacy and Numeracy Strategies (NLS and NNS – for details of these see Chapter 2) and the Primary National Strategy (PNS). It draws on an ongoing four-year (2003–2006) Association of Teachers and Lecturers (ATL) project involving revisiting a national sample of 50 schools throughout England that were researched a decade earlier (Webb and Vulliamy 1996). In its first phase this project comprised 188 tape-recorded in-depth interviews with primary teachers in these schools, supplemented by classroom observations of 51 lessons (Webb and Vulliamy 2006).

The project data show that the government's overriding concern to improve pupils' performance in literacy and numeracy continues unabated with its adverse effects on the primary curriculum, the school experience of children particularly those in Y6 and creativity in teaching. According to our interviews and observations the NLS and the NNS have brought about considerable changes in teaching methods, not only in literacy and numeracy but also across the curriculum. These may be further developed through the PNS, which was welcomed by teachers for freeing up the curriculum and thus supporting initiatives in curriculum development and alternative learning styles.

The impact of targets, tests and league tables

National targets in literacy and numeracy have become crucial to the government's standards agenda. In the *Five Year Strategy for Children and Learners*
(DfES 2004a: 43) the government predicts that by 2008 'we will have reached
and sustained our literacy and numeracy targets of 85 per cent of children
reaching the expected level at the age of eleven; and the proportion of schools
in which fewer than 65 per cent of children reach this level reduced by 40 per
cent'. Headteachers in the 50 schools described the unremitting pressure on
them exerted by these targets and how in turn they put pressure on teachers
to improve pupil attainment in their classes, particularly in schools with
lower than average test results, and teachers passed this pressure on to pupils.
In response to complaints by headteachers about the adverse effects on
schools and the curriculum of the unrealistic targets set for them by LEAs, in
2003 ministers told schools that they could set their own KS2 targets, which
LEAs were supposed to take into account when setting their own targets.
However, the headteachers in our sample complained that they were still
being pressurized into setting targets to fit in with LEA predictions. This
perspective was supported by 2005 figures from the DfES revealing that more
than one in four authorities in England had set targets for English that were
between 5 and 13 percentage points higher than their schools believed possible (Ward 2004).

For teachers 'testing has gone far too far' resulting in primary schools
being 'over tested, scrutinized and squeezed' with 'no allowance for your
professional judgement'. As expressed by one teacher: 'I mean in Year 6, I do
feel a great pressure – this "I cannot afford to miss a day of English or maths
before the SATs are coming up". You have to be very focused'. Osborn *et al.*
(2000) and Galton *et al.* (2002) concluded that the standards agenda focused
teachers' attention on curriculum coverage in literacy, numeracy and science
to the detriment of the rest of the primary curriculum, especially art, music
and PE and our research showed this situation remained unchanged. Preparation for the tests that completely distorted the curriculum in Y6 was an
established necessity in all 50 schools. Before the tests in the Spring term year
6 children were unlikely to engage in activities, such as residential fieldtrips or
class productions, which might disrupt their work on the core curriculum.
Schools provided booster classes, made use of standardized tests and QCA
optional tests for years 3, 4 and 5 and offered other school-specific initiatives
to support children's test preparation, such as homework programmes and
the after-school SATs clubs.

Pressure for schools to meet their targets and demonstrate improved
pupil attainment in the national tests was viewed as having a considerable
negative impact on the school experience of children. Year 6 teachers

explained that the concentration on tests was against their 'better judgement' but deemed necessary to reduce the stress involved for the children by thorough preparation and to enable them to do as well as possible for their own benefit and that of the school. Teachers tried to achieve a balance between getting pupils to realize the importance of doing their best but without making them over anxious. Pollard *et al.* (2000: 238) after interviewing 103 children across nine schools about their experience of taking the tests concluded that while the children's comments reflected both the reassurances of teachers and parents and the pressures of their expectations 'overall, the children seemed only too aware that whilst "trying" was worthy, "achieving" was actually the required outcome'. This perception was reflected in the accounts of the teachers that we interviewed of the responses of individual pupils to their test results:

> I whispered in each child's ear the results – outside the classroom so nobody else could hear – and when I came back in the classroom one lad, who had actually achieved a level four, which was what I expected him to achieve – he was crying. Nobody else had said anything to him but he just felt that level four wasn't good enough ... For him, that level 4 was a good result and, although I'd said so to him, his own self image couldn't let him see that. So, for children like that, and for children who do, plod on, and who still can't achieve a level 4, I do feel very sorry.
>
> (Teacher, June 2004)

Some confident, competitive, high-attaining children were regarded as finding the challenge of tests exhilarating but for many others, particularly lower achievers, the tests were demotivating, stressful and alienating. Also teachers in the 50 schools often commented on the inequitable nature and demotivating effect of SATs that rewarded ability often largely irrespective of effort.

Whereas classteachers held an overwhelmingly negative view of SATs and would like to see them abolished, only eight headteachers were completely against them. This was because most headteachers acknowledged that, whatever their concerns about the effects of SATs, these had played a crucial role in driving up pupil attainment in literacy and numeracy. However, they were highly critical of league tables and of the technical problems associated with the value-added version of these tables – criticisms that are substantiated by Easen and Bolden (2005) and Goldstein (2001). The tables were also perceived as being profoundly demotivating for teachers in situations where, firstly, a good performance at KS1 resulted in even the highest performance at KS2 meaning that a better than average value added score was not possible and, secondly, the achievements and progress of children with special educational needs were not recognized.

Schools were collecting and analysing increasing amounts of assessment data, particularly performance data, aided by the development of school management information and communications technology in order to make comparisons between: the school's results and those of other schools in the locality and nationwide; current and past cohorts of pupils; test results and TA or other assessment data; and pupils' results with their own previous results. Many of the 50 schools used QCA's optional SATs as the basis for such analyses – often administering them at the same time as the Y6 tests in order to instil quiet throughout the school, accustom all KS2 children to test conditions and emphasize to parents the importance of their child's attendance during 'test week'. While the focus of the analysis of performance data was the attainment and progress of individuals and groups of pupils and strengths and weaknesses in the coverage of literacy and numeracy, issues were necessarily raised about differences between teachers in the quality of teaching. Thus increasingly teachers were expected to set attainment targets for individual pupils and their performance was judged according to their ability to enable pupils to meet these attainment targets (see also Chapter 13).

The National Literacy and Numeracy Strategies

In our qualitative research project the use of a relatively large interview sample enables us to present, where appropriate, a broader quantitative picture of our interview responses to act as a context for the more nuanced qualitative analysis of key themes. Each of the 188 interviews was scrutinized for evaluative comments made about either the NLS or the NNS or both in terms of a threefold classification of 'strongly like', 'strongly dislike' and an intermediary category of 'mixed responses' where interviewees could not be firmly placed in either of the other two extremes. Twenty-three of the 119 interviewees who made such evaluative comments on both strategies strongly liked each of them – for example:

> I think that the National Numeracy Strategy and the National Literacy Strategy have been really, really big steps forward. I think that they have been excellent and I like the structure of them [Literacy and Numeracy Hours] and I think that is great for kids who do not benefit from just being given tasks and asked to finish them in their own time.
>
> (KS2 Co-ordinator, June 2003)

However, as can be seen from a comparison of Tables 3.1 and 3.2, the NNS was viewed very much more favourably than the NLS.

Table 3.1 Teachers' responses to the National Literacy Strategy (N = 124)

Strongly like	Mixed responses	Strongly dislike
19%	68%	14%

Table 3.2 Teachers' responses to the National Numeracy Strategy (N = 119)

Strongly like	Mixed responses	Strongly dislike
52%	45%	3%

Another indication of this differential response is that 7 of the 17 interviewees coded as 'strongly' disliking the NLS were coded as 'strongly' liking the NNS. In Earl *et al.*'s (2003) research into the early stages of the implementation of the strategies it was found that headteachers viewed them more favourably than other teachers. However, data from our sample suggests that at a much later stage, when the strategies had more firmly bedded in, the responses of headteachers and teachers were very similar. Finally, although other researchers have sometimes found that there are differences in teachers' responses to the 1990s reforms between those who had entered teaching before and after the implementation of the Education Reform Act 1988 (Osborn *et al.* 2000; Day 2002), there is only a very small tendency towards this in our sample.

Although not mandatory, the implementation of the strategies was forcefully recommended (DfEE 1997c). Teachers in the 50 schools, irrespective of their opinions on the advantages and disadvantages of the strategies, were highly critical of the government for imposing them 'in a such a way that "You don't have to do it, it is an option, but woe betide anybody who doesn't!"' The strategies were viewed as another expression of the government's lack of trust in the teaching profession and a public declaration that teachers lacked the required expertise, which further lowered morale and reduced teacher self-confidence. The pressure for compliance exerted on schools through Ofsted inspections and the LEAs was also greatly resented. The minority of schools that decided against implementing the strategies as specified and chose to modify the literacy and/or numeracy hour from the outset found themselves 'doing battle', 'fighting their corner' and 'defending the barricades against all the onslaught' from LEA strategy consultants and advisers. As argued by Jeffrey (2002: 541) 'the performativity discourse changed teacher-inspector relations from one of partnership to one of subjugation'. Consequently, the majority of teachers interviewed described how they 'toed the line' even if they had misgivings about what they were doing and, if they did deviate from recommended practice, they did not publicize the fact to colleagues.

All the 50 schools in our sample were adapting the strategies to some extent on the basis of their experience in order not only to tailor them to the needs of the children but also to take into account the strengths and limitations of the teaching staff, to abandon aspects considered unnecessary or unsuccessful and to bring back valued practices 'squeezed out' by the strategies. This process was facilitated by the perception that such adaptations were now acceptable, even expected of them (see, for example, Ofsted 2002a), although the majority of schools weary of change opted to proceed slowly. Not surprisingly given the criticisms of the NLS this was subject to much more adaptation than the NNS. Adaptation took a variety of forms ranging from 'modifications in small ways by different staff as they need to' to major changes in whole school policy, such as no longer teaching a daily dedicated literacy hour and incorporating aspects of the NLS across the curriculum (for details, see Webb and Vulliamy 2006). The perceived freedom to make changes engendered a sense of 'being back in control' that was crucial to the restoration of teacher confidence.

Benefits and limitations of the strategies

The main downside of overprescription in the strategies was that it negated spontaneity and meant that if, by choice or circumstances, a lesson did not occur 'you fell behind a day with everything knocked out', which was a source of anxiety. Teachers welcomed the increased flexibility: 'Just to be able to relax a little bit, to say "I didn't meet that objective but tomorrow I will" – things like that.' However, for many teachers a positive side of the prescription of the strategies was knowledge of exactly what ought to be covered in order to teach the basics thoroughly, especially for teachers lacking confidence in either literacy or numeracy who admitted that previously sometimes they struggled to come up with varied worthwhile activities. The majority of headteachers valued the strategies for encouraging continuity and consistency of teaching across the school so 'harmonizing what is going on in a much more clear transparent way'. Several referred to how they had used the strategies to monitor and support weaker members of staff to improve the quality of their teaching and to exert pressure for improvement where teachers were reluctant to change. However, a small minority of headteachers complained that such staff used the strategies as 'a crutch' and delivered literacy and numeracy lessons 'unthinkingly without taking into account the needs of the children'. Headteachers also reported that 'teachers don't change into other years now because they have got their resources all lined up', which made it difficult to spread expertise and good practice around the school and prevent weaker teachers being permanently located in years 3 and 4.

The strategies were generally viewed as very positive in that they ensured that children across England had access to the same content in literacy and numeracy and meant that children moving schools would have had similar experiences to their peers in their new schools. The strategies were also regarded as providing pace, structure and objectives that helped children to understand the purpose of their work and to work harder. In some schools the NLS was regarded as having brought about considerable improvements in the teaching of reading. However, this was also an area that headteachers often felt had been well taught before the NLS with many teachers declaring that to varying degrees they had always used phonics to teach reading. The most frequently cited major benefit was that 'it's hugely increased the number of genres that children are exposed to both in reading and in writing and that is an enormous plus' and 'gets children interested in all forms of literature'. The NLS was also regarded as having focused attention on trying to address the underachievement of boys in reading and writing.

However, interview questions about the NLS invoked very strong negative responses from a small minority of headteachers, who were dismissive of it in its entirety because they perceived its implementation as causing a fall in their schools' standards. Also, most teachers tempered their positive comments with criticisms of the limitations of the NLS, particularly the adverse effects it had on pupil writing and the overemphasis on technical language and grammar whereby 'it's still very difficult to be talking to the children in terms of subordinate clauses and phrases and punctuation when some of them can't even read properly'. Some teachers also referred to the negative effects on pupils' speaking and listening skills attributed to an overemphasis on teacher input, which 'they [those responsible for the NLS] should have known from the beginning – they don't necessarily know what's good for children.'

In comparison to the NLS, the NNS was regarded by most teachers as having mainly very positive effects. There was general agreement by teachers that 'the teaching of maths is better now than it was' as maths lessons comprised of individual work, such as those criticized by Ofsted (1999b), had been replaced by whole-class teaching at the beginning and the end, or throughout the lesson. Several favourably compared the level of numeracy of the children they taught with that of their own children and/or their own numeric competency on leaving school. Teachers generally reported growth in children's confidence in, and enjoyment of, mathematics and believed that their understanding of mathematical concepts had increased:

> I think the Numeracy Strategy's really worked, the oral and mental starter making children a lot more independent, a lot more knowledgeable, a lot more numerate – the ways of doing calculations are a lot more how your brain works. How maths was – we taught them a trick, but if they couldn't do the trick sufficiently well they had nothing, whereas now they are using a lot more common sense ...

and there are a lot more children enjoying maths than ever used to. They love the oral and mental starter and the class teaching. You can see them humming really, they're all there – so it's great – even the less able are far more involved now. I think that's been good.

(Headteacher, July 2005)

Most headteachers also considered that it had directly contributed to raising their school's maths standards. In order to investigate the effects of the NNS on attainment the Leverhulme Numeracy Research Programme and Nuffield Extension Study collected comparable test data on year 4 pupils before and after the NNS in 40 schools (10 in each of four varied LEAs). Members of the research team found a 'small but statistically significant change in attainment in relation to the changes in curriculum, in particular, the changed emphases and ways of teaching particular topics (for example, using a number line)' (Brown *et al.* 2003: 667–8). They stress that this challenges politicians' claims that it has been 'an indisputable success' in increasing attainment. However, in line with the perceptions of headteachers in our sample, they acknowledge that their data suggest that the NNS 'has been effective in improving teacher confidence, and in modernising the curriculum and the ways in which mathematical ideas are taught' (Brown *et al.* 2003: 670).

In addition to more whole-class teaching, another major change and break with the past introduced by the strategies was planning lessons to achieve specific learning objectives. These objectives were then shared with children so that they were clear about the purpose of a lesson and reviewed at the end to consider what they had learned:

I never would have thought a decade ago of actually telling them what I was going to do before we did it. At the end of the lesson too, something else I would never have done a decade ago is asking them 'well, what have you learnt in this lesson?' or 'do you think you have understood . . .' whatever the objectives were that we were trying to get across, you know, who feels that they have really got hold of that. I would never have thought of that ten years ago.

(Deputy head, June 2004)

Plenary sessions were viewed as very important for revisiting learning objectives, bringing the threads of the lesson together, diagnosing pupil understanding and planning the next steps in pupil learning. However, they were often experienced as problematic because they were rushed and overreliant on getting pupils to read out their work.

The impact of the strategies on teaching methods

For teachers trained since the implementation of the NLS and the NNS the teaching approaches advocated through the strategies were second nature. However, most teachers trained before the implementation of the strategies considered that their practice had been strongly influenced by implementing the strategies and as a result had changed and improved. They frequently referred to the new 'all singing all dancing teacher' who was continually engaged in lessons through explaining, questioning, directing and giving feedback to pupils. In their systematic review of the literature, Kyriacou and Goulding (2004) suggest that teachers may not be aware of the distinction between traditional whole-class teaching and 'interactive' whole-class teaching as promoted by the strategies, particularly in relation to teacher questioning and pupil responses. While some teachers in our study viewed whole-class teaching within the strategies as synonymous with traditional whole-class teaching, most viewed it as different because of its emphasis on maintaining pupil participation in lessons and cited examples, such as oral activities that required all pupils to respond, asking pupils to demonstrate skills in front of the class and pupils sharing and discussing their ideas.

Across the curriculum, as in literacy and numeracy lessons, teachers specified lesson objectives, did more whole-class teaching at the beginning and end of lessons or throughout, made use of instructional introductory sessions and rounded off lessons with plenaries. Consequently, teachers kept much tighter control over the direction and pace of lessons than previously. While a few teachers were concerned that pupils might become bored 'with too much sameness', others felt that the potential for this was overcome by including a variety of interlinked cooperative and competitive tasks and activities for individuals, pairs and groups throughout or in the central part of the lesson. Also as our observations showed, particularly in the foundation subjects, approaches to curriculum and classroom organization used prior to the implementation of the strategies have been subsumed within whole-class teaching patterns to provide opportunities for more varied, demanding and sustained work – for example, in the central part of lessons we observed children working in turn on a carousel of linked activities, carrying out cooperative group tasks and researching topics on the school intranet.

The changes resulting from the strategies were viewed by teachers as helping them focus on pupils' learning. Interestingly, a pilot study focusing on four teachers in Y5 and Y6 classes (Jeffrey 2003) found evidence from pupils for teachers' beliefs that such changes in practice were beneficial for pupils. He identifies explicating teacher intentions to pupils as a major development aiding pupil learning that is a direct result of the strategies. He found three significant factors contributed to the clarification of those intentions: 'These were clear teaching and learning objectives, the incorporation of a significant amount of direct teaching as opposed to in-dependent learning, and the highlighting of specific technical vocabulary and concepts attached to each subject' (Jeffrey 2003: 492). In particular, 'making learning objectives explicit, albeit an initiative of the reforms, opened the door to learners' awareness of teacher intentions' (Jeffrey 2003: 492). Such a development of 'learner-relevant pedagogies' contrasts with pupils' experi-ences prior to the strategies where Pollard *et al.* (2000: 178) found pupils 'had a relatively limited conception of these intentions, based on inference rather than confident knowledge'. Consequently, 'a concern for children was to find out as precisely as possible "what she wants" and to respond to well-known idiosyncracies'. Pollard *et al.* (2000: 178) also found that pupils 'had little or no language that helped them to discuss learning processes' whereas Jeffrey (2003: 493) observed the technical language to which pupils had been in-troduced within lessons being 're-incorporated in evaluations by learners and in some cases creatively'. However, he cautions that while the pilot project showed 'learners to be aware and articulate' there was little evidence of tea-chers taking account of learners' perspectives to evaluate their practice.

A further change in practice we observed was in relation to classroom seating arrangements. In our 1992–4 fieldwork, all the classrooms observed had pupil seating patterns whereby mixed-sex groups of pupils were seated together around separate tables as was found both in Galton *et al.*'s late 1970s fieldwork and in 27 of the 28 classrooms in their 1996 study (Galton *et al.* 1999). Of the 45 classroom-based lessons we observed (5 of the 51 lessons were in an ICT suite and one was a PE lesson in the main hall), only 26 (58 per cent) had pupils seated in groups around tables. In 18 classes the tables had been rearranged so that pupils were seated in rows and in one classroom the horseshoe formation of seating (McNamara and Waugh 1993) had been adopted. When group work (and especially group discussion activities) were required within a row-seating classroom this was achieved by asking the pupils in one row to turn their chairs around and face the row behind them. Teachers suggested two reasons for such changes. First, they felt that with more whole-class teaching with the teacher at the front, including the use of an interactive whiteboard at the front of the classroom, no pupils should have their sides or back to the whiteboard as would have been the case with the traditional group seating by table pattern. Second, they thought that pupils concentrated more and behaved better when seated in rows than when grouped around tables.

Before concluding this section, however, we need to acknowledge the argument arising from some published research studies on the impact of the strategies that the ensuing changes in classroom practice remain at a rela-tively superficial level rather than effecting deeper changes in pedagogy. Hargreaves *et al.*'s (2003) research into 30 primary teachers' approach to the NLS found a massive increase in the observations of teachers' questions and in the ratio of teachers' questions to statements by comparison with either the 1970s or the 1996 ORACLE studies (Galton *et al.* 1980, 1999). They also found that, whilst there was a very high frequency of lower order factual questions in KS1, at KS2 in contrast 'when compared with Galton *et al.*'s (1999) ORACLE made just before the introduction of the NLS, there was an unexpectedly high percentage of more demanding questions, i.e. those which a child answered with some explanation, reasoning, prediction or ideas' (Galton *et al.* 1999: 229). However, they found that KS2 teachers' greater use of higher order questions did not extend beyond their NLS teaching to their teaching of other subjects such as history or science. Moreover, 'even where more challenging questions were dominant in the Key Stage 2 classes, responses were rarely "extended" in either Key Stage' (Galton *et al.* 1999: 234). Consequently, they conclude that 'teaching in the Literacy Hour, having become "interactive" in a "surface" sense, has remained heavily teacher-dominated' (Galton *et al.* 1999: 234). A similar point is made in Brown *et al.*'s (2003: 668) research into the NNS. They argue that although teachers in interviews are overwhelmingly positive about the impact of the NNS on their teaching when the ways that teachers interact with children, are examined, 'it appears that in almost no cases have "deep" changes taken place'. In addition, F. Smith *et al.*'s (2004: 409) research into the NLS and NNS, using systematic classroom observation and discourse analysis to investigate the patterns of teacher-pupil interaction with a national sample of 72 primary teachers, concludes that 'traditional patterns of whole class interaction persist, with teacher questioning only rarely being used to assist pupils to articulate more complete or elaborated ideas as recommended by the strategies'.

The Primary National Strategy

The PNS (DfES 2003b) was generally welcomed by teachers in the 50 schools as 'a move in the right direction to get rid of all this narrowness in education' and to 'put the fun back' into the primary curriculum. It was regarded as a government response to the negative effects on the whole curriculum of an overemphasis on the NLS and the NNS. The government was also perceived as 'panicking' because attainment in literacy and numeracy was no longer improving. Teachers believed that ministers were now attributing this to the lack of spark and creativity in teaching that was resulting in 'a level playing field whereby highly talented teachers were being brought down' and able pupils 'being held back'. Consequently, teachers' perceptions were that the government recognized that creativity needed to be brought back into primary education: 'I think it's gone full circle and creativity and flexibility is being valued now, and a lot of the sort of constraints are being removed by the government because I think they've seen that a lot was lost because of that.'

The broad agenda of the PNS meant that its aims were viewed as 'all intermingled', 'diffuse', 'wide-ranging' and 'all encompassing' and therefore open to a variety of interpretations. However, it was regarded first and foremost as 'freeing-up' the curriculum and thus facilitating cross-curricular work and greater emphasis on the foundation subjects. In a few schools it served to legitimate the topic approach that they had modified considerably to accommodate the demands first of the National Curriculum and then of the NLS and NNS but had never completely relinquished. However, in the majority of schools, where the curriculum comprised mainly separate subjects, a move towards subject integration was approached with caution for fear that it might reproduce the characteristics of much-criticized topic work. In many of these schools cross-curricular work involving a broader range of subjects took the form of variously labelled theme/project/topic days or weeks with 'Europe' and 'healthy living' being recurrent themes. Schools were also reviewing their timetables to achieve a better balance of subjects and more opportunities for children to study aspects of these in depth. The 'blocking' of some subjects was already practised by over half the schools and in others it was being introduced or extended to other subjects. Schools already involved in their own or LEA wide initiatives to develop new approaches to teaching and learning – such as through the use of interactive whiteboards, philosophy for children, accelerated learning, visual, auditory and kinaesthetic learning (VAK) – saw these as a means to personalize learning and therefore as consistent with the recommendations of the PNS and appropriate to be classed under its umbrella.

For headteachers there was a tension between the government's drive for excellence through the standards agenda and the desire for schools to be creative and foster enjoyment. The performativity culture with its fixation on targets meant that schools felt pressured to concentrate on literacy and numeracy to the continuing detriment of the curriculum as a whole rather than reintroduce a broader curriculum and initiatives to promote creativity. Relaxing the emphasis on the basics and the achievement of targets was viewed by high achieving schools as a potential and perhaps unwarranted risk to their position in the league tables:

> It is whether or not you can actually afford to take that risk and I don't think that many people want to take that risk. It is just 'let's keep those standards up'. Certainly the inspectorate are very, very keen to keep those standards high. We are quite a flagship school in some respects I would say and it is important that we keep results high year on and year out. I am not altogether sure that we can do that if we are addressing other more important fundamental rights of children in terms of enjoying education.
>
> (Headteacher, May 2005)

Ofsted (2002a) argues that schools that are successful in achieving high standards in literacy and numeracy can also provide a rich and varied curriculum which does full justice to the foundation subjects; it does not acknowledge that there is an irresolvable contradiction between achieving excellence and enjoyment. While at the level of rhetoric these two aspirations are complementary and the 50 schools provided many examples of both excellence and enjoyment in their classroom practice, the interview and observation data provide evidence of the tensions between these experienced daily and the toll taken on pupil enjoyment and the primary curriculum by the government's narrowly focused target-obsessed standards agenda.

Conclusion

In our study, in answer to the question 'what keeps you in teaching?' the predominant responses were interest in children's learning, enjoyment of working with them and making a difference to their lives. It is therefore perhaps unsurprising that teachers attached considerable importance to the benefits for children that they considered were derived from the strategies. As a consequence they made changes to their practice and in many cases changed previously held values and established practices. Moreover, the teaching methods advocated by the strategies were increasingly being employed across the curriculum. Consequently much of importance in the focus, structure, pace and control of lessons appears to have changed as a direct result of the strategies and these changes seem likely to be enduring.

It should not, perhaps, be surprising that the ambitious aims of the use of 'interactive whole-class teaching' in the strategies to promote higher quality teacher-pupil dialogue and higher levels of pupils' thinking and understanding as yet show little evidence of having been achieved. However, the research studies providing this evidence (Brown *et al.* 2003; Hargreaves *et al.* 2003; F. Smith *et al.* 2004) were conducted within the first few years of the implementation of the strategies and since then teachers have become more confident in their approaches to them and they have blended the methods advocated with other aspects of best practice in their teaching. In addition, as witnessed in some of the observed lessons (Webb and Vulliamy 2006), our research suggested that both the greatly increased use of ICT – brought about by the introduction of computer suites in many primary schools and of interactive whiteboards in classrooms – and the increased classroom support provided by teaching assistants as a result of workforce remodelling, in combination with the strategies, can create conditions conducive to higher quality levels of teacher-pupil interaction (see also Chapters 7 and 12). The PNS also has potential to support such trends. However, the suffocating stranglehold of the performativity culture will need to be considerably loosened for teachers to feel confident, trusted and encouraged to experiment with teaching methods in order to make further strides to promote pupil learning.

4 From 'TA' to Assessment for Learning: the Impact of Assessment Policy on Teachers' Assessment Practice

Caroline Gipps, Bet McCallum, Eleanore Hargreaves and Alison Pickering

This chapter charts a journey in the development of policy and practice in assessment in primary schools. From the beginning of National Curriculum Assessment (NCA) to the more recent Assessment for Learning (AFL) initiative we will outline changes in teachers' assessment practice alongside these policy initiatives.

The journey started a little further back with a wide-scale study of teachers' use of standardized tests carried out in 1980/81 (Gipps *et al.* 1983). From this a picture emerged of testing (with reading tests, standardized maths and other tests, and teachers' own tests), record-keeping and marking of work as the teachers' repertoire for evaluating pupils' performance. Assessment involving teachers' informal assessment of pupils' attainment and understanding, based on observation and questioning, was not in evidence and is largely a post-1988 concept at primary level. Norman Thomas (1990: 111) had this to say about the status of informal assessment:

> Overwhelmingly, assessment is relatively detailed, informal and undertaken in the course of the day's work. Assessment of this kind is probably one of the most difficult parts of a teacher's job, but far less time is given to it in initial training and in in-service training than is given to discussing child development in general terms.

By 1991, however, Conner was able to produce a 180-page book on methods or techniques for informal assessment of primary-aged children (Conner 1991).

At that time, the general consensus seemed to be that much of the assessment made by primary teachers was intuitive. Given the absence of syllabus, benchmarks or criteria for teachers to focus on when evaluating pupils' performance, in the days before the national curriculum and assessment programme, a lack of articulation or systematic approach would not be surprising. The question that interested us as researchers at the time was how practice changed, if it did, when the national assessment programme came in.

The introduction of national assessment

In 1988 the blueprint for the national assessment programme was published in the Task Group on Assessment on Testing (TGAT) report (DES 1988). The national assessment programme required pupils to be assessed against the national curriculum attainment targets both through external tests (originally called Standard Assessment Tests (SAT) and by their teachers through Teacher Assessment (TA).

An important aspect of the TGAT framework was that teachers' assessments would be central to the system; teachers were to assess pupils' performance continuously using their own informal methods and this assessment information would provide both formative and diagnostic information to support teaching. The TA would be summed up at the end of each key stage and used as part of the reporting programme. As Lawton (1992) points out, a major achievement of the TGAT report was to make a significant change in professional and public thinking in relation to ongoing assessment and the teacher's role in this. Because of teachers' anxiety about testing young children and the fear of assessment at 11 bringing back a rigid 11+ testing system, the TGAT report was generally welcomed by teachers and educationists as it placed a firm emphasis on *formative teacher assessment* – assessment that was integrated with good curriculum and teaching practice.

Phase one: national assessment in primary schools

As a result of the research which the first two authors and Professor Margaret Brown carried out from 1990–4 three models of teacher assessment were proposed in relation to how key stage one (KS1) teachers made informal assessments; these were: intuitive, evidence gatherers and systematic planners (Gipps *et al.* 1995).

Intuitives objected to the imposed system of national assessment as a disruption to intuitive ways of working. There was a reliance on memory and lack of observable ongoing TA, and thus we were unable to describe in detail the process that this group was using to make assessments. One of the main characteristics of this group was its rejection of systematic recorded TA, which was seen as interference with real teaching.

Evidence gatherers had a basic belief in the primacy of teaching, rather than assessing. Their main method of assessment relied on collecting evidence, which they only later evaluated. They could be considered rational adapters in the sense that they have adapted in such a way as not to change their teaching: collecting evidence does not interfere with teaching practice.

Systematic planners – for this group, planning time specifically for assessment had become part of their practice (although this varied in the degree to which it was integrated with everyday teaching) and the planned assessment of groups and individuals informed future task design and classwork. For all systematic planners assessment was diagnostic.

National assessment in primary schools: phase two

In the next phase of the research (1994–7) the same team developed models for key stage two (KS2) teachers; these were: testers, frequent checkers, markers and diagnostic trackers (Gipps *et al.* 1996).

Testers are characterized by teaching a body of work relating to one or more attainment targets and then checking by testing children using assessment tasks that have been planned well in advance: assessment is essentially 'bolt on'. Levelled tasks kept as evidence feed into decision making and recording of levels.

Frequent checkers have some things in common with Testers in that, at the beginning of the year, they plan which assessment tasks they will carry out. This is usually related to school policy decisions that demand, for example, one assessment per core subject per term. However, frequent checkers do not confine themselves to these tasks; they give more short informal tests of spelling and tables, more self-designed assessment tasks (aimed at groups, year groups, or sets) or simply use graded worksheets on a much more regular basis. Thus their practice is characterized by more frequent task monitoring and setting than testers.

Markers make intuitive judgements using personal criteria and marking schemes, which later need to be converted into National Curriculum criteria before assigning a level. Work is aimed at the whole class, is based loosely on the National Curriculum programmes of study and may be aimed at one particular level. Work in books, rather than special assessment tasks/material, is used as evidence and for assigning levels. This is essentially a group of intuitive assessors who think of assessing as marking and say that a lot of assessment goes on in their heads.

Diagnostic trackers are characterized by detailed planning for different National Curriculum levels, day-to-day tracking of children as they cope with the work, and teacher assessment that uses techniques of research: questioning, observation and recording incidents as they happen (sometimes called qualitative assessment). These teachers aim to integrate assessment with teaching. They plan teaching very carefully to SoAs or ATs, differentiating the work for children on different levels at the planning stage. When they are teaching they collect data; they try to assess how each child is doing on the work set by purposely using techniques such as standing back, listening, asking open-ended questions and observing and making notes.

In comparing the practice of Y2 and Y6 teachers we found, not surprisingly perhaps, that giving informal and formal tests was much more in evidence among the junior teachers than infant teachers. As a result there was rather less integrated assessment and more evidence of summative or 'bolt-on' assessment, albeit linked to taught units of the curriculum. Another difference between Y2 and Y6 practice was a reduced focus on the individual child at Y6 (apart from diagnostic trackers) but more of a focus on the class or group, with curriculum differentiation rather than individual diagnosis as a theme. There was also more of a focus on the task at Y6, as though Y6 practice was between the 'teaching children' and 'teaching subjects' extremes. What is clear is that 'qualitative' forms of assessment, based on observation and questioning, *did* form a part of most of the Y6 teachers' practices: they did *not* rely only on testing and marks. Systematic practice was also evident to varying degrees in the Y6 models, lending support to our view that systematic practice is more a feature of personal style, and school practice than of age group taught or ideology.

The KS1 models of practice varied along three identified dimensions:

- systematicity;
- integration with teaching; and
- ideological underpinning.

We would identify the underlying dimensions at KS2 as:

- systematicity;
- integration with teaching;
- focus: individual or class/curriculum;
- approach: informal (qualitative) or formal (quantitative); and
- rationale: diagnosis or differentiation.

Comparing and contrasting the models of teacher assessment across the two age groups we can identify some underlying themes. A focus on the individual and assessment for diagnosis at Y2 shifts to a focus on assessment for curriculum differentiation for the class/group at Y6. The strong ideological views about what is appropriate (in both assessment and curriculum terms) for young children (Gipps *et al.* 1995) shift/soften to a rather more accepting view of the appropriateness of formal testing by age 11 (although the use of league tables is still not seen as acceptable – see Chapter 3). Along with the use of tests and assessment tasks there would appear to be more summative than formative assessment at age 11 and this assessment appears to be less integrated with teaching (Gipps *et al.* 1996).

Phase three: teaching, assessment and feedback strategies

The third and final stage of the research (1997–2000) focused on KS1 and KS2 teachers (in Y2 and Y6) who were identified as 'expert' from two contrasting LEAs (Gipps *et al.* 2000). We investigated their assessment and feedback practice as well as teaching strategies. We worked with six Y6 teachers in each of the two LEAs – 24 teachers in all. They covered a wide age range and years of experience in teaching, although only two were men. There were 20 schools involved in suburban, town, inner city and rural settings taking children from a broad range of family backgrounds.

It became clear that, over the course of the decade, primary teachers' assessment practices had developed quite significantly as a result of/alongside changes in government policy. The practices were more detailed and varied than we had found in previous research, so instead of developing models, we described the strategies used. Teachers used a wide repertoire of *assessment strategies*:

- **Those that involve teacher-pupil interaction:**

    - testing;
    - questioning – oral testing (requiring a specific answer);
    - questioning – delving (more open ended);
    - getting a child to demonstrate.

- **Those that involve the teacher in watching and listening:**

    - observing;
    - checking;
    - listening;
    - eavesdropping.

- **Those that involve the teacher in 'mentally' considering the evidence:**

    - using other teachers' records;
    - marking;
    - making a mental assessment note;
    - gauging the level – assessing general level of understanding;
    - gauging the level – judging progress;

- gauging the level – looking at range of work to make a summative judgement;
- working out why a child has or has not achieved. (Gipps *et al.*
  2000)

Overall, we found that by 1999 Y2 and Y6 teachers coincided more in
their assessment practice than they differed. Teachers of both age groups used
observing, oral testing, getting a child to demonstrate, marking, listening,
making mental assessment notes and working out why a child has or has not
achieved in the same ways and in the same contexts. Teachers of both age
groups described the process of 'gauging the level' of general understanding
in the class, of individual progress and of samples of work. We found that Y6
teachers were more likely to use standardized tests than Y2 teachers and in
general to do more testing.

A marked difference from the earlier studies was in relation to feedback:
by the end of the decade primary teachers were conscious of, and articulate
about, the role of feedback in classroom assessment. The *feedback strategies*
were:

- **Evaluative:**

  - Giving rewards and punishments;
  - Expressing approval and disapproval.

- **Descriptive:**

  - telling children that answers/work is right or wrong;
  - describing why an answer is correct;
  - telling children what they have and have not achieved;
  - specifying or implying a better way of doing something; and
  - getting children to suggest ways they can improve.

Teachers used *evaluative feedback:* to motivate children and boost their
self-esteem as people and learners, when they gave rewards and expressed
approval; or to discourage them from showing learning behaviour that was
not acceptable to the teacher, when they gave punishments and expressed
disapproval. In using *descriptive feedback* teachers were giving children more
or less information about the standard of their achievements (in relation to
more or less specific criteria and looking towards improvement). By telling
children they were right or wrong, teachers sorted the correct from the
incorrect so that children knew which paths to follow in future and which
they would need to think about again. Teachers then described to children
why their answers were correct in order to confirm the child's achievement
but also to inform the child about what an acceptable performance

consisted of. Teachers told children what they had or had not achieved in order to inform them what they had learned in relation to a specific goal. In relation to the areas where children had not yet achieved, the teacher could now feed back by specifying or implying a better way of doing something and then get the children to suggest ways themselves in which they could improve.

This conceptual progression from giving personal, evaluative comments for motivational or control purposes to inviting children to suggest how they could improve their own work with reference to specific targets reflects the range of feedback types represented in our original typology of feedback (Tunstall and Gipps 1996). Conceptually we describe this as progression from strategies dominated by the teacher's authority over a 'passive' pupil to those which rely on the pupil's engagement and initiation.

With all evaluative feedback (rewarding, punishing, approving and disapproving) the teacher is feeding back her own, personal judgement about work. With descriptive feedback where the teacher is specifying attainment or improvement, the teacher is *telling children [something], describing* and *specifying* and may refer the child to an outside authority, such as a learning target. Then the child may evaluate the feedback in relation to the target and recognize the gap between what is achieved and what is not yet achieved. This feedback type is one in which the teacher tells (and the pupil receives). With descriptive feedback where the teacher and pupil are discussing or *'constructing'* attainment or improvement *mutually*, the child's role is integral to the feeding back process itself. The child is being encouraged and supported in making a self-assessment or self-evaluation by reflecting on his or her performance in relation to the standard expected (and indicated by the teacher), and thinking about how performance can improve. This end of the feedback spectrum therefore involves children in using *metacognitive* strategies, whereby they monitor or regulate their own learning. They are now *supported* by the teacher rather than *dependent* on her, in deciding on the value of a performance and how it could improve (Gipps *et al.* 2000).

Assessment for learning

What we describe above is an early version of assessment for learning. The concept of assessment for learning was first developed by members of the Assessment Reform Group (ARG). Following this Paul Black and Dylan Wiliam reviewed studies of formative assessment published in English since 1988 to synthesize evidence of its impact. They found that formative assessment strategies do indeed raise standards of attainment, with greater effects for children of lower ability (Black and Wiliam 1998; ARG 1999).

> The Assessment Reform Group defines assessment for learning as:
>> the process of seeking and interpreting evidence for use by learners and their teachers to decide where the learners are in their learning, where they need to go and how best to get there.
>
> (ARG 2002)

The key elements are: making essentially informal assessments on a regular basis; evaluating the evidence from the assessment, against clear learning outcomes or objectives; and feeding back to, or negotiating with, the learner the next steps.

The publication of Black and Wiliam's review and the ARGs' work have had a considerable impact on classroom practice. The 10 principles of effective teaching and learning identified by the ARG are now posted on the QCA web site (2004) and form the basis of current approaches to learning and teaching in many classrooms. The systematized approach to planning, teaching and assessment is now extended to include teaching approaches which will enhance assessment for learning. So what does this look like now in the primary classroom?

Current primary practice

Routinely, learning objectives are shared with pupils at the beginning of a lesson but now the teacher provides criteria on how to achieve these goals and reiterates them at intervals throughout the lesson so that the children are constantly working towards the intended learning outcome. It is also quite commonplace to see a system of traffic lights in place where the children indicate by using a red, gold or green dot against the objective according to whether they have not, partly, or fully understood the concept. This not only acts as a tool for pupil self-assessment but as a guide for the teacher as to the effectiveness of the lesson. This approach to assessment moves pupils on from being passive recipients of the teacher's comments to being informed appraisers of their own progress.

The use of open questioning is stressed so that children can offer their own opinions and that these opinions are a valid response. This is directly opposed to a closed questioning technique where only one response is deemed 'correct' by the teacher, which leaves the children guessing what the teacher wants to hear rather than basing their response on their own ideas.

Closely linked to the use of open questioning is allowing pupils thinking time. The children are given a question and the teacher tells them to think about their response for a certain period of time before replying. This is a marked change that encourages the children to think more deeply about the question and can enable the use of higher order thinking skills. Recent research shows that:

Increasing the wait time can lead to more students being involved in question-and-answer discussions and to an increase in the length of their replies. One particular way to increase participation is to ask students to brainstorm ideas, perhaps in pairs, for two or three minutes before the teacher asks for contributions. This allows the students to voice their ideas, hear other ideas and articulate a considered answer rather than jumping in to utter the first thing that comes into their head in the hope that it is what the teacher is seeking.

(Black *et al.* 2003: 35)

This focus on the quality of children's responses was highlighted by Barnes (1976: 71) who said that the quality of discussion in the classroom depends on 'the nature of the task, their familiarity with the subject matter, their confidence in themselves, their sense of what is expected of them, all these affect the quality of the discussion, and these are all open to influence by the teacher'.

Another positive development is the involvement of pupils in their own assessment and peer assessment. This allows the children to reflect on their own work, acknowledging problems in a supportive environment. The evaluation of other pupils work has also been shown to enhance their own understanding of the task particularly at KS2.

As the research in Phase Two and Three above showed, elaborated feedback allows learners to see ways in which they can improve their own work through constructive feedback linked to clear criteria. There is recognition of the need to make time for this feedback to be read and acted upon immediately to make most impact on pupil learning. This has implications for KS2 classrooms where previously marking was often done after school and returned by the teacher with no follow up. It is now seen as a vital part of the lesson as indeed it has always been at KS1. So teachers of KS2 children must make time for pupil discussion about their work, which may mean a reduction in time for other parts of the lesson.

From the above it can be seen that this approach to assessment for learning has built on and improved upon much good practice already in existence in KS2 classrooms and it has confirmed the desirability of an ongoing dialogue between pupil and teacher. It also transforms pupils from passive recipients to active participants in their own learning.

Reflections

Looking back to concerns about National Assessment in 1994 in *Look Before You Leap?* (Pollard 1994) what is most telling is how the concerns about the downgrading of TA and the negative impact of formal testing have been played out over the 10 years. The work of Pollard, Broadfoot and colleagues in the PACE project charted with great rigour and insight the impact of formal testing on children as learners, their motivation and self-esteem (Pollard *et al.* 1994). As they moved through the first two years of KS2 the pupils in Pollard and colleagues' study became increasingly aware of teacher power and were very aware of the extent to which their activities were evaluated by teachers (Broadfoot and Pollard 1996). Their preferred orientation was pleasing the teacher rather than learning *per se*, and there was a growing preoccupation with avoiding failure (Broadfoot and Pollard 1998) – see also Chapters 5 and 6.

Torrance and Pryor's (1998) work, closely observing very young children engaging in formative assessment, argues that informal assessment in the classroom can be construed as a key arena for the negotiation of classroom relationships and we would agree. They used the example of assessment of children aged 5 (on entry to the first stage of schooling) to show that it is by no means just an assessment activity but part of the child's earliest initiation into the rituals of schooling. While the teacher attempts to encourage the pupils' responses by praise, smiles and so forth, in their example she is also determined to exercise control over the pupils in order to accomplish her agenda.

In traditional teaching the assessment relationship is directive and hierarchical: the teacher assesses and the pupils receive judgements. However, if teaching is aiming towards the development of good learning strategies in pupils, including the development of autonomy (taking some responsibility for one's own learning) and the ability to evaluate one's own work and progress (becoming a self-monitoring learner) then the teacher-pupil relationship needs to be more open and enabling, or constructing, than directing.

Royce Sadler, whose work on formative assessment has been seminal, points out that teachers bring to the classroom a more elaborate and extensive knowledge base than their students, including: skill in assessments, a deep knowledge of criteria and standards appropriate to the assessment task; evaluative skill in making judgements about student performance; and expertise in framing feedback statements. Sadler argues that some of these skills need to be shared with students, because:

> . . . ultimately the intention of most educational systems is to help students not only grow in knowledge and expertise, but also to become progressively independent of the teacher for lifelong learning. Hence if teacher-supplied feedback is to give way to self assessment and self monitoring, some of what the teacher brings to the assessment act must itself become part of the curriculum for the student, not an accidental or inconsequential adjunct to it.
>
> (Sadler 1998: 82)

This is just as important for young learners as for older learners. Douglas Barnes, as early as 1976, wrote about the importance of equal status and mutual trust between teacher and pupil in order to allow and encourage risk taking (Barnes 1976). We also know from the work of psychologists and classroom researchers about the importance of classroom climate in enabling children to feel 'safe' and to take risks in learning. American psychologists Ames and Ames (1984) described how learning environments can be differentiated in terms of specific cues that influence the ways in which children process information and come to understand their performance. Their argument is that certain classroom structures can influence goal orientation in children. Positive structures include assessment (or evaluation) strategies that: focus on individual improvement, progress and mastery rather than comparison; make evaluation private, not public; recognize and reward student effort; provide opportunities for improvement; and encourage a view of mistakes as part of learning (Ames 1992: 267).

Conclusion

Research in England shows that since 1988 primary teachers' assessment practice has shifted very considerably from one based on standardized testing, marking and record keeping to one in which regular informal assessment coupled with constructive feedback to the learner is more in evidence. As this chapter shows, TA and other forms of teacher assessment have become absolutely central to primary school practice.

The importance of teacher assessment at primary school level is also well recognized in Scotland and Wales. In Wales the National Assessment Programme initially followed the same structure as that for England (and Northern Ireland) but publication of primary school leagues tables was ended in 1999. More recently the Welsh Assembly has accepted the Daugherty Report (ACCAC 2004), which recommended phasing in broader testing for formative purposes in year 5; this will guide teaching in year 6 when there will be TA to support transition to secondary school.

In Scotland there have never been key stage tests in the same way. A sample-based national monitoring programme (similar to the APU that ran in England from 1975 to 1990) reports on national standards. At school level teachers use tests and tasks from a National Assessment Bank to support and confirm teachers' professional judgements; measuring improvement in overall attainment through a sample based Scottish Survey of Achievement, rather than relying on the annual 5–14 survey (which aggregates tests results). These tests and tasks are given by teachers when pupils are felt to be ready, so although they are formal tests they are used in conjunction with, and supported by, teacher assessment (SEED 2004).

The direction of government policy in England, on the other hand, has been to control and define much more tightly teachers' practice (see also Chapters 3 and 13):

> Teaching as an activity now comes with a much stronger official frame around it ... firmer definitions as to the purposes of teaching, clearer specifications of the what and how of teaching, more rigorous and assertive vetting and regulation procedures and a 'fixing' of positions and functions within the structure of the occupation. In short teaching as an activity has become much more tightly bounded, and this tighter bounding is externally defined and imposed.
>
> (Mahony and Hextall 2000: 84)

With the government's latest initiative *Excellence and Enjoyment* (DfES 2003b), there is more emphasis on assessment for learning. To support this approach in primary schools the DfES have produced a set of professional development materials DfES (2004e), which are to be used as part of whole school continuing professional development. The materials are based around the research findings of the Assessment Reform Group (2002) and, although lesson objectives are closely planned around national initiatives, much of the advice about assessment for learning is soundly based on research (DfES 2004e: 10–11). The problem with this, as with the literacy strategy, is that once again teachers are being told what to do and how to do it.

> Regardless of rhetoric, from government and other sources, which claims that teaching should be a research-based profession, recent policies have tended to construct professionalism in teaching as technical skill; and the relationship between educational research and classroom practice as a process in which teachers select and apply only those research findings which are relevant to their immediate teaching.
>
> (Poulson 1998: 430)

Black *et al.* (2003: 119) in their research project to ascertain how research findings can be put into classroom practice found that: 'the basis of research results ... could only provide stimulus, challenge and support for the work of teachers in inventing new practical knowledge about classroom work.' There has been no consultation with professionals in the classroom in developing these particular professional development materials and it is difficult for KS2 teachers to reconcile these sound pedagogic practices with the formal high-stakes assessment required by the SATs. This concern by teachers about the impact of SATs on their pupils was acknowledged in the findings from the PACE Project (Pollard *et al.* 1994), which documented the enormous efforts of teachers to 'mediate' the impact of National Curriculum assessment, to minimize its adverse effects on pupils, with the result that this demonstration of perceived 'professionalism' compromised the standardization of assessment practices in the SAT testing (Sammons *et al.* 1994).

There appears, however, to be a difference in approach to the implementation of these strategies according to the experience of the teacher. Newer teachers who have never known the era before the National Curriculum or The National Literacy or Numeracy Strategies seem to accept more readily these imposed curricula. Troman (1996) refers to two kinds of teacher, one he calls the 'old professional', who believe that teachers should have control of their work and resist control by either headteachers or politicians. The second type of teacher he calls the 'new professional' who accepts guidance from government but who in so doing defines their own professional practices in a semi-autonomous and often progressive way.

So what are the implications for the future? From discussions with both 'old professionals' and working directly with 'new professionals' what is clear is that 'Teacher professionalism ... can be defined as the ability to reach students in a meaningful way, developing innovative approaches to mandated content while motivating, engaging, and inspiring young adult minds to prepare for ever-advancing technology' (http://students.ed.uiuc.edu/vallicel/Teacher_professional). The evidence of our research is that many KS2 teachers have adopted and adapted classroom-based and formative assessment and developed approaches to constructive feedback. It is probably safe to say that, given proper support and respect as professionals many will also take on the best of assessment for learning practice.

5 Pupils' Views of the School Experience

Cedric Cullingford

Introduction

When the previous volume on the curriculum at key stage two (KS2) was published (Pollard 1994), the National Curriculum was still comparatively new. The title, *Look Before you Leap?* could still suggest that it was not too late to warn the policy makers of some of the inadvertent effects, just as previous books had done (Haviland 1988). We now live in different conditions in which the seemingly relentless series of reforms are heading in the same inexorable direction. There are criticisms but there is also a sense of inevitability in the instrumentalism of the prevailing view of schools, of targets, testing and inspection. The direction of policy and, perhaps more importantly, its underlying tone have remained unchanged. Whilst reforms are constantly being introduced, the experience is a familiar one. What is clear is the 'instrumental and pragmatic view of education held by teachers and pupils' (Nias 2000: xii). The research that has explored pupils' experience has been essentially about the effectiveness of policies, using their views as the basic instruments of research (Pollard *et al.* 2000). There is a growing awareness of the social world of children, as in the work of Pollard and Filer (1999) so that listening to the pupils' point of view has been recognized as increasingly important.

The problem with this is that, although pupils are starting to be allowed a voice, this does not mean that anyone is listening to what they are really saying (Pugh 1997). The nature of the school curriculum, the position of teachers and the pressure to teach in particular ways (for example, literacy hours) means that the pupils are listened to in certain conditions and with certain assumptions (Smith and Hardman 2001). The National Curriculum remains intact and is even being tightened up with ever more emphasis on literacy and numeracy. Even the titles of the books that invoke pupils suggest that they can be involved as a way of helping them adapt to the demands of schooling (for example, MacBeath *et al.* 2003). 'What's in it for schools' (Flutter and Ruddock 2004) has become an accepted condition for the exploration of pupils' attitudes, and even before key stage three (KS3), the sense of compliance in the model of education runs deep (Sammons *et al.* 2004).

The research on which this chapter is based attempts something rather different. It does not focus on a particular reform or new policy initiative. Indeed, its concerns predate the Education Reform Act. Nor does it limit itself to the pragmatics of the curriculum and the particular styles in which it is 'delivered' and assessed (Pollard with Filer 2000). Government initiatives might come and go or they might be moving relentlessly towards a philosophical goal but, from the point of view of pupils, schooling remains a distinct experience, one that is only part of their lives and to which they bring many hidden perceptions and where they are influenced by many private and complex sources (Harris 1998).

For pupils the essential experience has not changed over the years, even if the experience of teaching has. The statements of pupils that illuminate the theme of the chapter are drawn from semi-structured interviews that have taken place over a number of years. Whilst these interviews were not confined to KS2, the kinds of information gathered has relevance to any age, because the attempt is to see 'outside the box', to hear what pupils say beyond the instrumental necessities of the everyday. The main interviews were 215 in 1991, 110 in 1992, 195 in 2000, 52 in 2002 and 68 in 2005. The research instrument mainly used (amongst several) was the semi-structured interview. I have discussed elsewhere some relevant methodological issues concerning this research, such as informed consent (Cullingford 2002), the notions of 'structure' (Cullingford 2000) and the uses and analysis of evidence (Cullingford 1999). These issues are not new (Spradley 1979) but there are certain underlying themes that are important. The conditions of the interviews are of anonymity and confidentiality, with respect (the non-judgemental, almost laconic stance) and following the thought patterns and directions of the individuals. The structure is there to make sure that all the samples cover similar topics so that there are no lacunae in the data for which one is attempting validity and reliability. The samples include, in every case, a wide spread of socioeconomic circumstances (unusually wide) and, as it happens, an expansive geographical spread. The illuminative statements made here all come from pupils at KS2. When pupils know that they are not being tested and when they are not attempting to guess what they ought to say, they are both articulate and analytical. They connect to other research in the field and should be familiar to practising teachers.

Young children possess a strong desire to learn. The research studies that demonstrate their strong intellectual capacity also reveal their motivations (Pinker 1997; Cullingford 1999). The need to make sense of the world is constantly manifest and the curiosity to understand the big issues such as 'why we become as we are' continue to be apparent even in their early experiences of school. We only need to overhear the conversations that pupils have with each other informally to appreciate the depths of curiosity, the ability to explore ideas and the urgency of their attention to, and observation of, their environment. These private dialogues are rarely part of the formal school day and have no place in the curriculum but they substantiate pupils' deep love of learning.

This all contrasts with the emphasis in the National Curriculum on subject content, the acquisition of knowledge, the tests and the closed questions that are at the centre of the education system. When pupils wish to satisfy their curiosity they want to do so in their own way, pursuing ideas and sharing these ideas with others. They love the metaphor of stories, the excitement of relating their own experience to others. They seek their own agendas. When they are faced with the need to conform to someone else's set tasks, a rigid timetable and measurable outcomes, some of that motivation to learn is at once diminished.

In all the research I have carried out listening to what children say and trying to understand their implications, several strands consistently emerge. These include the juxtaposition between what they need and what they receive, their resilience in the face of great difficulties and the refusal of the system as a whole to take their views into account. I say the 'system' as opposed to teachers themselves who do a heroic job in the face of great difficulties.

When pupils see the formal curriculum as an edifice of facts to be learned, skills to be demonstrated and outcomes to be measured, they perceive their task in school as not so much to think as to guess what it is that the teachers want. Their intelligence is diverted partly into hiding from ideas and partly into second guessing what is expected from them. Schools are early on envisaged as the locus of teachers in which pupils are temporary, ephemeral and of low importance. Instead of being a companion with whom ideas are shared, teachers are put into the position of being imposers of facts, controllers of the subject and organizers of the day.

Interactions and relationships with teachers and peers

The role of teachers as organizers of classes and large groups means that they are observed very closely by their pupils. Pupils note the different styles of teachers and, as the work stemming originally from the ORACLE Project (Galton *et al.* 1980; Galton 2000) makes clear, the need to learn to adapt to them:

> If our teacher's away another teacher comes in and says you don't do it that way, you do it a different way, you've been doing it wrong. The teachers might think you're not good at work if you're untidy. (Girl)

The two key notes struck here are both the necessity of adapting to the requirements of teachers and the emphasis on presentation.

Pupils pass on information about teachers to each other and quickly detect how they should manage them (Pollard and Filer 1999; Measor and Woods 1984). For manage them they do, working out their idiosyncrasies, how to please them and how to avoid detection. Teachers are expected to be in control of the pupils and themselves:

> I don't mind her being strict because she is kind. Mrs B was terrible. She used to take it out on us. (Girl)

The ones who are appreciated are those who show themselves to be human and approachable, even if firm. The phrases for this quality are typically:

> He always makes jokes and things. (Boy)

> The teacher makes it nice because she joins in with things with us. (Girl)

> If anything happened to me, she'd care. (Boy)

Children want firmness, consistency and integrity, balanced by genuine human warmth. This is demonstrated by concern for individuals, the ability to explain and the most personal of connections, humour. Being able to joke with a teacher is the personal connection to strive for an opportunity soon lost on leaving the primary school and even there not one that is taken up by many (Pollard *et al.* 2000). Joking is individual and mitigates the feeling of being 'picked on'. What pupils constantly report is the desire for a sense of security. Nothing is more disturbing than the sense of 'unfairness', of inconsistency of judgement. Having favourites or enemies, or having changes of mind is disturbing, but so are changes of mood and lack of consistency:

> It's not fair on them and you never know who he's going to pick on next. (Boy)

> He screams at you – he doesn't just shout 'Don't do it – he screams at you and like afterwards ... he started like being more friendly and saying 'I'm your friend'. I don't think that's right – you go crawling back to a child. (Girl)

The personal relationship with a teacher is an intellectual one, a sharing of ideas and a feeling that an individual adult is interested in what you are learning. This is distinct from the realization that teachers have individual personalities and idiosyncrasies. Indeed, pupils often express the kinds of forgiving psychological patronage made so apparent in the fiction they read:

> She is going through a bad patch. (Girl)

The real relationship that constitutes shared learning, so often an ideal, is hard to achieve and pupils miss it.

When one reads the pages of the *Times Educational Supplement* on memories by individuals of their best teachers one gains some insight into what stands out from the normal routines of schooling. The remembered teachers are not necessarily exceptions in their teaching; more flamboyant or more organized or more imaginative. They are the ones with whom the pupils have struck up an individual rapport. There is a sense of personal connection, of a relationship that is with an individual over time rather than with someone playing a role. Pupils long for special and sustained relationships with adults, and they find this difficult to achieve given the school system. Teachers are analysed as part of a clear hierarchy of control and power. They are very busy and have little time and, in a culture of fear, risk-taking like going on field trips is often avoided. The implacable demands of the paperwork and the sheer number of pupils makes relationships with everyone more demanding even in the classroom setting. When pupils are asked about what they feel they have most missed at school the most significant matter is personal acquaintance with individual teachers, getting to know them as people, sharing a joke and, most important of all, sharing personal experiences with one person (Cullingford 2000).

One of the reasons for longing for gentler and more sustained relationships is that pupils see schools as a particular version of society as a whole. They feel they have only an insignificant part to play. They see the important decisions being made for them and learn to accept the fact that schools are run for teachers who are expected to impose their will upon them. The way that pupils think about discipline in schools makes this clear. Pupils accept both their own intransigence and the imposition of rules. They want order but have learned to assume it necessary to be strict:

> If you didn't have rules in the school, everybody would be just running riot ... they may have some kids who turn out to be really naughty, so you'll need more rules. (Boy)

> The children would be bad if there wasn't rules ... and everybody would do just what they wanted to ... they'll have to be stricter because they've got a lot more people to keep an eye on. (Girl)

Discipline is a matter of authority and the enforcement of rules. This in itself demonstrates the sense of opposition, of the pupils opposed to the essential weight of the school. The fact that the pupils say they need rules, that it is by implication the result of their own natural naughtiness, only reinforces the essential estrangement.

In the routines of discipline and order and in the impersonal relationships that result, the desire for relationships is fulfilled naturally enough by the peer group. Because of the nature of schooling, friendship with peers becomes not an addition to other relationships but an alternative experience to that of the formal curriculum. The private worlds of conversation, of changing friendships and mutual interest develop beneath the surfaces of the routines. As the experience of school develops, the juxtaposition between the public and the private worlds becomes stronger. This estrangement begins early and the telling answer to the question 'What did you do in school today?' 'Nothing' denotes the attempt by pupils to keep their home life outside the school gates and vice versa. Nevertheless they take a great deal of private matter with them into school. The private friendships and knowledge acquired through their computers and the media link to their personal interests. After a time, as pupils generate more homework and rely more on their home ICT, school becomes a place not just to hand in work but to see their friends (Cuthell 2002).

Inclusion

There are two aspects to the concept of inclusion: experience and understanding. The experience of inclusion is being made to feel a central part of an organization, valued and respected. Understanding entails an appreciation of the feeling and thoughts of others, without prejudice. The latter, which is hardly mentioned in the primary school curriculum, is something children seek from early on and to which we will return in discussing their views on the curriculum. Inclusion as an experience is what children would like to feel is central to schools. They wish to feel safe:

> I just like our class. It's a nice place. It's a bit more safe than being outside. Plus it's much more warmer. It's a good place to work and it's more comfortable. Normally we can laugh. (Boy)

Every pupil has favourite places in the school and not just in the classroom. Sometimes a lobby or a library is the place they feel most secure.

Conversely, every pupil associates parts of the school with threat. More significantly, they all experience some sort of bullying. Being 'picked on' is what pupils dread. Sometimes it is the teacher who singles someone out but the playground is the usual locus of conflict. The distinction between rough play and bullying is a very fine one (Boulton 1997). The most distressing experiences are verbal rather than physical abuse. Friendship groups are formed and disbanded with merciless ease. Each child has the experience of being ostracized. The same competitiveness that permeates the experience of learning is inflicted on friendship. And just as those that stand out from the norms of the pace and standards of lessons are those who are most likely to be 'picked on' so are those who stand out physically or in terms of character. The same pressure towards conformity is felt in the suspicions held against the self-conscious or those with special educational needs. Young children have a natural sympathy for others (Dunn 1988) but the experience of school seems to diminish this. Instead, an intolerance of others and a prejudice against them is bred in the groupings and disciplines of school. The suspicions of the outsider and the vying for power creates an atmosphere in which some survive by trying to be invisible, keeping out of the way (Pye 1989).

Most of the bullying that takes place in school is hidden and ignored. Nor is the most heartfelt pain the result of a deliberate infliction of cruelty. It is the inadvertent remark, so easily made by the teacher, that hurts. The opportunities for being humiliated are many, from the inadequacies of performance in the classroom to being the last one chosen for a team in sport. The experiences of pupils and the way they report them when they are questioned substantiates the impression of schooling as generally unpleasant when it is not boring.

The curriculum and its purpose

For pupils the most important task is to keep up with the demands, to understand what they are and make sure that there is no trouble. There is rarely a sense of excitement or wonder. School is a matter of keeping up with routines, with teachers and with fellow pupils. The sense of boredom is often mentioned:

> Its so boring ... the practical is all right but the ... lessons 'really boring'. (Boy)

Keeping up with the routines set by the teacher is central, but so is the competition with other pupils. Every one of them knows their own place in the achievements of the class; who is clever and who isn't. There are two imperatives for the individuals in the class. One is not to hold up the general work by being slow. The other is not to stand out too much by being seen as clever. The aim is to get gold stars and effort marks but if anyone is outstanding then there is a sense of resentment. The middle way, doing just enough to keep up and doing it neatly to please the teacher, is what counts. This underlines the sense of routine in the school, of steady repetitive work, with testing that diminishes any sense of collaboration or really helping each other. The potential for disenfranchisement goes deep and when teachers recognize this, which is not common, they find it difficult to rectify because the whole system of education is geared to the curriculum, the teaching styles, the hierarchies of control and the routine disciplines of order.

If rules are so central, underpinned by the perceived alternative of chaos, the pedagogy of the school is similarly understood as imposed. There is an implacable sense that the secret of survival is to adapt not only to the rules of behaviour but to the disciplines of subjects. Pupils soon acknowledged that each subject is in a hierarchy of significance as demonstrated in its timing during the day or the week. Literacy hour, for instance, is not placed, like art, in the afternoon. The core curriculum dominates, increasingly. Pupils also acknowledge that the curriculum has to be delivered, that teachers have a set amount to get through. The sense of submission is pervasive, however many creative interludes individual teachers manage to conjure up.

The control of learning is dictated by the urgencies of the curriculum and the needs of tests. The subjects begin to be liked or avoided according to how well the pupils find themselves doing in them:

The thing I'm best at. Maths is the easiest for me. (Girl)

It's my favourite because I can do it very well. (Boy)

Achievement and pleasing outcomes, like praise, displace any sense of exploration. Indeed, the formal curriculum is accepted as something imposed, to which they have to adapt. It is not only the core curriculum that dominates but the assumption that these subjects are the only ones to develop the skills on which pupils will be judged.

From pupils' points of view school does not have to be boring or threatening. The agenda of targets and standards and tests, with which all have to comply, is at variance with the expressed wishes of the pupils. They are rarely asked what they think. When they are, they are so accustomed to compliance and to closed questions that they will at first give polite, non-committal answers. The most they will say is that school is alright:

It's alright. Well, I don't enjoy it but it's alright. (Boy)

When we compare the experience of school with the pupils' ideal curriculum we see that there is a great gap. The question is whether this contrast is a necessity or a natural one, or the result of sheer inadvertence and habit. The curriculum, as presented to pupils, is something in the hands of the teachers. The pupils have no sense of ownership of it. This is the great dilemma for teachers and, at the same time, acknowledging this is the secret of good teaching. The pupils may well be polite about teachers and what they are taught but beneath this surface we detect signs of displacement. The teaching and learning process is one that is seen as an accepted routine, carried out because it is part of the way that society operates. Pupils are aware of legislation and the framework of inspection. They are not sealed off from political awareness, and know the significance of league tables. They are even more aware of the importance of SATs and all the other tests that drive them. This places teachers in a difficult position. The system is concerned with measurement and with accountability. This necessarily leads to a concentration on what can be measured. Pupil's love of learning and curiosity is an open-ended one. They ask big questions of each other and of adults. They are full of speculation and the willingness to guess and make interpretations in their own idiosyncratic way (Harlen 1985). Their speculation and their internal logic is the heart of creativity.

The contrast between open and closed questions could not be greater. The open question is exploratory and fearless and demonstrates the instinctive capacity for critical and philosophical thinking. In contrast, the schools present an implacable face of closed questions; answers are either right or wrong. Pupils know that they have to learn what they are supposed to say or guess what the teacher wants to hear. This contrast between pupils' desire for certain kinds of experience and realities of a monolithic school system can be illustrated in two ways. The first is the way in which pupils understand the purpose of schools. Given the desire to learn on the one hand and the awareness of what they ought to say to please the teachers on the other, one should expect them to extol the virtues of learning, and the excitement of the accumulation of knowledge. Instead we find a strong awareness of the significance of testable skills, of subject disciplines ('What are you writing?' 'I'm doing English') and of outcomes ('That looks lovely; what do you hope to get from doing that?' 'I'll get a "C"'). Learning is secondary to being taught. The sense of submission comes about because they see the real purpose of schools as being to fit them for the future, to adapt to employment. The purpose of schooling is clear:

> Learning so that when you grow up you'll learn how to find a job and add things up that are quite hard. It's for exams. (Girl)

> If I didn't go to school I'd know nothing and wouldn't be able to get a job or nothing. It's really for people to learn things you didn't know before and when you are older you'll have so many GCSEs you can get what you want. (Boy)

Given all that pupils hear about the nature of schooling, the importance of a skilled workforce, the competition for university places and the significance of examinations, let alone the imperative to survive in the struggle against others, such interpretations are not surprising. They are reinforced by the ways in which pupils see schools operate, with their management systems, the external controls and the carefully structured literacy and numeracy hours. Such a set of assumptions about schooling is not necessarily what teachers would wish to endorse. The most dedicated and the most confident have a different agenda but they know they are placed in this context of systems and they need to be aware of just how deeply their own pupils are affected. Within the classroom there will be moments of joy, of shared excitement, of bursts of activity but in the back of the pupils' minds remains the awareness that these are exceptional and not the norm.

Pupils' needs and the realities of school

Pupils take schools for granted up to a point. They have little choice. Given the pressures on pupils, the 'drop-out' rates or failures are surprisingly small. For schools would not be as they are if they were designed around pupils' needs. Given the perceived demands of the state and the apparatus of policy, schools have three contradictory aims: to enhance autonomous academic excellence; to ensure the mentoring of worthy, obedient and skilled citizens and to develop the personal emotions, self-expression and wellbeing of the individual (Egan 1997). Pupils have to live through this contradiction every day.

If the pupils' viewpoints were listened to, schools and the curriculum would not be the same. Pupils come to school with the instinctive desire to learn and explore all the big questions of life, all centred around the question of who we are and why. Their early curiosity is not just about the physical world but about people. The need for categorization is the need for understanding. The curriculum, for them, would be centred on the fundamental open questions as a starting point for unlimited and demanding exploration in which facts would accumulate in the service of understanding rather then getting the better for it. The idea of subject disciplines would be far less serious and the demand to go as far as possible in seeking out knowledge would be encouraged. The notion of society (what later is the tokenism of citizenship) would be central: how it operates and why. This would necessarily make the school itself come under scrutiny.

The desire to express their critical thinking skills would inevitably lead to the extension of philosophy and all the means by which people try to understand the world: art, literature, music and all the other expressions of the cultural and social world. The real excitement of stories and of literature generally – stories as the narrative basis of learning – would give such a purpose to the curriculum that the explorations of the physical world as well as the cultural would subsume the need to undergo the mechanical skills of reading and writing because they would not be detached from their *raison d'être*.

Such an expression of interest in a moral, meaningful world where all is related to the adult experience without inhibiting the freedom of energy would itself suggest a different way of learning, with the emphasis on the individual pupil's explorations of interest rather than on their being taught. Such an alternative can only be hinted at here but all the ideas, and more, derive from the pupils. They have a clear point of view but this is denied them. They have an urgency to understand but this is displaced. They long to be listened to but their voices remain unheard. The difference between the needs of pupils and what happens to them could not be greater. The result is that they learn many things we would not want them to – insecurity, lack of self-belief, loss of motivation, indifference, selfishness and cynicism. We are, however, so accustomed to the way the system operates that this finding appears extreme.

In one sense any such summary must be extreme. However, it is mitigated by two factors. One is the resilience of the pupils. The system might be inflexible but the pupils are not; the majority find their way through, damaged but not distraught. The other factor is the teachers. Teachers continue to do their best despite what is demanded of them. They are often brilliant as well as courageous in the way that they go on teaching the pupils. The fact that pupils would like things to be different is not to blame the teachers. It is, however, important for teachers to remember the real point of view of their pupils, not just the accumulation of evidence summarized so briefly here, but the individuals in their class. The very fact of listening and acknowledging their learning, rather than their resentment at being taught, will have a transforming influence.

6 Learning to Love Learning? – What the Pupils Think

Yolande Muschamp and Kate Bullock

Introduction

In this chapter we use research evidence from our classroom study of year 6 pupils as they complete key stage two (KS2) and move through year 7 to examine the experiences of children who have received their primary education since the introduction of the National Curriculum and national assessment. This cohort of pupils began primary school when the first National Curriculum was in its infancy and left as yet another initiative, the National Primary Strategy, was introduced. As a framework for our analysis we return to the research evidence of *Look Before You Leap* (Pollard 1994) to identify how, within the national policies for primary education, learning was discussed in 1993, and how this rhetoric has shaped the policies of today. We find during this period that the concept of learning has been dramatically redefined and that one concern of 1993 relating to the curriculum, that of 'match', although equally transformed, has remained central to the policies of today. We build on the findings of the PACE project of the 1990s, which documented the child's experience in terms of competence and performance (Pollard and Triggs 2000) and the ORACLE studies of pupils' experiences (Galton *et al.* 1980, 1999) and examine the call for 'bespoke' support within the Primary National Strategy (PNS) (DfES 2003b), which places the individual child at the centre of this new focus on learning. This repositioning provides the framework for this chapter as we examine the pupils' understanding of the learning process, their views on the challenges they face, and the extent to which an emphasis on the individual has supported their independence.

Even with the benefit of hindsight it is difficult to explain why discussion of primary pedagogy has moved from the process of teaching to the process of learning. In 1994 the problems facing KS2 teachers in relation to their pupils' learning were identified and conceptualized in terms of their responsibilities as teachers to match task to pupil capability, to cover the whole curriculum and to engage in whole-school planning. Although these problems still preoccupy teachers, they no longer receive the attention in research studies or policy debates that they did then. The need to provide differentiated activities within KS2 to meet (or match) pupils' prior achievement became embedded in planning the curriculum. The introduction of the National Literacy Strategy, which required teachers to divide their classes into five ability groups in an attempt to reduce the need for individual support, consolidated this practice. Primary policy continues to prescribe teacher activity, yet, ironically, it is the term learning alone that has become the focus of policy rhetoric.

One concept from 1994, that of 'match', has, however, developed to encompass both teaching and learning. The pedagogic imperatives implied in this concept of differentiated activities tailored to meet the needs of individual children have continued and are now to be found in the call for challenge. Pupils are believed to be challenged when they learn independently and take responsibility for their own learning. There is, however, a recognition that independent learning is primarily contingent on clear guidance and support from teachers to underpin student activities (Bullock *et al.* 2002). It is the equilibrium when moving from support to challenge that is the crucial factor in effective learning (Vygotsky 1962; Wood 1988; Claxton 1999). Within this scenario, an understanding of how children themselves experience the balance between support and challenge is important. We begin with an analysis of the ways in which pupils describe the learning process, including their views of themselves as learners and their perceptions of the support they receive, and then explore their views of challenge and enjoyment within their learning. The children's views provide a valuable insight into the reality of 'learning to love learning' in the primary school.

Learning to learn

Campbell, in Chapter 2, shows how the difficulties of ensuring curriculum coverage, identified by research into the implementation of the National Curriculum and discussed in *Look Before You Leap* (Campbell and Emery 1994; see also Muschamp *et al.* 1992; Gipps 1992), has given way to concerns relating to breadth and balance (Pollard and Triggs 2000). The swing of government policy towards a 10-subject curriculum and back to a focus on three core subjects has recently begun to return once more to an emphasis on curriculum breadth. The introduction of the national strategies for numeracy and literacy have, however, reinforced the dominance of the core subjects. Within the PNS, 'learning to learn' has emerged as the curriculum imperative of the 'back to basics' in the National Literacy and Numeracy strategies with the claim that enjoyment in what they do will ensure that children 'learn to love learning' (DfES 2003b). Implicit in the PNS is a view that this focus on the individual will ensure that children will learn about learning in order to sustain the possibility of lifelong learning.

Since 1994, learning has been reconceptualized. The theoretical accounts remain the same (dominated by Vygotsky and Bruner) but there is now a much greater emphasis on the promotion of such programmes as thinking skills, learning styles and brain gyms (Smith 1998; MacGilchrist and Buttress 2005). Whereas much of the content of these programmes is at the level of study skills, strategies for memorizing and concerns for learning environments (for example, the availability of drinking water) some aspects of the programmes represent fundamental changes in the ways in which teachers discuss learning (Claxton 1999; Coffield *et al.* 2004; Bullock and Muschamp 2006). At worst some of these programmes have become faddish; most have encouraged teachers to reflect on their current practice and at best they have led to creative ways in which to engage children in learning. Our classroom research allows us to examine how pupils believe they have fared under this changing view of learning. Have they 'learned to learn' during KS2 and have they 'learned to love learning'?

Our study was based on semi-structured interviews with 24 pupils before and after their transition from primary to secondary schools in 2003. A first set of interviews was carried out with year 6 pupils in four different primary schools within the same local education authority (LEA). Six pupils in each school were interviewed individually. One boy and one girl were selected by the class teachers from three levels of achievement within the recent national tests (SATs) for mathematics, English and science. Twenty of the pupils were interviewed again at the end of their first term in year 7 when they had progressed to two secondary schools. Each interview lasted approximately 30–40 minutes and was audiotaped and transcribed. The data from the pupil interviews were complemented by field notes taken during and after visits to the schools, by notes from discussions with the class teachers and the senior manager of each school and by discussions with local education authority advisers to the schools.

We were mindful in our analysis of the pupil surveys from the much larger PACE project of the 1990s (Pollard *et al.* 2000). We present our data here and then show below how our pupils of the following decade have had very similar experiences, although there is evidence that they are developing a slightly different account of learning. Most of the pupils understood the instructional discourse of the primary classroom as an intervention where they were told what to do and how to do it. Their accounts are dominated by description of the day-to-day organization and activity of the classroom, illustrated by the accounts of Jamie and Emma:

> Mostly the teacher will go over what they want you to do. Like if there are things you haven't learnt before they will go over that and then they'll ask you to do a piece of work in a workbook in that subject. Usually you're asked questions and sometimes you have to

> copy a piece of work, a passage from a book and let's say it's in the first person and you have to edit it so that it's in the third person. So that's the sort of thing we're doing at the moment. (Jamie)

> Well we've got these books. I can't remember what they're called, but we work with them and at the beginning of the lesson our teacher gives out equipment and maths things and we've got a whiteboard, and then he writes a bit about what we're meant to do in the book and then we do the work in the book. But sometimes we have investigations and he writes the investigation on the board and then we have to do it, find out and write what we've found out and like a conclusion. (Emma)

These two accounts were typical of the acceptance that children expressed of the daily routines. However, not all the children were so accepting and some expressed their frustrations, like the three children here:

> I had this teacher and she's the one that explained it and then said 'Here we go, do it, you've got a deadline'. And she was a proper bossy boots. I don't want to mention her name ... the teacher will often say 'I'm going to put some sums on the board and you've got exactly half an hour to do them.' It makes me kind of think 'Oh no, I don't really have a choice'. (Ben)

> Well I like some English, like the explanations texts and the instruction texts, but I don't like stories that much because I find it hard. If they set a title, I find it hard to imagine quite quickly. I have to be able to set my own title, otherwise I find it hard. (Faye)

> Well sometimes you've got to work out how you do it and how you did the experiment, but you don't really know why you did it. You just do it. (Sophie)

It is clear that many children did not believe that they had control over their own learning in terms of choice of the activities within the core subjects and only a limited choice in the methods that they used in their work. Despite this, the children's responses suggested that they recognized that they had to take responsibility for their own learning and that they were all able to describe the strategies that they could use. They recognized who it was that supported their learning in school and at home and many had clear views on how effective this support was:

> Most of the time I think you do what the teacher tells you. We don't really have much choice. The teacher tells us what we have to do. (Jamie)

> I think it depends on how the teacher teaches you, to see how strict or kind or nice they are or if they're pleased with your work. Then you can actually produce more nice work and they'll be quite kind about it. (Emily)

> My mum usually reads through my stories ... Sometimes I go on the computer and that's quite good. That's how I get all my spellings right. (Ben)

> I ask the person sitting next to me ... we have groups depending on how good you are at learning ... Yes I tend to ask the person next to me. (Alex)

> Sometimes it gets really boring because you have to do like ... and it's really hard because everyone is waiting for the answer and the teacher is asking and you've got the answer but you don't know if it's right or wrong. So the people who aren't confident just wait and it's scary. Because if you say the wrong answer some boys tease you and when they get the wrong answer we don't tease them. (Hayley)

It seems that some of the responsibility felt by the pupils is the responsibility to be right (see also Chapter 5). While it is acceptable to be wrong talking to Mum or a friend, offering a wrong answer in front of the whole class is, for most, intolerable.

We found the children varied in the extent to which they could explain the learning strategies they used. We found some children who had a sophisticated understanding of their learning, which suggested that they had reflected on what was involved. A few had grasped the transferability of knowledge and skills:

> You've got to focus on stuff the teacher is saying, not chatting and mucking about with your friends and just persevere if you can't do anything. Just try. (Hayley)

> Well our teacher has told us to ask him when we get stuck straightway so you don't just sit there and start getting worried about not knowing what you're doing.
> *Are there any things you do other than ask the teacher?*
> Well sometimes you can ask the person next to you. Sometimes you sit down, read the question again and see if it makes it any clearer. (Emma)

I think they have to listen and think for themselves and think out-side the question. So if you like just read the question and think outside it kind of and realise what you could use from other things that you've learnt to answer the question and stuff. (Faye)

I don't know. I like working it out in my head but sometimes I like using a calculator because it makes it easier. (Abbie)

Challenge

The Primary Strategy document states that in the best primary schools children are 'engaged in learning that develops and stretches them and excites their imagination' and 'every child is supported and challenged' (DfES 2003b: 9). We continued our analysis of children's understanding of the learning process by examining the extent to which children feel supported and believe that they are challenged. Identifying support was relatively straightforward in our discussions with the children. Many of the classroom activities that the children described gave accounts of the ways in which they were supported by the teacher. Asking and waiting for support was a routine aspect of class-room life as in the description by Jack:

> In some tasks we worked in partners but some we had to do individually.
> *Anybody else help you?*
> Not really. If you're stuck you'd go up and ask Mr. D**.
> *How do you know it's a good piece of work?*
> We get a class point from Mr. D**. He marks them and probably I'd be impressed with my work.
> *You yourself?*
> Yes. Before he marked it.
> *So you knew something about it was good. What makes it good?*
> The standard, punctuation. Good standard of whatever, just like writing.
> *How do you know how to improve your work?*
> I don't know. Just try harder, just kind of whatever – ask the teacher and he'll show you how to make it better.

Assessing the children's perception of challenge however is more problematic. In our earlier discussion we suggested that one aspect of challenge is the extent to which activities 'match' the level of achievement of each child. In its simplest form the children expressed an understanding of 'match' by their use of terms such as 'hard' and 'easy' as in Emily's comment below.

When they didn't use these terms, it was clear that they understood the level of difficulty by their references to the time taken to complete the task, as in Emma's comments, and the need for support as described by Hayley and Josh. Hayley reminds us that children do not necessarily have the same access to support while Josh has clearly identified a range of supporting networks to draw on:

> Well, arithmetic is like easy, but sometimes when we do stuff that we just start or we haven't really focused on a lot yet, I sometimes find that hard unless I get it straightaway. (Emily)

> Normally you'd feel pleased with it. You've read it and if you've done it in the time limit and you've written what you've been taught to do, like figurative language and things like that. Then you know that you've written that and it sounds good. (Emma)

> I ask my mum, but sometimes she don't know the answers and I get really stuck and if I take it back to school I forget it and I feel I'm going to get really told off, but sometimes my mum couldn't help me. She doesn't do the work for me. She says you have to work out some parts because I'm not at school and you have to work it out. (Hayley)

> I look in books, I ask my friends if they know or I ask the teacher or if it's the end of the day I ask my mum and dad at home. (Josh)

Other children attempted to explain what made work more difficult with references to the complexity and length of tasks. Josh is describing his expectation of maths at secondary school:

> Similar things, just more complex.
> *And maths?*
> Probably the same with maths as well, but the teacher says that as we're getting older, when they tell you the answer you have to find out how it works.
> *So you'll be doing more for yourself.*
> Yes, but here it's basically 'You've got to find out what the answer is.'
> *And what will it be like there?*
> It will be more reversing the answer to find out how you do it.

Enjoyment

It is commendable that in the PNS enjoyment has been identified as an essential component of the curriculum. Most of the children we talked with identified areas of schooling that they enjoyed. Only one boy stated categorically that there were no subjects or activities that he enjoyed. The imperative to teach children to love learning resonates with earlier calls to ensure that the primary years were the foundation for lifelong learning. No explanation is offered of how to ensure children learn to love learning. The suggestion that this can be brought about through support and challenge was investigated further as we analysed the extent to which children actually enjoyed challenge. We found that children associated enjoyment with subjects that they found easy as in the comments made by Faye, Ben and Ross:

> Well I like some English, like the explanations texts and the instruction texts, but I don't like stories that much because I find it hard. If they set a title I find it hard to imagine quite quickly. I have to be able to set my own title, otherwise I find it hard. (Faye)

> I have to say I've always liked science and English. English because I just find it so easy and story writing is my favourite. Science I have to say I like because I like doing experiments and recording down my results. But maths, I don't entirely like it that much. I am good at it but not as good as I could be and I don't like it all that much anyway. (Ben)

> Well I like some subjects like science and PSHE, but I don't like maths as much because I think I struggle with that more and I like literacy. I especially like story writing. (Ross)

Jamie sums up the relationship clearly when he says:

> I don't want to be too full of myself but I think I'm OK at it, quite good at it. If you're good at something you like it more.

Conclusion

In returning to our original question 'have children learned to learn by the end of KS2?' we are able to conclude that the 24 children in our study had many insights into the learning process. They were able to identify and evaluate those people who supported their learning, had a view of the level of the activities and a range of strategies (beyond the scope of this chapter – see Bullock and Muschamp 2006) to support their learning. The dependency on the teacher was, however, quite striking and perhaps problematic at the end of a period of schooling that would be followed by a complete change of procedures and practices when they moved on to secondary school. The children clearly had learned to identify themselves as responsible for their learning and yet rarely reported having any control or choice over activities. This echoes the findings of Pollard and Triggs (2000: 283) in the PACE project of the 1990s where two thirds of the pupils reported that there 'was "not much" or "no" choice of curriculum activity'. It does appear that the failure, identified by Pollard and Triggs (2000), to excite pupils with a broad and balanced curriculum is still evident in pupils' attitudes to their work. The pupils looked forward to the possibility of authentic experiences in science laboratories, art studies and drama halls that appeared to be on offer in the secondary school.

Hard work was uniformly reported as worrying and unpleasant. Our pupils, again like those in the PACE findings, were 'increasingly aware of the weight of subject content and the pressure to perform' (Pollard and Triggs 2000: 283). In contrast, however, our children did enjoy the subjects in which they performed well, unlike the pupils in the PACE project who were observed often to appear 'in flight from an experience of learning that they found unsatisfying, un-motivating and uncomfortable' (Pollard and Triggs 2000: 288). Our case study children as a whole had developed the belief that effort was the main contributor to success and, like the PACE pupils, associated success with enjoyment. This suggests that they would fit Dweck's (1999) category of master orientation associated with the belief that intelligence is malleable and thereby helping them to develop the resilience they need for effective learning (Claxton 1999). The enjoyment in achievement in our findings suggests that enjoyment and excellence may in fact be appropriate aims for the primary years.

The warnings of a primary education dominated by a performance cul-ture expressed elsewhere in this book (see Chapters 2, 3, 13 and 15) must, however, be taken seriously. If the achievement of pupils at the end of KS2 continues to be represented by norm-referenced tests there will always be a large proportion of children who do not achieve the highest levels and who therefore may not enjoy their schooling. The pupils can show us an alter-native primary strategy. They also had clear views on their hopes for sec-ondary school as they anticipated enjoyment of the 'grown up' real life activities. They looked forward to taking greater responsibility for their work. Kalechstein and Nowicki (1987) demonstrate that children who believe that they are in control of what occurs in their life are more likely to select chal-lenging tasks. The challenge for schools is to match the responsibility, that pupils believe they have, with a degree of control or autonomy for them. For this group of schools a good foundation already exists in that the pupils showed that they believed achievement was the result of their own effort. They attributed their achievement to an internal cause over which they could exercise control (Weiner 1986; discussed in Pollard and Triggs 2000). Perhaps the challenge for the next 10 years is now to ensure that it is the teaching and learning that results in enjoyment rather than the achievement in national tests.

7　New Technologies and 'New Teaching': A Process of Evolution?

Gary Beauchamp

> ICT in education can motivate all pupils, particularly the disaffected. But the potential of ICT is much greater than this. It can transform the way that education is delivered and open the way to a new pedagogy.
>
> (DfES 2001c: 23)

In recent years primary teachers have been working in an environment of increased government intervention that has moved beyond telling teachers *what* to teach to telling them *how* to teach it (see Chapters 1 and 3). The impact on classroom pedagogy in England has been significant, particularly in the areas of literacy and numeracy. Although influential, such moves must nevertheless be seen in the larger context of an evolutionary process in classroom teaching – even though some may see the current trends as looking more to the past, than the future – in which there are many other potential influences on teachers' pedagogy, including:

- teachers' personality;
- teachers' experience;
- teachers' knowledge;
- ethos of their school;
- age and ability of their children;
- resources available to teachers. (Kennewell 2004)

Advances in both the availability and capability of new technologies, specifically in the area of information and communications technology (ICT), have ensured that it is becoming an influential resource for both pupils and teachers. Research evidence suggests that ICT can have an impact on pupil learning outcomes (BECTA 2001, 2002; Cox and Abbott 2004) – a fact not lost on governments or their agencies – as well as improving motivation (BECTA 2003). Indeed, the literature on the motivational role of ICT is 'significant'

(McFarlane and Sakellariou 2002) and most pupils react favourably to the use of computers in the classroom (Cox 1997).

Before this can have any impact on the classroom, however, teachers must incorporate the use of ICT into their pedagogy – summarized here as 'any conscious activity by one person designed to enhance learning in another' (Watkins and Mortimer 1999: 3) – and schools must be equipped with appropriate resources. As investment in such resources increases, driven by much government rhetoric about the potential to improve pupils' learning (DfES 2003c), increased pressure is exerted on schools to 'deliver' results. There seems to be an inherent assumption in government initiatives that teachers will welcome such initiatives provided they are given sufficient resources but it is important to remember that 'computers, of themselves, are not transforming' (Somekh and Davies 1991: 153). Neither are they 'a medical cure to be prescribed or a mediating agent to change teachers; they are tools to support learning and learners' (Abbott 2001: 119). As with any tool, it takes time to learn how to use ICT to good effect and some will use it better than others. As 'microcomputers' have been a feature of primary schools since 1982 it might be assumed that some progress has been made, yet there is evidence that many teachers still regard ICT as 'new' and 'rapidly changing' (Loveless 2003). There are even some suggestions that ICT remains a 'marginal force' in primary school education (Robertson 2002) and that 'educational computing has yet to find its own voice' (Watson 2001: 252). Loveless (2003: 315) takes this further and contends that amongst teachers there is still 'a lack of consensus and understanding of the conceptual framework for ICT in education'. Research evidence, summarized in a report to the DfES by Cox and Webb (2004: 3), suggests that:

> the teacher's own pedagogical beliefs and values play an important part in shaping technology-mediated learning opportunities. It is not yet clear from the research literature whether this results in technology being used as a 'servant' to reinforce existing teaching approaches, or as a 'partner' to change the way teachers and pupils interact with each other and with the tasks. Teachers need extensive knowledge of ICT to be able to select the most appropriate resources. They also need to understand how to incorporate the use of ICT into their lessons; they may need to develop new pedagogies to achieve this.

These findings provide the focus for this chapter, which will concentrate on the potential of ICT, highlighted by the DfES (2001c), in their White Paper *Schools Achieving Success* quoted at the start of this chapter, to both transform teachers' existing practice and develop new pedagogy. The discussion will explore whether teachers will need to develop a single ICT pedagogy, whether they can incorporate ICT into their existing pedagogy (either to consolidate or improve the learning opportunities they provide for pupils) or whether the varied curriculum of the primary school will generate a similar variety of new pedagogies.

Pedagogy or skills: where do we begin?

From the outset it is acknowledged that teachers might find themselves in a 'Catch 22' situation where they have to resolve two questions:

> 1) How can you decide how to use new technology if you have no experience of what it can do?
>
> 2) How can you gain experience of what new technology can do if you do not know how to use it?
>
> (Dawes 2001: 68)

It is thus important that teachers develop their confidence and basic skills in using ICT resources (Goodison 2002) as this is a prerequisite for a greater synergy of ICT with pedagogy (Beauchamp 2004). In doing so, they will need full access to computers (Dawes 2001) both in school and at home (Williams *et al.* 2000). If this is not provided it is hard to see how teachers can avoid looking for features of the technology that can be assimilated into their existing pedagogy (Eraut 1991), rather than allowing the capabilities of the technology to lead them to new approaches. In other words, teachers will not develop a new teaching style, but rather they will perpetuate their old style in a new way. It is also imperative, however, that debate is not limited by the ultimately surmountable practicalities of providing opportunities for, and funding of, the necessary training and resources to enable teachers to resolve the above dilemma.

A new pedagogy: a risk worth taking?

In every area of the curriculum, any fundamental change in pedagogy will involve risks on the part of teachers and their schools. Harris (2002) reports on examples of schools where these risks have been taken in developing 'innovative pedagogical practices' using ICT (such as all-day access to their own PC for every pupil; writing for a purpose: email between pupils and employees at a local factory; using a database to monitor and set targets; schools working collaboratively on a Web site to solve crosscurricular problems and challenges) but stresses the importance of a school ethos that is 'one of collaboration and mutual support' (p. 458). Ideally this would be situated in, or even pre-empted by, a political climate where 'initiative is applauded within a no-blame culture' (Hammersley-Fletcher *et al.* 2004: 3). Even within such a context there are demands on teachers, both personally and professionally. Not only are they being asked to develop technical skills in ICT but they may also need to 'accept changes in their role and in the interactions they [have] with students and they also [have] to support children as their roles [change] too' (Harris 2002: 457).

This situation is complicated by the fact that much previous staff development has focused on either technical skills or background knowledge of ICT rather than its pedagogic use (McCarney 2004). Nevertheless, the potential for ICT to allow the teacher's role to change to coach, observer and facilitator arises as they transfer greater responsibility for learning to their pupils (Selinger 2001; Smeets and Mooij 2001; Jedeskog and Nissen 2004). Thus, teachers may need to move away from the model which puts themselves as a central feature of the classroom, to one where the ICT is the central focus with teachers *enabling* access to, and facilitating relevant skills for, its use. In fact, the teacher becomes one of the tools and resources available to the pupils in the school context. There is evidence that some teachers are not confident that their pupils have the ability to be responsible for their own work and learning (Jedeskog and Nissen 2004), but there is considerable evidence that moving towards pedagogies which allow full interaction, collective reflection and the development of consensual knowledge may help improve learning and attainment.

Unfortunately, in the current climate the pressure of imposed 'top-down' pedagogic guidance is encouraging teachers to concentrate on the more superficial features of interactive teaching, such as pace and structure, at the expense of the deeper aspects of pedagogy (Tanner *et al.* 2005). The same may also be true of the imposition of new technology but at least the availability of greater ICT resources allows teachers the opportunity to reassert their professionalism. It is in orchestrating the 'affordances and constraints' (Kennewell 2001) of ICT in the classroom that teachers can develop opportunities for, and the ability of, children to interact with appropriate resources in new learning situations and hence develop new pedagogies.

If new pedagogical reasoning does not allow pupils to develop more independence in learning it is unlikely that teachers will take advantage of the capacities of ICT to deliver such opportunities. Equally, if their approach to classroom management centres on the dominant teacher *control* model, it is again unlikely that the ICT will be used to its full potential in promoting independent learning (Goodison 2002). This is not to say that teachers will lose control in the classroom but rather that they will 'learn to interrelate creatively with computers in educational events. The machine becomes an expression of human endeavour and growth; its opportunities are exploited, it is not in control' (Somekh and Davies 1991: 154). If this approach is also inculcated into children's attitudes to learning, all those in the classroom will be working with a common understanding of the role, purpose and owner-ship of ICT.

At present, Watson (2001) asserts that teachers only use ICT when it resonates with their pedagogic or subject philosophy and those teachers who do not use ICT may take this approach for sound professional reasons. This is presented as an argument against ICT use but it could also lead to greater ICT use if teachers were to change their pedagogic or subject philosophy in favour of new technologies. However, changing teachers' philosophy of education, particularly without the impetus provided by legislation, can be a long and complicated process. This situation, together with the proposition that 'the development of new pedagogies need nurturing and encouragement' (Law *et al.* 2002: 425) would seem to suggest that significant moves to ICT-based pedagogy are only going to happen in the longer term in a supportive culture – both within schools and from governments. Although it could be con-tended that externally enforced changes in practice, such as those associated with the National Literacy Strategy (NLS) and National Numeracy Strategy (NNS), can bring about change in attitudes in a shorter period of time (for example, if the enforced strategies can appear to bring about increased achievement), the evidence above suggests that such attitudes may be driven by pragmatism rather than philosophy.

Teachers are increasingly faced with a more immediate dilemma as schools and governments invest in ICT resources: should ICT be a *tool* to use in current practice (which may allow things to be done better, quicker and save time – aren't most primary teachers at this stage?) or should it provide the *foundation* for a new pedagogy? To answer this question, we need to examine briefly the features of ICT that make it a suitable medium to justify such a potentially radical change in practice for a significant number of tea-chers – as it should be remembered that some may already have made this transition and, perhaps, that some never will!

ICT and 'interactivity'

Loveless (2002: 11) identifies five features of ICT which 'make it distinctive from other media, tools and resources':

- interactivity – see below;
- provisionality – ability to make changes, try out alternatives and keep a 'trace' of the development of ideas;
- capacity – allows access to huge amounts of information in many forms;

- range – access to huge amounts of information in many forms;
- speed – in storing, changing and displaying information as well as calculating, spell checking, graphing and so on.

The first of these is the feature of ICT that has perhaps been advocated most widely and evidence from the research literature suggests that 'the use of ICT has a limited impact on teaching and learning where teachers fail to appreciate that interactivity requires a new approach to pedagogy, lesson planning and the curriculum' (Cox and Webb 2004: 3–4). Unfortunately, there appears to be neither consensus on the precise meaning of the word 'interactivity' in primary ICT teaching and learning, nor consistency in its usage. This is particularly worrying given the prominent place of 'interactive whole class teaching', and even 'interactive teaching programmes' (http://www.standards.dfes.gov.uk/primary/publications/mathematics/itps/) in the English National Literacy and Numeracy Strategies. F. Smith *et al.* (2004: 409) examine this process and conclude that 'teachers have no clear concept of what interactive whole class teaching is, or shared vocabulary to discuss it'. This is supported by the views of Moyles *et al.* (2003) who 'dig deeper' into possible meanings of interactivity but conclude that there is no clear definition of what constitutes interactive learning in the primary schools (see also Chapter 3). Burns and Myhill (2004: 47) support this assertion and as a consequence claim that the 'current overuse' of the term 'interactive' is 'perhaps unhelpful'. They further contend that classroom interaction 'is largely a case of pupils participating on request' with little constructive meaning making and 'rather too many classroom discourses where teachers, as experts, control the knowledge in an inflexible authoritative manner'.

If this is the case, there is a danger that learners are not being allowed to engage with the learning process at a 'deeper', cognitive level. Inherent in any interactive teaching is the ability of the learner to understand, and even take control of, the learning process. If teachers are restricting interactivity to a 'traditional' triadic structure of initiation, response and feedback (Tharp and Gallimore 1988) they are not allowing pupils opportunities to co-construct knowledge and understanding by contributing ideas and exploring them with both teachers and their peers (see also Chapter 8). This latter approach is likely to be facilitated in a classroom where pupils have a high degree of control over learning, including the use of ICT. There are, however, factors that may prevent such a shared pedagogy developing. In terms of ICT, the availability of technology that is physically capable of performing the required tasks is of paramount importance as this could affect the speed, capability and collaborative nature of interaction (Tanner *et al.* 2005).

The nature of ICT resources

Could it be, therefore, that features of the ICT resources available are by their very nature limiting teachers' ability to teach 'interactively'? In primary schools, most recent investment, led by government initiatives, has moved beyond individual classroom personal computers (PCs) to other resources, including computer suites, tablet PCs, pocket PCs and increasingly the interactive whiteboard (IWB). However, by their very nature all these resources need a tactile act to invoke a response (which may or may not involve cognitive engagement): personal computers generally have a keyboard to input data, whereas interactive whiteboards and pocket PCs are normally accessed or controlled with a pen on the screen, or again via a keyboard. Although ICT can provide a degree of 'interactivity' by giving 'immediate and dynamic feedback and response to decisions made by the user' (Loveless 2002: 11), a potential problem with developing an effective ICT pedagogy is the inability of a computer, compared to the teacher, to assess whether this response has involved any cognitive effort or engagement – an essential part of the learning process.

In addition, although computers are often claimed by manufacturers to be intuitive, they are in reality restricted to preprogrammed responses. Even software that claims to be predictive has a limited effect in educational use as children are rarely predictable! Nevertheless, computers are also able to provide such responses much quicker than teachers and do not get bored in having to do so endlessly. The computer itself allows teachers to combine in one place a variety of otherwise disparate resources – video, flash movies, text, audio files, Web sites, scanned images (such as pages from a big book), images from peripheral devices (such as electronic microscopes) and conventional curriculum resources – to demonstrate a given point. This can be done with access to stored materials or in real time and in a variety of formats to meet either particular learning styles or special educational needs.

This capacity does mean that teachers can plan and provide lessons that move away from a linear transmission model of lesson construction. The ability to switch between different programmes and the use of hyperlinked text and images, allows lessons to explore a variety of tangents, whilst easily returning to the central learning outcome. This may allow teachers to develop a significantly different pedagogy but to achieve it they will have to invest significant time in software preparation to engage the pupils at an appropriate cognitive level and enable the technology to respond to them in a way that furthers their learning.

The interactive whiteboard

The interactive whiteboard (IWB) is perhaps the best resource for teachers to demonstrate this range of capacities. It is a large, touch-sensitive board, which is connected to a digital projector and a computer. The projector displays the image from the computer screen on the board – which can come in a variety of sizes. The computer can then be controlled by touching the board, either directly or with a special pen. There is evidence that primary school children are very enthusiastic about the versatility, multimedia capabilities, fun and enjoyment afforded by the use of IWBs (Hall and Higgins 2005). The British Educational Communications and Technology Agency (BECTA 2003) summarized the main research findings and have identified the following benefits for pupils:

- Increased motivation
- Greater opportunity for pupils to participate and collaborate
- Pupils are able to cope with more complex concepts as a result of clearer, more efficient and more dynamic presentations
- Increased capacity to cater for different learning styles
- Enables pupils to be more creative when making presentations to fellow pupils
- Pupils do not have to use a keyboard to engage with the technology, increasing access to younger children and pupils with disabilities.

Evidence suggests that the IWB can present a 'fluid medium through which teachers can deliver not just ideas, but also challenges, opportunities and open-ended frameworks for pupils to develop metacognition' (Beauchamp and Parkinson 2005: 102–3) and influence teachers' pedagogy (Kennewell and Beauchamp 2003). Although there is currently a paucity of evidence about the actual impact of the interactive whiteboard on attainment (Smith *et al.* 2005), the capacity of ICT in general and the IWB in particular, to help the teacher illustrate and 'transform' (Shulman 1987) concepts (to re-present ideas in a variety of all the different forms) is very powerful. Such an approach is beneficial in initiating discussion and in facilitating teacher-pupil interaction. This is particularly so if applied in early years settings where Siraj-Blatchford *et al.* (2002: 10–11) have shown that:

> adult-child interactions that involve some element of 'sustained shared thinking' or what Bruner has termed 'joint involvement episodes' may be especially valuable in terms of children's learning ... When it does occur, it has been shown to extend children's thinking. Our investigations of adult-child interaction have led us to view that

periods of 'sustained shared thinking' are a necessary pre-requisite for the most effective early years settings.

Opportunities for 'sustained shared thinking' may be developed as children progress through the primary school where they can be provided with opportunities to use ICT to initiate, explain and discuss their own ideas. Such a relatively simple change in pedagogy can have quite a profound impact on pupils' self-confidence and their perception of themselves as learners. It could also be argued that such a move to encouraging children to articulate their methodology, reasoning or understanding within a structured framework provided by work on ICT resources, especially the IWB, can also be helpful to teachers in assessing whether learning objectives have been met or how misconceptions may have arisen – as well as giving pupils the opportunity to have greater responsibility for their own learning and that of others.

The interactive whiteboard is very efficient at sharing ideas with larger groups of children but its main drawback is that its size and the need to stay aligned with its projector ensure that it can only be used in a fixed position in the classroom. For ICT to have a further impact on teacher pedagogy it needs to be available to individuals and small groups in different settings and locations.

Wireless mobility

Recent advances in the use of wireless technology have the potential to make a significant impact on pedagogy. Central government commitment to the 'e-confident school', which will combine the increasing use of wireless networking and a profile shift in computer provision in favour of more mobile 'kit' (DfES 2003c), will ensure that teachers face new challenges but also provides many new opportunities. This move away from static computers attached with cables and the use of smaller laptops and even personal digital assistants (PDAs) will ensure that more children will have access to ICT resources in a variety of learning contexts. It will mean that children can work anywhere in the classroom and these devices can even be used outside of the school building both as stand-alone machines (for example, to log data, write a story or store pictures from a digital camera) and as part of a network – as long as they are within their own range of the network. It also means that teachers can allow access to the Internet and a wide variety of stored resources on a central network without moving children to a computer suite or even from their desk. If pedagogy is regarded as any conscious activity by one person designed to enhance learning in another, it is hard to believe that creative teachers will not see a growing number of different activities that this change would provide. As this technology becomes widely available, many primary teachers will see the potential of changing the way they teach across the curriculum and it may have a significant impact on pedagogy.

The primary curriculum and pedagogical subject knowledge

It is in assessing the potential to develop 'new teaching' that the role of pedagogical subject knowledge becomes an important consideration. It is generally accepted that different pedagogic techniques are necessary for the effective learning of different forms of knowledge, skills and understanding (Siraj-Blatchford 1999). This 'pedagogical content knowledge' (Shulman 1987) includes knowledge of how to represent a subject, how pupils learn within it, and how to sequence concepts effectively within a curriculum (Wilson et al. 1987). Shulman's (1987) model of pedagogic reasoning and action is based upon the ability of teachers to comprehend what they are teaching ('to teach is first to understand', Shulman 1987: 14) before transforming it for the comprehension of others. Given the fact that primary teachers are teaching at least 10 subjects within a National Curriculum (11 in Wales) and that it is unlikely that they are 'experts' in all of them, this may be another consideration which will affect their ability to develop new pedagogies involving ICT. Thus it may be possible that the pedagogy will only be developed in areas in which teachers have specialist subject knowledge or as part of an imposed generic teaching pedagogy across the primary curriculum.

In the current political climate, it is argued that opportunities for 'new teaching' are most likely to evolve outside of the current numeracy and literacy straitjacket. The greater pedagogic freedom enjoyed by both science and the foundation subjects may provide a better forum for the development of new teaching – although some research suggests that teachers are transferring pedagogy to other curriculum areas (see Chapter 3). However, in some primary curriculum subjects, especially those such as physical education and games, which take place predominantly outside the classroom environment, it is perhaps unlikely that ICT will have a significant impact on pedagogy in any form. In other more practical subjects, such as music and art, it may be that ICT will provide a stimulus for creative ideas (such as musical compositions) or, with the use of digital images, video and sound recordings, a means to appraise work undertaken both within and outside of the classroom. By using computers or the interactive whiteboard it is possible to share work not only with other classes and the school but with classes around the country and indeed the world. It is the capacity of ICT to *record* in a variety of formats, *transport* this information at high speed and then enable it to be *shared* with others that may have a significant effect on teacher pedagogy. Indeed, it may be that the very act of sharing ideas and classroom activities between teachers will develop networks of good practice, which can help in the mentoring of other teachers, in providing valuable learning experiences for pupils and in sharing new pedagogy.

What of the future?

This chapter began with a view that the use of ICT could 'open the way to a new pedagogy' (DfES 2001c: 23). It may be that we are still waiting for a 'transforming pedagogy' (Somekh and Davies 1991) for ICT, but perhaps the most important message from all that has proceeded is that in primary schools there may not be a single pedagogy for ICT, which will suddenly arrive with the introduction of specific ICT resources or through government edict. The diversity of the primary curriculum leads to a potential diversity in pedagogy. Evidence is emerging (Beauchamp and Bicknell 2005) that teachers are strongly influenced in their use of ICT by the pedagogic demands of a particular subject area and the age of the children concerned. They consequently make informed choices about how and when they use ICT (if at all), based on the demands of a subject rather than responding to a generic exhortation to use ICT across the curriculum. It could be argued that greater high-quality subject-specific advice may have a greater impact on the use of ICT in the primary school, than attempts to impose a single pedagogy.

Even if the above approach was adopted, it is perhaps inevitable that individual teachers and schools will continue to respond in different ways, with varying degrees of success and at different speeds. There are many variables that may affect the speed of change – including teacher confidence, their pedagogic subject knowledge, the degree of control they pass to pupils and the availability of suitable ICT resources – and it is possible that this may vary between subject areas across the curriculum. As in any process of evolution, change in ICT pedagogy in the primary school is likely to be gradual and based on 'fitness for purpose'. Nevertheless, instead of limiting expectations to a 'new pedagogy', the potential synergy of both pupils and teachers using new technologies to adapt and explore new roles and interactions in the classroom may lead to a diversity of new pedagogies and 'new teaching' across the primary curriculum.

8 Pedagogy at Key Stage Two: Teaching through Pupil-Teacher Partnership

Peter Silcock and Mark Brundrett

Introduction: two challenges

At key stage two (KS2) English primary school teachers face two different though related challenges. First, the primary national strategy (DfES 2003b) and stance on 'personalized learning' (Miliband 2004) admit (as many have long taken for granted) that schools should enrich pupils' personal lives as well as teaching publicly acclaimed knowledge and skills. The emotional and personal dimensions of school life are seen as no less crucial to school success than are the academic. Second, KS2 pupils are expected to move gradually towards the more formal studies that they will meet at key stage three, to be prepared for phase 'transfer': the 'key stage' designation marks the transition (DES 1987). Both challenges, it is suggested, create potentially conflicting priorities and therefore real difficulties for teachers. In each case, paying due attention to the talents, emotional states and personal ambitions of pupils may compromise teachers' efforts to fulfil conventional expectations (and vice versa: see McNess *et al.* 2003).

This chapter examines KS2 teaching in the light of such a conclusion while promoting a form of pupil-teacher partnership especially designed to deal with conflicts of priority. It starts by spelling out some basic principles of KS2 pedagogy.

Pedagogy at KS2

What is pedagogy?

As educational situations change and teaching purposes alter (for example, between key stages), classroom practices should presumably alter too. Pedagogy at KS2 will have its own features born of its main purposes. However, the assumption that teaching is professionally tailored to suit varied ends and is not, for instance, shaped more by classroom circumstance than by design *is* an assumption. Our 'impoverished' knowledge of the subject does not at first sight guarantee it (Edwards 2001: 161; see also Watkins and Mortimore 1999; Alexander 2004). Levine (1996: 95) calls pedagogy 'our missing concept'.

Fortunately, Lingard *et al.*'s (2003: 417–18) definition of pedagogy as practices that 'teachers have accrued to their professional identities and to some extent hold outside the state's purview' is helpful in a number of ways. It is consistent with other definitions, such as that of Edwards (2001), and is easily allied to views on teachers' professional development that root it in experience (for example, Schon 1995; Hogan 2003). It avoids narrowly restricting pedagogy to strategies validated by 'scientific' research (Simon 1994) yet sees it as much more than a synonym for teaching (Watkins and Mortimore 1999; discussed in Edwards 2001: 162; Katz 2002: 6–7). It also calls into question the rather complex business of carving up classroom practice as 'typologies' (Alexander 1995) or 'styles' (Bennett 1976). If pedagogy is an out-and-out professional enterprise rather than trial-and-error strategies needing to be labelled or 'typed' its practices will have built-in values and purposes and be to a fair extent self-regulated; they should not be tagged as better or worse ways of reaching the same ends (Hogan 2003). A further merit of making pedagogy professional by nature is that it implies that teachers will necessarily take account of wider theoretical and cultural influences impinging on their professionalism (see Alexander 2004).

Another benefit from grounding different forms of pedagogy in teachers' professional expertise is that to do so helps explain what is sometimes called the 'process-product paradox or dilemma' (Katz 2000, 2002; Brundrett and Silcock 2002). This paradox has it that means and ends in education are invariably bound together; altering means to any significant degree usually alters ends (and vice versa). The point is that one would expect the dilemma to apply if teachers' practices by their nature change along with their purposes. In other words, the process-product paradox tells us that a potential for professional practices to reach intrinsic ends is their *raison d'être* rather than having to match to criteria for reflectivity, ideological correctness, measures of general effectiveness, competence or whatever.

Such arguments suggest that 'KS2 pedagogy' can be regarded as professional practices with purposes and features separable from others. The brief discussion above is worth summarizing in terms of principles that will prove useful later:

- Pedagogy is the contrived 'means-end' practices of professional teachers.
- Important features of these practices alter between phases as teachers' purposes do (for example, influenced by changing demands from differing groups of pupils). Teachers design or pragmatically shape distinct forms of pedagogy through necessity.

- Types of pedagogy (or 'pedagogies') are best grouped either by purpose (within key stages or value-orientations perhaps – child-centred/subject-centred and so on) or by main feature (formal/informal; reflective/technical-rational and so on) where purpose and feature are conceptually interdependent.
- Because different kinds of pedagogy have built-in values and purposes with linked features it is somewhat fruitless to search for a *single* generic formula for effective teaching or 'best practice' (see Campbell *et al.* 2003 and 2004 for related discussions).

Teaching at KS2

As introduced, a KS2 phase of education was meant to ease 'bridging' between primary and secondary schools (DES 1987). Yet it has to share the wider brief of primary schools to educate young pupils in ways suited to their experiences, age and capabilities. The special features of upper primary teaching should therefore, at a minimum, reconcile two different kinds of needs – those characterized in terms of the normal development of young pupils (intellectually, socially, emotionally and so forth) and those characterized in terms of transfer between phases. Broadly speaking, KS2 teachers look in two directions at once – towards the generalist, child-centred world of the traditional primary school and the subject-centred world of early adolescence.

Unfortunately, as far as we can see from research findings, the key stage designation seems to have made little difference to school transfer. Research over decades (Nisbett and Entwistle 1969; Measor and Woods 1984; Gorwood 1994; Rudduck 1996; Galton *et al.* 1999; Galton 2000) finds the move between phases almost 'intractable' (DfEE 2001b: 40) with no obvious improvement during recent times. Primary and secondary schools still plan without reference to each other (Gorwood 1994: 294). Secondary school teachers still have 'many other things to do than to ponder over the records of new pupils' (Blyth, cited in Gorwood 1994: 297). Galton (2000) regrets that a full decade of legislation has neglected teaching at KS2, echoing Alexander's (1995, 2004) complaint that politicians' reforming zeal has left classroom teaching untouched. Noyes (2004: 189) blames poor transfer on 'structural limitations inherent in our school system' but thinks radical changes in the 'climate' of school classrooms are needed as well as changes within society generally.

The reasons for poor primary-secondary transfer are undoubtedly complex (Galton and Hargreaves 2002) but to some extent the main culprit for whatever goes wrong has to be unsuitable teaching at one or both phases. This is not to deny government policies at KS2 their success. As Fitz (2003: 234) reports, a 'proportion of 11-year-olds achieving benchmark standards in literacy and numeracy (rose) by 19 percentage points, and 20 percentage points respectively, in the period 1996 to 2002'. Yet aims for the age-phase must be more ambitious than to help pupils do well in national tests. It could be that straining for high scores at eleven conditions pupils' states of mind in such a way as to impair what happens later. Longitudinal studies (Galton *et al.* 1999; Pollard *et al.* 2000) hint that undue stress on 'performativity' (Jeffrey 2002) has damaged the emotional climate of primary school classrooms, affecting pupil performance subsequently (see Chapter 3). Confining public interest to the instrumental aims of education over past decades has neglected the expressive, putting its aims further and further out of reach (McNess *et al.* 2003).

Effective KS2 teaching must satisfy demands from changing curricula and from developmental and contextually linked circumstances *at the same time*. Regarding the first, one side effect of curricular reform has been the increasing subject-centred or transmission teaching of preadolescent pupils (Ball 1999; Pollard *et al.* 2000; McNess *et al.* 2003; Osborn *et al.* 2003), which has already transformed classroom life. Children no longer have much say in what they study (Pollard *et al.* 1994); they are grouped differently from before (Kutnick *et al.* 2002; Hallam *et al.* 2004) and work within increasingly autocratic organizations dedicated to content delivery (Fitz 2003). Such cultural and organizational changes are prefigured in primary-phase teacher education where discipline-based study has replaced many programmes on pedagogy. They also explain why KS2 teachers are often fixated on test results because tests at 11 are 'very high stakes indeed given the publication of results on a school-by-school basis in newspapers' (Shorrocks-Taylor *et al.* 2003: 52).

Aiding transfer by making the upper primary school like the lower secondary ignores (for many pupils) the other defining feature of any KS2 work that it reflects pupils' developmental needs. Very simply, however much adults might want preadolescent pupils to learn the content of subject-based curricula and be tested against measurable targets (that is, conform to formal, academic criteria), young children will not universally be capable of such learning. Some will be; a number, poorly advanced intellectually, socially or emotionally, will manage – at best – through rote memorization and surface conformity. Primary school teachers are probably well aware of such matters, using transmission teaching because it is the best way to deliver set content not because they are professionally sold on its effectiveness (Gipps *et al.* 1999; McNess *et al.* 2003).

Prawat (1989) points out that transmission teaching is 'dramatically different' from teaching for understanding (cited in Wallace and Louden 2003: 545). Prawat suggests that ensuring comprehension is at the heart of constructivist ideals and recommends a social constructivist pedagogy for schools, as do Galton (1989), Silcock (1999), Brundrett and Silcock (2002), Hartley (2003) and Wallace and Louden (2003). His argument resonates for the upper primary phase. Making content-retention signal success rather than a secure grasp of knowledge gives pupils on the threshold of secondary education a poor start to discipline-based work.

Theoretical and empirical support for partnership teaching

Murphy and Ivinson (2003) argue for the need to challenge the dominant discourse surrounding pedagogy in many countries which, they suggest, is predicated on individualistic accounts of achievement and solutions to enhance achievement. This discourse takes little account of the relationships between thinking and the cultural, institutional and historical situations in which it occurs, leading to what has been termed a 'hegemonic pedagogy' that 'perpetuates power/knowledge inequities' (Hildebrand 1999: 2). What is excluded from such pedagogy is any understanding of the microinteractions between learners, and between learners and teachers, and their social and cultural mediation, which is the essence of a sociocultural view of pedagogy. Within such revaluation it is argued there are complex, socially situated, everyday processes that surround subject knowledge reconstruction.

Thus pedagogic interventions are required that challenge knowledge representations in order to extend participation for individuals by making space for and, therefore, providing a sense of belonging for a range of social identities. They legitimize the knowledge that learners bring to classroom settings and create curriculum from the perspective of the learner (Lave and Wenger 1991). From a sociocultural perspective, interaction and emergent processes play a constitutive role in learning and the transformation of identity and cannot be reduced to generalized structures (Hanks, cited in Lave and Wenger 1991). Such theorizing frequently avers to the centrality of social mediation in the work of Vygotsky, and the more recent work of Rogoff (1995) is also often cited.

These theoretical constructs are supported by a growing body of research affirming the co-construction or partnership approach to teaching and learning. The advisability, if not necessity, of co-constructing the early childhood curriculum has been noted by Anning et al. (2003: 181) who cite Pramling's phenomenographic research incorporating adult-child metacognitive dialogues to increase children's awareness of their learning. Anning et al. (2003: 187) go on to argue that misinterpretations of Piaget's research led to a de-emphasizing of the role of the teacher. They suggest that issues of quality in early childhood education can only be framed when the teacher is 'placed back' in the teaching and learning context. In a separate paper, Cullen (1998: 2–3) offers the development by Te Waariki of the Early Childhood Curriculum Guidelines in New Zealand as an example of a national initiative re-emphasizing a developmentalist philosophy. In 1996 these guidelines adopted a more socially constructed view of learning in accordance with the dynamic perspectives on child development promoted by Vygotsky. Cullen points out that under this more dynamic form of learning teaching becomes a process of co-constructing knowledge through shared learning experiences. Such innovations build on and engage with research which reveals that young children engage in a range of peer interactions, which are a major source of learning about classroom life (Cullen and St George 1996).

Further, a major study conducted by Siraj-Blatchford *et al.* (2002) noted that if learning comes from a process of cognitive construction that is only achieved when a child is motivated and involved then it is entirely consistent to treat the part played by an effective educator in the same way. Cognitive construction in this case is mutual, where each party engages with the understanding of the other and learning is achieved through a process of reflexive 'co-construction'. In these circumstances it is a necessary condition that both parties are involved and, for the resultant learning to be worthwhile, that the content should be in some way instructive. Siraj-Blatchford *et al.* believe that their analyses of the qualitative and quantitative data substantiate this model and that research has also shown how adult-child interactions involving some element of 'sustained shared thinking' or what Bruner has termed 'joint involvement episodes' may be especially valuable in terms of children's learning. Thus the most effective settings encourage 'sustained shared thinking', a sadly infrequent occurrence (Siraj-Blatchford *et al.* 2002: 10).

This movement in theory and research is not confined to early childhood education. For instance Beebe and Lachmann (2003) interlink research on infant learning and adult treatment in order to demonstrate how participation in dyadic interactions can reorganize relational processes in both analyst and patient in ways that are both consonant with and different from adult-infant interactions. Recent innovations in information technology have leant particular impetus to the development of collaborative or co-constructed learning environments and such work frequently emphasizes the communicative and participatory nature of learning (Schweinhorst 1998). The necessity to make and remake in the ongoing communicative process and therefore the need to co-construct both people and worlds has also been found in the field of organizational theory (Bass and Hoskins 1999) and the literature on educational leadership (Brundrett 2002).

Partnership teaching at KS2

Within a co-constructed learning environment where teachers and learners are sensitive to each other's mental and emotional states, there is some chance that KS2 pedagogy can bridge from generalist work to the more specialist studies of secondary education. However, there are many kinds of collaborative teaching (see, for example, Cowie *et al.* 1994; Slavin 1995; Blythe and associates 1998; Hopkins and Reynolds 2001; Brundrett and

Silcock 2002; MacDonald 2003) giving differently balanced roles and responsibilities to teachers and pupils. The critical divide is probably that separating pupil-teacher partnerships for the sake of purveying standard curricula from those treating 'knowledge not (as) a commodity owned by the expert teacher but ... something which can (at least in part) be constructed, developed and criticised by the group' (Cowie *et al.* 1994: 47). Arguably, only the latter approach is a 'true' partnership – that is, sanctioning learners to adopt, develop and extend *their own* positions *vis-à-vis* what is standard.

When pupils and teachers share decision making to ease curricular delivery rather than to inform and extend existing pupil-positions, naive assumptions about how conceptual change occurs may apply. Much literature on classroom collaboration (for a review, see Slavin 1995) justifies these by the virtuous processes fostered – talk, sharing, confidence building, moral thinking, democratic decision making, recursive role taking and so on. Yet it is quite possible for pupils to cooperate freely with each other and with teachers while working in ways and on tasks wholly prepared for them by others. Benefits may certainly follow but what this approach shirks is a consistent attempt to develop that more personalized, 'richly-textured' understanding (Davis 1995, 1999) on which progress towards higher order concepts and skills surely depends. Davis (1995), Blythe *et al.* (1998), Prawat (1989) and Wallace and Louden (2003) remind us that pupils who truly understand what they learn see its relevance to already known situations – that is, there is a continuity between *existing* experience-based conceptions and any new studies.

Implications of this argument are that KS2 classroom decisions should respect two 'givens': a written curriculum (a sociocultural framework) and pupils' already established cognitive and affective states of mind. Partnership teaching at KS2 is accordingly bipartisan. It acknowledges the *distinctive* yet equally valid individual and sociocultural positions of pupils and teachers, noticing that individual pupils' starting points for learning may differ from all others. As Dewey (1900, 1902, 1976) insisted school curricula must engage children's personal preoccupations if what is taught is to be meaningful for them. Curricula that do not respect pupils' beliefs, ideas, values, attitudes (most do not, according to Katz 2000, 2002) can alienate rather than capture pupil interest (see also Chapter 5). A first step towards reconciling teacher-pupil views is to recognize the distinctiveness and legitimacy of each.

Illustrations: from principle to practice

Illustrations of KS2 partnership pedagogy refer to

- lesson content and curricular organization;

- teacher input; and
- task setting and assessment.

It is important to note that these illustrations only illuminate principles. They do not provide a blueprint for practice (see Brundrett and Silcock 2002 for fuller guidance).

Lesson content and curricular organization

Lesson content for older primary pupils should, from the start, respect standard curricular positions (built into subjects) and pupils' own starting points – interests, ideas and aspirations. This suggests that teachers will be reasonably familiar with curricular science, maths (and so on) and with the personal and social worlds of their pupils, because one is to be interpreted in terms of the other. However, it is not so much that teachers should be expert in all curricular areas or have the insight into pupil minds of a care worker or social scientist but that their teaching impels pupils to access personal and public *milieus* equally. The work of neo-Piagetian action researchers like Resnick *et al.* (1992) and Adey and Shayer (1994) has just that dual intent. Maths and science students debate their experiences and intuitions among peers before being challenged by more public or standard views. Pupils explore two contrasting worlds *together* – the academic world of given (evolving) ideas and pupils' own tentative opinions, hypotheses, beliefs.

Immediately, one sees how curricular organization at KS2 benefits from a policy that ensures *by rule* a regular transaction between the personal and public knowledge bases that 11-year-old primary pupils must bridge. It is not that teachers gradually introduce more subject-based work because this is required of them. A process already in train moves forward irresistibly. Individual pupils increasingly place themselves relative to standard debates (as Driver *et al.* 2000 say they must) while steering whatever courses such debates follow in personal ways. Obviously, there is no point at which one might say that pupils are properly prepared for secondary education (no-one would argue that all 11–12-year-olds could be ready at exactly the same time!). Rather, the partnership principle implies a graduated evolution in ways of thinking and understanding, moving from one position to another, however these positions are characterized.

Teacher input

A main problem for partnership teaching is that pupils' inner worlds are privy to pupils and one can never with certainty know exactly what pupils need, expect, think, in anything but a hit-and-miss way. But pupils themselves can 'scaffold' teachers understanding of what is and is not useful for them to learn (in terms of their own perspectives) while teachers 'scaffold' pupils' thinking towards what is and is not publicly valued. Such dual tracking is hard in that it requires teachers to assess how well they are moving in two separate yet complementary directions. Yet it is exactly this judgement that informs teachers' planning and input. It helps them decide which curricular issues to explore and how these might be presented as propositions to be discussed or argued about (not provisional ideas masquerading as certainties).

It is still a tough question as to how to make teaching input vulnerable to interpretation from the full range of perspectives existing in the school or classroom community. Yet it is not an impossible question to answer and a few illustrations help. Teaching the 'language' of a subject not as a technical accomplishment but as a means for pupils to gain new perspectives on their own expressed and explored experiences is a paradigm instance of a twin-track strategy. Discarding a textbook lesson on 'the Victorians' in favour of one opening up the period via issues, problems, questions, themes to be explored in diverse ways and from diverse starting-points, is an equally *bona fide* ploy. A PSHE lesson where pupils explore their own emotional states before studying how artists, musicians, writers explore theirs is solid partnership work insofar as the two types of exploration blend. Geographic, mathematical or scientific insights gleaned from children's studies of familiar environments are already applied to more distant settings. Such lessons are in most primary school teachers' repertoires. What matters is that they are seen as instances where a bipartisan principle applies and so the same principle continues to be applied, consistently and rigorously. Lesson input must *invariably* arise according to a dual principle of selection where one criterion is a set of unique pupil positions enriched by standard ideas and the other a set of evolving perspectives taken on what is standard and public.

Learning tasks and assessment

Task setting within a pupil-teacher partnership engages standard curricula while allowing pupils to venture further into their own developing understandings and interests. At present, the key criterion applied to task setting is often that of cognitive ability – tasks are differentiated intellectually (DfES 2003b; Miliband 2004). Yet differentiation by emotional capacity and personal preference matters just as much if education is about awakening and refining pupils' values as well as helping them pass tests and exams (Silcock and Duncan 2001; McNess *et al.* 2003). Making such differentiation is hard not just because measuring specified skills and abilities is easier than assessing emotional capacity and personal commitment but because the latter judgements are only properly made by pupils themselves.

There are a number of workable strategies geared to pupil choice that teachers already use, suited to partnership work. These are most easily situated within general topics (sometimes – perhaps misleadingly – opposed to subject-based teaching: Alexander *et al.* 1992; Alexander 1995) because within a single theme pupils can be encouraged sensitively to move between areas of study. A child whose first choice of activity is to paint a steam train can without too much pain be nudged towards historical, geographical, scientific tasks (and so on). Learning science by stealth is still learning science. For teachers who believe their pupils cannot (for whatever reason) properly commit to work believed desirable or appropriate, individual or group negotiation allow standard ideas to be tackled from highly differentiated standpoints of interest. The integrity of pupil and curricular position is preserved.

Finally, and as an endpiece on *assessment*, a feature of partnership teaching is that each pupil 'constructs' his or her own unique position relative to common curricula. This may seem to impair any shift towards formal assessments at key stage three in that fair comparisons between unique and standard positions across pupils may seem impossible. Yet pupil progress can always be assessed against common criteria insofar as a central aim is to enable pupils to interpret standard ideas, albeit in personal terms. The point is that standard assessments are not the only ones that count. Teachers should assess, too, students' growing commitments and likely personal benefits from what they study (enthusiasm and interest are observable if not measurable psychometrically). It is in the light of the two interdependent criteria (personal and public values reflecting each other) that KS2 teaching should be judged.

Conclusions: summarizing partnership pedagogy

Partnership pedagogy at KS2 respects both a written curriculum and the diverse, developmentally linked learning needs of pupils, inviting a distinctive pupil 'voice' into important areas of decision making. It bridges routinely between formal studies meant to lead pupils towards phase transfer and more individually defined interests, points of view, ambitions and so forth.

The main principles can be summarized briefly:

- Important teaching decisions should respect two worldviews: that built into publicly sanctioned curricula and that (often culturally situated) informing learners' more personal interests and aspirations. *This is a partnership principle.*
- Classroom practice roots itself in differences arising between *general* curricular positions and *particular* pupil preoccupations. Reconciling these via discussion, debate, problem-solving tasks and so on prepares fertile soil for both public and personal improvement

(sounding boards for each other). *This is a conceptual change or bridging principle.*

- Although – even in close partnerships – one partner may have to act in the absence of the other, all classroom decisions can in some sense be democratically rule-governed to serve multiple ends. Partnership teaching should nurture democratic environments. *This is a democratic or contextual principle.*

Guided by these three principles, teachers can help older primary-age pupils invest interest and energy in their studies, building academic progress on emotionally secure foundations. The expressive and instrumental aims of education are realized together, through a bipartisan pedagogy which acknowledges that there is more to KS2 teaching than pressing pupils into textbook exercises whether they wish it or not. Pupil-teacher partnership is by its nature suited to reconciling conflicting loyalties and demands facing pupils on the brink of secondary education.

9 Promoting Inclusive Education: from 'Expertism' to Sustainable Inclusive Practices

Elias Avramidis

Inclusive education is now firmly established internationally as the main policy imperative with respect to children with special educational needs or disabilities. In this chapter I intend to consider the recent policy initiatives promoting inclusion in England and examine the extent to which they have resulted in the development of a more inclusive educational system. In so doing, I highlight the tension between the widespread expressions of support for the principle of inclusion and the continuing maintenance of special segregated provision as portrayed within the ongoing ideological debates between commentators in the field. Following a brief review of the factors contributing to inclusive developments, I shall discuss the two main barriers to promoting inclusion, namely the competitive policy environment, which renders mainstream schools unfavourable places for vulnerable pupils, and the inadequate preparation of teachers to meet the needs of an increasingly diverse pupil population. In addressing these issues, I shall consider an alternative perspective which argues that inclusion requires a shift away from pathological-deficit models of 'need' and a discourse of 'expertism' towards 'productive pedagogies' in which issues of social justice and equity are foregrounded. Such pedagogical practices are, in turn, dependent on reflective professional development that facilitates systemic changes conducive to the needs of *all* pupils.

Developments in education policy and enduring debates

The achievement of an inclusive education system is a major challenge facing countries around the world. Such efforts form part of a broad human rights agenda, which can be traced back to the Salamanca World Statement on principles, policy and practice in special educational needs (SEN) issued by the United Nations Educational, Scientific and Cultural Organisation (UNESCO 1994). The declaration, which was signed by delegates representing 92 governments (including the British government) and 25 international organizations, asserts the fundamental right of every child to education and advocates the development of inclusive mainstream schools, which 'are the most effective means of combating discriminatory attitudes, creating welcoming communities, building an inclusive society and achieving education for all' (Clause 5, second paragraph).

In England, the Green Paper, *Excellence for All Children*, published in October 1997 (DfEE 1997a) and the subsequent *Meeting Special Educational Needs: A Programme of Action* (DfEE 1998a) vigorously support the principle that children with SEN should wherever possible be educated in mainstream schools and demonstrate the Labour government's commitment to place inclusive education at the heart of a policy addressing the wider agenda of social inclusion. The Labour government also issued statutory guidance to schools and local education authorities (LEAs) detailing ways of removing barriers to learning and participation that hinder or exclude pupils with SEN (DfES 2001a). The principles upon which this document is framed are further strengthened through the new Special Educational Needs Code of Practice (DfES 2001d) and the Special Educational Needs and Disability Act 2001. The latter anti-discrimination legislation, which came into effect in January 2002, has marked a major sea change in provision as it makes it unlawful to discriminate against pupils on the basis of their disability, and thereby makes real the right to education in mainstream schools for *all* pupils.

However, as Farrell (2001), Evans and Lunt (2002) and Lindsay (2003) have all noted, the development of policy towards inclusion in England is well advanced, but not all-encompassing. Specifically, the ambiguities contained in the Green Paper (DfEE 1997a) and in subsequent documents over whether 'inclusion' refers to *all* or simply *most* pupils have resulted in a variety of interpretations and applications across different local education authorities (LEAs) (Ainscow *et al.* 2000; Croll and Moses 2000a). This is vividly illustrated in the series of surveys by the Centre for Studies on Inclusive Education (Norwich 1997, 2002b), which showed a slow but steady trend towards inclusion but remarkable variation between the extent of segregated provision across LEAs. Such variation essentially means that there have been many instances of children being educated in mainstream schools who, if they lived in another area, would be in a special school. In 2001, for example, a disabled pupil in Manchester was more than seven times as likely to be placed in a segregated special school than a child in the London Borough of Newham; Manchester had 2.64 per cent of 5–15-year-olds in special schools, whereas Newham, which has actively pursued a policy of inclusion for 18 years, had just 0.35 per cent (Norwich 2002b). More recent statistics released by the centre (Rustemier and Vaughan 2005) at the time of writing have indicated that little progress towards inclusion was made during the period 2002–4, with one third of LEAs increasing segregation of disabled pupils over the 3 years and with similar disturbing local variations in placement recorded across England. A critical view of this continuing variation between LEAs might suggest that the promotion of a policy of inclusion is still insufficiently strong and that an absolute commitment to total inclusion is necessary.

While the retention of separate special school provision does not sit comfortably with efforts to promote inclusion, prospects for its abolition seem highly improbable in the immediate future (Lindsay 2003). Indeed, the recent government working party on special schools concluded that the latter are part of a spectrum of provision for SEN and therefore should be retained (DfES 2003e). This tension in education policy has sparked theoretical debates between commentators in the field adhering to antithetical ideological stances. Whereas some authors have been critical of a 'full' or 'purist' model of inclusion embracing a more 'cautious' and 'responsible' form of it (Hornby 1999; Croll and Moses 2000b; Wilson 2000), others firmly entrenched within a human rights discourse have challenged not only the moral-ethical basis of special schooling but also the evidence in support of retaining segregated provision (Gallagher 2001; Slee 2001; Thomas and Loxley 2001). In their comprehensive critique of the intellectual foundations of special education, Thomas and Loxley (2001), for example, have cogently argued that much of the knowledge about special education is misconceived, if not erroneous. More importantly, overreliance on such traditional frameworks has at best, distracted attention from alternative understandings for children's failure to thrive and, at worst, necessitated segregated provision for a significant minority of children since their education supposedly requires specialist knowledge and expertise not available in mainstream environments.

A more balanced stance has been adopted by Brahm Norwich who, amongst others, sees educational practice in general and special needs education in particular as characterized by 'dilemmas' (Norwich 2002a; Norwich and Kelly 2005). Such dilemmas arise because the practice of education is a complex venture that attempts to respond to essentially conflicting imperatives – to extend the capacities of the most able, for instance, whilst making provision that is equitable for all children, or to respond to children's particular interests and motivations while enabling them to acquire common bodies of knowledge and skill that are socially valued. By extension, the rights of children to have maximum access to mainstream education need to be balanced by their right to an effective education appropriate to their needs often available in segregated provision. Seeking a resolution to such contrary rights and values implies some inevitable loss, which, in turn, suggests that there can be no pure version of inclusion. The dilemmatic perspective is therefore a model that draws our attention to the value bases of dilemmas and calls for a positive acknowledgement of multiple values, the balancing of values and thus the acknowledgement of ideological impurity. This model, however, while powerful in analysing complex educational policies, does little to advance our understanding of how more inclusive practice can pre-vail. Such insights gained from research studies rooted within a school ef-fectiveness/improvement tradition are presented next.

Factors for successful inclusion

Without losing sight of the theoretical debates about the 'necessity' of seg-regated provision for pupils labelled as having SEN, it is generally agreed that the move towards a more inclusive education system requires substantial reform of mainstream schooling. Indeed, a large body of research in primary (Rose 2001) and secondary (Florian and Rouse 2001) settings has sought to identify organizational structures and practices that may be associated with facilitating or impeding the development of inclusion. Interestingly, a range of different studies conducted in different countries and using different methodologies, have reported conclusions that show substantial overlap. Ainscow (1995), for example, drew on findings from the UNESCO Teacher Education Project *Special Needs in the Classroom* in identifying conditions necessary within a school if it is to restructure so as to provide effective education for all:

- effective leadership, not only by the headteacher, but spread throughout the school;
- involvement of staff, students and community in school policies and decisions;
- a commitment to collaborative planning;
- coordination strategies;
- attention to the potential benefits of enquiry and reflection;
- a policy for staff development.

Along similar lines, in the US, Lipsky and Gartner (1998) identified seven factors based on a national study in 1000 school districts. These were judged to be consistent with the factors identified in a smaller study of 12 schools as follows:

- visionary leadership;
- collaboration;
- refocused use of assessment;
- support for staff and students;
- funding;
- effective parental involvement;
- use of effective programme models and classroom practices.

However, such lists of factors (which are applicable in both primary and secondary settings) are very general and tend to overlook the ambiguity, tensions and complexity of schooling. Further, being descriptions of inclusive schools, it remains unclear whether these factors are causal of inclusive development or simply defining characteristics of inclusive schools. Nevertheless, the recommendations offered by these researchers can be viewed as 'levers for change' or organizational actions that can move school systems in an inclusive direction. Such institutional actions, however, can only bring sustainable development if wider (policy) factors that hinder progress are also addressed. It is towards discussing in more detail two recurring themes in the literature concerning barriers to inclusion that we turn next.

Major barriers to the implementation of inclusion

Perhaps the most often cited barrier in the inclusion literature is the competitive policy environment in which schools are operating. Several commentators (Lloyd 2000; Loxley and Thomas 2001; Evans and Lunt 2002) have argued that the legislative and policy framework of the 1990s, which was underpinned by a market-place philosophy based upon principles of academic excellence, choice and competition, is at odds with a policy of educational and social inclusion. Rose (2001: 148–9), for example, drawing on his research in primary schools notes that:

> the emphasis upon an outcomes-driven curriculum, where success is measured only in academic terms and school performance is judged through performance tables, is a direct impediment and a disincentive to schools. The latter see pupils with special needs as presenting a challenge to the image of the school in the wider educational community.

Moreover, in today's competitive atmosphere where schools are expected to raise their standards and vie with each other for students and funding it should not be surprising if they become unfavourable places for pupils considered by many teachers as challenging. The continuing trend for considerable numbers of pupils with emotional and behavioural difficulties (EBD) to be excluded (DfES 2004d) is also indicative of the reduced tolerance of mainstream schools.

The clash between the principles that underpin market-based reforms and the principles that underpin the development of inclusive forms of schooling has clearly produced a set of tensions between such notions as 'equity' and 'excellence'. Schools are expected to become more 'inclusive' or 'equitable' at the same time as they pursue a standards agenda based on narrowly defined notions of 'excellence' within a context of increased public accountability and government control. Here, however incompatible the concepts of 'equity' and 'excellence' might appear, they are not mutually exclusive. In fact, the literature contains examples of schools that do not see the tensions as bipolar, either/or opposites from which they have to choose one extreme or the other. Instead, they have found creative ways to become more inclusive while achieving high academic standards.

Brookside Primary School, for example, is a mixed, community, 4–11 school in Stockport that has acquired a reputation for providing an excellent education while having developed towards an inclusive direction. Brookside is one of five primary schools in Stockport to be receiving additional funding (resource provision) to provide extra teaching and support staff for children with severe or profound learning difficulties. Currently, there are eight children with severe learning difficulties as well as others with special educational needs who have come to the school because of its inclusive philosophy. The school prides itself for pursuing a fully inclusive approach with tremendous benefits for every member of the school community in terms of understanding, achievement and confidence. As is mentioned on the school's Web site:

> At Brookside, we have a huge range of attainment and achievement; all is valued and celebrated ... Performance of Stockport children in the annual Year 6 SATs tests is ranked and published annually. Children at Brookside perform very well indeed, many attaining above the national average and our 'value added' score (the progress made between Infants and Juniors) is excellent. As mentioned, all achievement is valued. All of our children are included in the league table (including those with severe learning difficulties) which lowers our ranking in the table.

It is worth noting that an Ofsted inspection in 2001 rated the school's practice as excellent, while its reputation was further enhanced that year through participating as an exemplar of inclusive education in the Channel 4 documentary *Count Me In*.

Notwithstanding such exemplary cases, it is generally agreed (Farrell 2001; Dyson *et al.* 2003) that most schools continue to resist the pressure to become more inclusive because they are concerned that to do so will have a negative effect on the academic progress of other pupils and/or lower academic standards. This concern is directly linked to an often-cited inability of mainstream schools to become fully inclusive. Views reflecting such preoccupations were elicited in a large-scale study by Croll and Moses (2000b) investigating professionals' views of inclusion. Interviews with education officers and headteachers of both special and mainstream primary schools in

11 LEAs revealed support towards inclusion as an ideal but considerable reservation about the feasibility of inclusion based on the types and severity of children's difficulties and the insufficient capacity of mainstream schools to address them. Specifically, children with moderate learning difficulties and children with sensory or mobility problems were regarded as most appropriately integrated in mainstream settings, while children with severe and complex difficulties and children with emotional and behavioural problems were most frequently regarded as exceptions to the principle of inclusion. Moreover, there was widespread agreement that some children presented such complex difficulties (for example, autistic children) that it was impossible or unreasonable for them to be catered for within regular settings mainly due to the lack of appropriate resources and teaching expertise; the latter were seen as essential by many mainstream heads if they were to operate more inclusive schools. Similar findings were reported in another small-scale study eliciting primary teachers' perceptions of the necessary conditions for greater inclusion (Rose 2001). In this study, respondents strongly felt that inclusion required additional classroom support, substantial training, extra time for collaborative planning, a restructured physical environment and sympathetic parental attitudes. The absence or inadequacy of any of the above was seen as rendering the inclusion project unfeasible.

The teachers' anxiety voiced in the Rose (2001) study could be attributed to the respondents' lack of confidence both in their own instructional skills and in the quality of support available to them. Indeed, another frequently cited barrier in the inclusion literature is the inadequate preparation of teachers to meet the needs of a wide range of pupils with special educational needs. Research indicates that many newly qualified teachers entering the professional arena perceive themselves as ill-equipped to teach these pupils (Garner 1996; Avramidis et al. 2000a). This is partly due to the increased school-based element in initial training, which does not normally allow adequate consideration of approaches to the teaching and learning of these pupils. Experienced teachers have also been reported in the literature as lacking the necessary knowledge and teaching skills to support the inclusion of pupils with complex needs while working effectively to raise standards for all pupils (Avramidis et al. 2000b). Further, the limited opportunities for professional development have resulted in the perpetuation of negative teacher attitudes towards pupils with special educational needs and scepticism towards the feasibility of a fully inclusive education system. These negative attitudes are shared by primary and secondary teachers alike (Avramidis and Norwich 2002).

However, as it transpires from the relevant literature on inclusion, there is a strong demand on the part of teachers for more training with a narrower focus on specific or distinctive groups of learners. This is fundamentally paradoxical in the absence of sufficient empirical evidence to substantiate the existence of distinctive special pedagogies. This was reflected in a recent literature review conducted by Norwich and Lewis (Norwich and Lewis 2001), which examined whether differences between learners (by particular special educational needs group) can be identified and systematically linked with learners' needs for differential teaching. In challenging the claim that distinctive teaching strategies are needed for children with special needs, the authors concluded that the notion of 'continua of teaching approaches' is useful as it captures the appropriateness of more intensive and explicit teaching for pupils with different degrees of learning difficulties. This notion also makes it possible to distinguish between the 'normal' adaptations in class teaching for most pupils and the greater degree of adaptations required for those with more severe difficulties in learning, those designated as having SEN. These are adaptations to common teaching approaches and have been called specialized adaptations, or 'high density' teaching.

Despite the scarce empirical evidence to substantiate a specific pedagogical distinction for pupils labelled as having SEN (see also Chapter 10), the latter continue to be seen by mainstream teachers as 'someone else's problem'. My research in primary (Avramidis 2001) and secondary settings (Avramidis *et al.* 2002) has identified a culture where teachers, pressurized by a 'standards agenda', feel that they are responsible only for the learning outcomes of 80 per cent of the children in their classes, the remaining 20 per cent being the responsibility of the SEN teacher. Such a culture emanates from a psycho-medical paradigm (Skidmore 2004), which relates 'needs' to notions of personal pathology, disorder or deficit that require a 'specialist' pedagogy not readily available in mainstream schools. In such cases, the underlying assumption has been that children defined as having special needs belong to a different pedagogical category and thus cannot be taught by ordinary teachers. The psycho-medical paradigm gives rise to a 'discourse of expertism' – a phrase loosely used here to denote overreliance on professional 'expert' knowledge and practices – which results in the exclusion of challenging individuals, thus relieving mainstream schools of the pressure to respond to their needs. Without disregarding the needs of some disabled students for technological aids, particular adjustments, or medical care (for example, a deaf student requires hearing aids and a physically disabled student requires an accessible environment), we must ensure that teachers undertake responsibility for the vast majority of pupils with SEN without overreliance on professional 'expert' knowledge and practices. Unfortunately, the failure to strike this balance currently perpetuates and even strengthens a divisive ideology that impinges upon efforts to create more inclusive schooling environments.

In the remainder of this chapter I address the critical changes needed to transcend the discourse of expertism and to move towards the development of genuinely inclusive forms of schooling. In so doing, I will briefly refer to Allan's (2003) appeal for the adoption of 'productive pedagogies', before outlining in detail my recommendations for the kind of professional development required to support such systemic changes.

The way forward: the formulation of 'productive pedagogies' through critical professional development

In exploring the challenges of developing an inclusive education system, I have come to agree with Julie Allan (2003) who advocated the need for a significant shift in thinking away from notions of including particular individuals or groups of children towards constructing environments that include *all* children. Her argument draws on recommendations from two large-scale studies undertaken in Queensland, Australia, and Scotland, which critically examined the respective education systems. The Queensland School Reform Longitudinal Study (Luke *et al.* 1999) identified a set of 'productive pedagogies' in which issues of social justice, equity and inclusion are placed at the centre. Specifically, the pedagogies recommended in this study involved 'heightened intellectual demand on students, connectedness to the students' lives outside the school, a supportive classroom environment and recognition of difference' (Allan 2003: 175). These were accompanied by further suggestions for fair assessment, professional development, inspiring leadership and a greater recognition of equity issues in the school. Similar changes aimed at establishing an education system for all were recommended by the Scottish Parliamentary Inquiry into Special Needs (Scottish Parliament 2001). These emphasized the importance of listening to the voices of children and their parents; the adoption of pragmatic child-centred approaches to provision; the need to rectify inequalities created by conflicting policies (for example, inspection and target setting) and the need to support professionals through offering substantial training opportunities.

In reviewing this research, Allan notes that both studies identified as one main obstacle to achieving an inclusive education system the continuing emphasis on individual deficits, which distracts attention from structural and attitudinal barriers within institutions and society at large. Such 'destructive' practices can only be overcome through the adoption of 'productive pedagogies' involving major systemic changes in schools. The latter presuppose the adoption of a self-reflective stance on the part of professionals and the continuous examination of their practices. Rather than prescribing a 'recipe for inclusion', that is, a single set of recommendations or action points, Allan (2003: 177) posed the following questions as starting points for reform, which I quote here in full:

1. How can teachers be helped to acquire *and* demonstrate the necessary competence to qualify as a teacher and to understand

themselves as in a continuous process of learning about themselves and others?

2. How can teachers develop as autonomous professionals *and* learn to depend on others for support and collaboration?
3. How can teachers be supported in maximizing student achievement *and* in ensuring inclusivity?
4. How can teachers be helped to understand the features of particular impairments *and* avoid disabling individual students with that knowledge?
5. What assistance can be given to teachers to enable them to deal with the exclusionary pressures they encounter *and* avoid becoming embittered or closed to possibilities for inclusivity in the future?

All the above questions call for teacher development in the sense of assisting them to overcome their fears and scepticism in relation to the inclusion of children with significant needs. Clearly, pre- and in-service (INSET) training to enhance regular educators' knowledge and skills in teaching students with learning difficulties and disabilities is warranted. Teachers may not hold 'negative attitudes'; rather they may not see solutions to problems that they feel are outside their competence or control. Consequently, if they are guided and supported through careful and well-planned training courses, then it can be anticipated that tremendous attitude change can be obtained resulting in genuinely inclusive practices. What is required here is a radical rethinking of professional development away from low (INSET) level technical responses to specific 'needs' or 'syndromes', towards longer term reflective training (Bayliss 1998; Tilstone 2003). Such critical self-reflective courses result in the acquisition of 'generic' teaching skills that allow teachers to modify their practice in ways that are conducive to meeting the needs of *all* learners within 'inclusive' (holistic) frameworks.

Similarly, Initial Teacher Training (ITT) courses should provide training on the psychological principles of teaching and learning as well as a critical understanding of the educational process. Central to ITT training should also be, amongst others, topics such as differentiating the curriculum, assessing academic progress, managing behaviour, developing IEPs, and working collaboratively with colleagues to enable prospective teachers to respond creatively to the challenges of inclusion. The assumption here is that if teachers receive assistance in mastering the skills required to implement an innovation such as 'inclusion', they become more committed to the change (and more effective) as their effort and skill increase.

However, at a deeper level of analysis, what underlies this line of thinking is a presumption of 'efficiency'. If teachers are more efficient, defined in terms of professional knowledge, expertise and energy, then inclusion can 'happen'. This reductionist analysis assumes 'super teacher' status, whereby a diverse group of learners can be supported within an ever-increasing range of pupil abilities, learning styles and motivational states, to achieve narrowly defined standards of attainment. Given the current professional context in which teachers are embedded, it becomes problematic that any one teacher can sustain the pressures of performativity (see Chapter 3) while implementing inclusive forms of schooling. In searching for a way out it is all too easy to rush towards proposing significant shifts in education policy (that is, putting an end to an emphasis on narrowly defined notions of academic 'excellence' and league tables) as the first point of departure. However appealing, such moves towards more equitable forms of schooling presuppose a substantial, if not complete, abandonment of many recent market-based initiatives. In reality, however, it is highly unlikely that governments will entirely abandon the standards-based reforms in which they have invested politically and financially in recent years. Further, traditional approaches to professional development may not produce any change in teachers' attitudes and, consequently, in mainstream schools' 'praxis'. That is because such courses tend to reinforce the popular conception that inclusive education is about special children and special educators who will prove problematic as they are resettled in mainstream settings (Slee 2001).

A more promising way forward involves challenging the way teachers conceptualize difference and educational failure in particular, through offering critical training that questions 'taken for granted' understandings and practices. Such courses explicitly challenge the processes of pathologizing 'difference' (and ultimately excluding individuals) currently operating in schools, while instigating reconstructed educational thinking and practice. Similarly, at the pre-service level, Slee (2001: 210) advocates that 'teacher education faculties might consider the possibility of interdisciplinary studies of exclusion and inclusion with a view to weaving the preparation for "inclusive" teachers right across the fabric of their teacher-training curriculum.' Such an approach, far from viewing teachers' attitudes toward inclusion as immutable and inevitable, has the potential of providing practitioners with a vision and skills to operationalize that vision in genuinely inclusive ways.

Finally, it is imperative to ensure that the self-reflective stance that teachers are likely to adopt as a result of their participation in 'critical training' is maintained in their schools, since a continuous questioning of their practices is needed. For such a stance to be sustainable, encouraging institutional conditions are required. The notion of 'communities of knowledge' formulated by Olson and Craig (2001) offers such possibilities. Within this framework, facilitating teachers' development and learning involves long-term opportunities for collaboration, autonomy and reflection (see also Chapter 14). As I have argued elsewhere (Poulson and Avramidis 2003), communities of knowledge can be established in primary schools by creating sustained opportunities for teachers to make practical knowledge explicit to themselves and others, to make connections between practical and theoretical knowledge, and to engage in activities beyond their own school. Moreover, such communities encompass all school constituencies including the SENCO, teachers, and teaching assistants, who constructively share experiences and stories about their work leading to the formulation of a rich knowledge base that could inform innovative school practices. More importantly, such communities also bring together school practitioners and external professionals such as teacher educators, LEA advisers, educational psychologists and researchers, thus allowing theory and practice to mingle and inform one another. Such an arrangement is dramatically different from the prevailing theory-practice relationship where 'experts' confront practitioners with ready-made answers or technical solutions to complex problems.

10 Teaching Strategies for Pupils with SEN: Specialist or Inclusive Pedagogy?

Ruth Kershner and Lani Florian

Introduction: understanding special educational needs at key stage two

Teachers commonly identify particular pupils who seem to find learning difficult in school for one reason or another, and some of these pupils come to be seen as having *special educational needs* (SEN) compared to their peers. The Primary National Strategy notes that '(a)ll children benefit from the kinds of approach once seen as the province of SEN', although some pupils with SEN may have additional needs for access to the curriculum, further examples, extra practice, and general opportunities to build depth and confidence in learning (DfES 2004c: 17). In this chapter we discuss research findings about teaching strategies for pupils identified as having SEN in the context of a UK education system that is increasingly concerned with the principles and practice of inclusion. We also discuss what, if anything, is 'special' about teaching pupils with SEN.

There are increasing external demands on schools, teachers and pupils in key stage two (KS2). Many primary schools now test pupils' progress each year, and as Year 6 approaches attention is increasingly given by pupils, parents and teachers to the end of KS2 tests and the imminent move to secondary school. Yet pupils' different rates of academic progress can result in wide variation of attainment within each KS2 year group, acknowledged in the National Curriculum framework as likely to range from Levels 2 to 5 (DfEE/QCA 1999). This range of attainment levels reminds us that KS2 can be a challenging time for many pupils. The transition from Year 2 to Year 3 (which can also involve transfer to a new school) has been associated by Ofsted with a general 'dip' in academic performance (Ofsted 1993b). In a study of this phenomenon Doddington and Flutter (2001) found that both teachers and pupils recognized year 3 as an important milestone for learning, with significant changes to the curriculum, routines and ways of working in school. Particular differences found in entering Year 3 may include increasing

opportunities and expectations for pupils to work independently and collaboratively, and to express and explain their own knowledge and ideas. The
pace of work increases and there are likely to be fewer opportunities for play
built into the timetable. As a result, there are increased demands on young
children to integrate different areas of their academic, social and personal
development sometimes facing apparently contradictory expectations.

While some pupils have identified SEN and associated special provision
from the early years of education, the heightened expectations at KS2 often
result in new assessments and referrals by teachers. The rate of incidence of
pupils identified with SEN but without statements in primary and secondary
schools peaks at age 8 to 9 years (around 20 per cent). For pupils with statements the rate is similar between 10 and 15 years (around 2.5 per cent),
peaking at 14 years (DfES 2005b). This suggests that a high number of primary
pupils identified with SEN may be seen to need additional in-school support,
with increasing numbers of formal statements of SEN (DfES 2001d) being
made at the primary-secondary transition period. This applies particularly to
pupils who fall behind their peers in literacy, or whose behaviour deteriorates
in the context of increasing classroom demands for concentration, effort,
academic achievement and social skills.

Herbert (2005) notes that the experience of primary education, including
transitions between KS1 and KS2, and from primary to secondary school, can
be the time when children may experience personal difficulties. These may be
diagnosed as anxiety disorders and the specific syndromes of selective mutism
and school refusal. Identifications of obsessive compulsive disorders, autistic
spectrum disorders and attention deficit hyperactivity disorder can also occur
prompted partly by the age-related expectations of pupils in primary school,
as do increasing concerns about specific learning difficulties and specific
language impairments. Herbert also remarks on the potential educational
impact of certain physical disorders at this stage of childhood, including
bronchial asthma, motor disorders and epilepsy, as well as the full range of
sensory impairments from mild hearing loss and short-sightedness to more
significant conditions of deafness and blindness. However, not all of these
difficulties lead to a designation of SEN, nor can SEN be described as clearly
associated with specific conditions or causal factors. In primary schools the
most prevalent type of primary need identified for pupils without statements
of SEN is 'moderate learning difficulty (MLD)' (32 per cent) (DfES 2005b).
However this generic MLD designation is of questionable educational value
because it is defined differently in different local education authorities and it
can present dilemmas in the identification of certain pupils as different from
others in a context of educational and social inclusion (Norwich and Kelly
2005).

The categorization of different 'types' of SEN does not sit easily with
primary teachers' day-to-day responsibility of helping individual pupils in

their classes to participate actively in worthwhile learning activities and make progress in relation to the curriculum. All pupils have a basic entitlement to the National Curriculum, and the last few years have seen a series of government policies and guidelines making the details of teachers' responsibilities more explicit with reference to SEN and inclusion. One of the most significant documents is the SEN Code of Practice (DfES 2001d), which sets out the expectation that the majority of children will learn and progress within the ordinary school arrangements for responding to the wide range of pupils' 'abilities, aptitudes and interests' (DfES 2001d: 44, para. 5: 3). It asserts that 'all teachers are teachers of children with special educational needs' (para. 5: 2), while acknowledging that further support may be needed for certain pupils whose needs are identified as *additional to* or *different from* their peers. The revised National Curriculum (DfEE/QCA 1999: 30–7) incorporates a general statement on inclusion. This sets out principles for 'setting suitable learning challenges', responding to pupils' 'diverse learning needs' and 'overcoming potential barriers to learning and assessment for individuals and groups of pupils', including pupils who are learning English as an additional language (who will not necessarily have identified SEN).

The current government strategy for SEN *Removing Barriers to Achievement* (DfES 2004f) confirms the expectations for primary (and secondary) schools to meet the needs of all pupils successfully. However this focus on developing inclusion requires an understanding of pupils', teachers' and parents' diverse views about the nature of SEN and the appropriate educational provision. The National Curriculum Statement on Inclusion (DfEE/QCA 1999) integrates the familiar primary teaching activities of differentiated planning and teaching for pupils in general with what have often been seen as more specialized approaches required for pupils with identified SEN and disabilities. Yet for many primary teachers these remain distinctively different activities, and some primary teachers believe that there are limits to what can be achieved with certain pupils without specialist expertise, help and additional resources. The government's policy on inclusion itself retains a role for special schools in providing education for children with the most severe and complex needs and in sharing special school teachers' expertise to support inclusion in mainstream schools (DfES 2004f: 26).

Teaching strategies: the question of specialist pedagogy

So what, if anything, is 'special' about teaching pupils with SEN? A recent review of research tackled just this question and came to the conclusion that whereas certain teaching strategies, programmes and materials for pupils with SEN may look rather different in the classroom, they are likely to share basic principles of teaching and curriculum design. The key difference lies in the intensity and deliberateness of their application – which may vary for different individuals and groups of pupils (Lewis and Norwich 2005: 216). The uses of different teaching strategies are best seen as part of teachers' overall 'pedagogy', which may be defined as 'the broad cluster of decisions and actions taken in classroom settings that aim to promote school learning' (Lewis and Norwich 2005: 7). Davis and Florian's (2004) review of research on teaching strategies for pupils with SEN concluded that there is little evidence for a separate SEN pedagogy, but that teachers' 'SEN knowledge' may be seen as an essential component of pedagogy, which guide teachers as they try out and reflect on different approaches. The main interest here is in how teachers use their knowledge to understand pupils' educational needs and apply combinations of teaching approaches for different purposes.

The body of published research on teaching pupils with SEN is complex and varied in approach, from individual case studies to large-scale overviews of published research findings in different contexts. The basic concepts and terminology can be particularly problematic, with significant international differences. In using the term 'pupils with SEN' in this chapter we mean pupils who have been identified as having special educational needs in the UK context, normally through the staged, multiprofessional assessment procedures set out in the SEN Code of Practice (DfES 2001d). This includes the four areas of need identified in the UK Code of Practice: communication and interaction; cognition and learning; behavioural, emotional and social development; and sensory and/or physical needs. It is acknowledged in the SEN Code of Practice and more widely in current academic and professional literature that pupils' special educational needs are frequently interrelated (DfES 2001d: 85, para. 7: 52). Indeed there is strong evidence that it is hard to separate the areas of need conceptually or practically. Nevertheless, this type of SEN categorization (with a related list of subcategories) is in administrative use in education and such terms are often used by researchers as an organizing device for gathering and analysing evidence about appropriate teaching strategies. Yet pupils cannot be solely understood in terms of their apparent educational difficulties, and for this reason we consider whether some of the principles and aims for primary pupils in general, including those that are embedded in recent developments like the Primary Strategy (DfES 2003b) can help us to view the teaching of 'pupils with special educational needs' in a new and productive way.

Research evidence about teaching strategies for pupils with SEN

The following sections draw on a survey of research literature carried out in 2003–4 by a team of researchers from the Universities of Manchester and

Cambridge for the DfES. The review was initially structured in terms of the four 'areas of need' identified in the SEN Code of Practice (see above), which were called 'strands' in the review. Each 'strand report' identifies the groups of children who experience difficulty in the relevant area of need and it gives an overview of forms of evidence available about teaching strategies and principal theoretical perspectives. Full methodological details and strand reports on the different areas of SEN are provided in the project report (Davis and Florian 2004). Some of the main findings are summarized below. However it is important to note that it is only possible here to provide a brief indication of the wealth of research evidence available. Most references have been deliberately omitted to allow clarity in presenting the key findings but specific research findings can be followed up via the references in the original research report or in other key reviews such as the one recently edited by Lewis and Norwich (2005).

Communication and interaction

A wide range of communication and interaction needs may be identified in pupils, and there is much diversity in the terminology used. The relevant research findings tend to focus on three broad groups of children whose identified needs may be best addressed in different ways:

- *Children identified with speech, language and communication needs* (sometimes referred to as specific speech and language difficulties/impairments) – these children do communicate as effectively as their peers, but the difficulty cannot be directly attributed to physical or sensory impairments or to profound learning difficulties. For these children most of the research evidence points to the value of highly individualized programmes of teaching best carried out in the form of additional support in a mainstream school.
- *Children identified with communication and interaction difficulties associated with severe and profound learning difficulties* who may use idiosyncratic, non-verbal or assisted means of communication (for example, symbols). For these children the move recently has been away from highly structured skill-based programmes of teaching towards approaches that place more emphasis on opportunities for peer interaction, meaningful experiential learning, multi-sensory learning environments, intensive interaction, and enabling systems of communication developed in the whole-school setting.
- *Children identified with autistic spectrum disorders (ASD)*, a term that covers a range of pervasive developmental disorders presenting difficulties in communication, social behaviour and cognition. For children identified in this way, there is a very wide range of

interventions in use. Most of these approaches are supported more by professional experience than by systematic research backing, except for some studies on the effectiveness of certain highly structured programmes of applied behaviour analysis and more holistic classroom-focused approaches like TEACCH (Treatment and Education of Autistic and Communication Handicapped Children). Practice tends to be rather eclectic in different schools and the choice of approach is often mainly influenced by the particular experience and expertise of the staff and parents involved.

In the primary years, there is research evidence of the long-term effectiveness of programmes like TEACCH (and others) for children identified with ASD, and explicit language teaching for children with speech, language and communication needs. Early identification and intervention has strong research support, as does a focus on supporting the generalization of learning with varying degrees of structure according to individual needs. However, a central problem lies in the ongoing assessment of pupils' progress, as assessment procedures tend to be primarily language based. This affects the assessment of pupils' attainment across the curriculum, not just their development in language and communication. In the future more research evidence is needed in such areas as the appropriate timing and intensity of existing intervention approaches on how to enable access to the whole curriculum for pupils with difficulties in communication and interaction, and on the specific needs of pupils identified with Asperger syndrome who often face subtle language difficulties, which may be misinterpreted as behaviour problems.

Cognition and learning

Difficulties in cognition and learning are central to the identification of pupils with SEN, and it can be hard to separate learning difficulties from associated physical, sensory, social, emotional and behavioural difficulties. However there is a great deal of research focusing primarily on children with primary difficulties in academic learning, typically in cognitive aspects of attention, memory, problem solving, reasoning, language and literacy. Certain pupils are seen to have specific learning difficulties in culturally and educationally important areas of learning, notably literacy (where the complexities of the irregular English language also present particular problems).

The main body of research evidence relates to literacy. The findings suggest a need for the comprehensive and integrated teaching of reading, with explicit reference to the sounds of language, grammar and meaning and to the connections with spelling and writing. 'Ordinary teaching' is not sufficient for certain pupils who will not make progress without repetitive and cumulative learning opportunities and collaborative support networks at school and home. There seem to be some promising approaches in use for certain pupils with specific literacy difficulties, such as multisensory teaching. However very broad group labels such as 'dyslexia' are usually too general to identify individual needs and they can lead to inflexible, prescriptive teaching. One of the main research interests now lies in the development of procedures for the assessment of pupils' needs through their responses to teaching – a form of 'dynamic assessment', which contrasts with the traditional psychometric test approaches that assume a fixed level of ability (Elliott 2000).

Another set of research findings focuses on the use of generic approaches for developing pupils' awareness and control of learning strategies ('metacognition'). These range from the use of devices for promoting transferable thinking and learning skills, such as writing frames and story mapping, to the types of teacher-pupil dialogue that support pupils' higher order thinking. There are also some 'thinking skills' packages in increasing use for pupils identified with learning difficulties, focusing particularly on speaking and listening rather than the literacy skills that can present such a barrier to learning. Further research evidence points to general aspects of the classroom learning environment that support cognition and learning, including new developments in ICT and other learning resources, cooperative group learning, and attention to relevant aspects of the physical space, seating and organizational routines.

Many of the findings about supporting pupils' cognition and learning emerge from research at primary school level but there is little research evidence about the effectiveness of particular strategies at different phases of education. It is more that the focus of research varies by age. In the primary years the research focus tends to be on literacy and numeracy, speaking and listening, metacognition, social development and relevant aspects of classroom behaviour, self-concept and motivation. Some of the research emphasis found more at secondary level could usefully be extended to KS2, including the investigation of learning difficulties in subject areas across the curriculum. There is also a need at all phases of education to gather systematic evidence about the increasingly popular but little researched areas of learning styles, exercise programmes and nutritional interventions like fish oils to assess their impact on pupils' cognition and learning.

Behavioural, emotional and social development

The research literature in this area tends to focus on two main groups of pupils:

- *Children identified with social, emotional and behavioural difficulties (SEBD)* – a wide-ranging term including children with emotional/

psychiatric problems and those whose behaviour is more reactive to their current circumstances and the social environment of school, families and peer group. Forms of behavioural difficulties may include acting out, withdrawal, self-harm, substance abuse, crime, and so on.

- *Children diagnosed with attention deficit/hyperactivity disorder (ADHD)* – a syndrome focusing on behavioural signs of inattention, hyperactivity and impulsivity.

Both of these groups are contentious in the field of SEN, partly due to the continuing debates about causality and the difficulty in identifying particular behaviour problems as a form of SEN. In the field of SEN, the 'medical model' locates the problem within the child in the form of biological or psychological (cognitive and emotional) factors, whereas the 'social model' focuses on the child in context, sometimes examining the influence of wider social and cultural factors extending beyond the school (for example, gender stereotypes in society and the impact on boys' behaviour in school). As in other areas of SEN, the assumed cause tends to influence the type of intervention recommended in the literature. However, in the case of children's behavioural, social and emotional difficulties it has been acknowledged that particular difficulties apply to inclusion (Evans *et al.* 2004) and there can be significant problems of blame, stress, conflict and guilt for all involved.

Much of the research in this field focuses on children in the primary years of education. The findings suggest some promising approaches in involving peers in the development of pupils' social skills, managing behaviour and reducing peer rejection. The active involvement of parents, and some programmes of parental training have also been shown to help. 'Cognitive-behavioural' interventions that help children to monitor and regulate their own behaviour have been shown to increase on-task behaviour and reduce antisocial behaviour, as have certain uses of behaviour management (for example, rewards, reprimands, redirection and 'response cost' – when something important is taken away). It has been suggested that certain strategies for involving peers and for developing self-regulation are more effective for adolescents than for children in the primary years. However, the research evidence about this is rather mixed and contradictory. One of the main gaps in the literature is on the sustainability of improvement. Much of the research concentrates on short-term outcomes and there is need for more long-term studies following up children over two or more years. There is also a need to extend the research perspective to include the educational/family/peer system as a whole and to take account of the views of the children and young people whose behaviour is identified as problematic in this context.

Sensory and/or physical needs

As in the other areas of SEN discussed previously, the terminology used to describe children with sensory and physical needs can be problematic. There are not only international differences (for example, 'hearing impaired' in the UK versus 'hard of hearing' in the US) but the terms may also have a wider political and cultural meaning – as shown by the capitalization of 'deaf' to 'Deaf' to indicate identification with a Deaf community with its own language and culture. Research generally focuses on the following groupings of children: *visually impaired (VI), hearing impaired (HI), multi-sensory impaired (MSI),* and *physically disabled (PD)*, although these are by no means hard-edged categories and each incorporates a wide variety of children with differing educational needs. Indeed many children with severe and complex MSI have more in common with children identified with severe, complex and multiple learning difficulties than with other children with sensory and/or physical needs. There can also be related medical needs to take into account, and certain chronic medical conditions are known to have educational implications (for example, epilepsy).

This is inevitably a complex field of research and it is notably supplemented by considerable professional knowledge that may not have been systematically evaluated and disseminated. The whole range of evidence suggests some promising teaching strategies and approaches, which focus on different aspects of the child in context. Much research is conducted with children in KS1 and KS2, and the evidence supports early intervention in the preschool years (although more is needed on the effectiveness of early intervention for children with more complex needs or disabilities). Some approaches focus directly on the systematic learning of certain skills (for example, using a protractor for a child with VI), or on the adaptation of the learning environment to facilitate children's participation and learning (for example, classroom amplification programmes; physical access). New technologies are particularly relevant in this area, including computer software (for example, for pupils with VI), hardware (for pupils with PD), and cochlear implants for those with HI. However, more generally, there is a diverse set of approaches that emphasizes the importance of providing opportunities for children to develop skills of social interaction, to gain access to the local environment and to develop independence. These include certain types of curriculum development (for example, in physical education) and extra-curricular activities and the use of alternative means of communication as well as emotional development, personal choice and target setting. The focus on social experience and independence partly reflects the traditional experiences of many children with sensory and physical difficulties in being taught separately from their peers and having little opportunity for social interaction and self-determination. There is also a particular problem for children with more severe MSI in gaining sufficient experience of exploration, play and other forms of social interaction to develop language, symbolic thinking and learning. For children with less severe sensory and/or physical impairments (and for older children and young people) research tends to emphasize access to the curriculum rather than specialist teaching. However there is a need for further research on the actual quality of their participation in lessons and evidence of learning.

Combining strategies for teaching pupils with SEN

One of the common findings about teaching children in all the areas of SEN is the need to use a combination of teaching strategies. For example, in the area of cognition and learning, there are clear research findings that the most effective teaching interventions use a combination of approaches for complex areas of learning in subjects like English, mathematics and science. In reading, for instance, it works well to combine 'direct instruction' for decoding words with 'strategy instruction' for comprehending texts because these 'lower order' and 'higher order' reading skills interact with each other as reading develops. In the area of behavioural, emotional and social difficulties we also see the apparent value of combining different approaches (for example, cognitive-behavioural training for self-regulation together with family therapy). 'Multi-modal', interdisciplinary approaches are promising for pupils identified with ADHD – an area that has been overdominated recently by the use of medication alone. In the area of communication and interaction there is promising evidence about the use of visual strategies to support verbal approaches in developing language, and with regard to children with sensory and/or physical impairments, a combined approach is similarly beneficial. Nelson and Cammarata (1996) suggest the need to replace single strategy solutions with 'tricky mixes of instructional strategies' that address the unique learning needs of deaf pupils.

Understanding research evidence in the wider context of primary practice

One of the main challenges for primary teachers in using published research findings is how to link the conclusions with their own ideas about 'what works' for pupils and apply new ideas in their own classrooms. Surveys of research evidence about teaching pupils who experience different patterns of SEN can be very powerful ways of providing teachers with a set of initial hypotheses about what may be likely to work with certain pupils whose needs are clearly identified. However, as mentioned earlier, there is considerable overlap and interrelationship between different areas or types of difficulty.

Teachers are in danger of losing a sense of each pupil as an individual if the focus is primarily on the categorization of SEN. Though skilled activities like teaching would be impossible without the selection and organization of knowledge about pupils, such as what a 'year 5 class' is like, human limitations are also evident in the potential operation of bias, stereotyping and inappropriate expectations. The potentially negative outcomes of labelling certain pupils have been well researched (Chaplain 2000). There is a continuing tension between knowing individual pupils and 'knowing a disorder', which can falsely separate pupils identified with SEN from their classroom peers. Yet we must also acknowledge the increasing emphasis in the last decade by many parents and teachers on the 'specialness' of certain groups of pupils, such as those identified to have syndromes like dyslexia, dyspraxia, attention deficit hyperactivity disorder (ADHD) and autistic spectrum disorders (ASD).

One way to form a more coherent and inclusive view of all pupils is to look more widely at primary education. In the last decade there have been some striking developments in the ways we understand primary pupils, some of which are embedded in the current Primary Strategy (DfES 2003b; DfES 2004c) and other initiatives such as those relating to 'personalized learning' (http://www.standards.dfes.gov.uk/personalisedlearning/).

These include:

- pupils as learners: attending to how pupils learn and their individual differences in handling information and developing knowledge;
- pupils as citizens: acknowledging pupils' opinions, rights and responsibilities, giving rise to efforts to listen to 'pupil voice' and promote pupil autonomy;
- pupils as human beings: connecting learning with pupils' personal, social, emotional and moral development and their lives beyond school;
- pupils as active members of a learning community: focusing on the social nature of pupils' participation in classroom learning, including the ways in which pupils may cooperate and help each other to learn;
- pupils as innovators: understanding pupils as leading and well informed users of information and communications technology, and as creative participants in the arts, humanities and sciences.

These different ways of knowing pupils apply equally to pupils designated as having SEN. For example, we know that friendships become very important to children in KS2, and the pupils themselves can identify when friends may either support or hinder their learning and confidence (Doddington and Flutter 2001). Friendships are equally important to pupils identified as having SEN, as Norwich and Kelly (2005) found in their study of year 6 and year 9 pupils designated as having MLD. They found that this is not just a matter of enjoying the company of friends and learning together; the awareness of other pupils' responses can also affect pupils' preferences for receiving learning support and other special educational provision either with or separately from the class.

Cooperative group learning has strong connections with positive social and academic outcomes for pupils in general, although currently there is mixed research evidence about the direct academic gains for pupils with specific learning difficulties (McMaster and Fuchs 2002). Pupils with core difficulties in group learning, such as those with Asperger syndrome have been shown to benefit from particular social strategies such as turn-taking games, social stories, role playing, social skills training in language and gesture, and regulating the social routines in school. Other pupils are central to the experience of learning in school, and it has been found that peer monitoring and 'buddy systems' can have a very strong effect on improving social skills and reducing peer rejection for pupils identified as having social, emotional and behavioural difficulties (McEvoy and Walker 2000).

Much of the current emphasis on learning processes applies equally to pupils identified with SEN (DfES 2004c). Active learning is intrinsically motivating and enjoyable, and there is evidence, for example, that active participation in learning activities can in itself have a positive impact on the social and behavioural development of pupils with visual impairment (Davis and Hopwood 2002). This also applies beyond the school setting. For instance research has also shown a connection for deaf children between their participation in extra curricular activities and their social and emotional development (Luckner and Muir 2001). The nature of pupils' classroom learning is a crucial area for further research given the need to understand the costs and benefits of inclusion in the current educational system and decide how best to move forward. With reference to deaf pupils, Greenberg and Kusche (1998) emphasize the need to create an atmosphere that encourages the integration of pupils' emotional and social development with academic and cognitive growth, which means looking closely at the elements of the primary classroom environment that promote pupils' participation and access to learning. This only involves technical adaptations such as classroom amplification programmes for hearing impaired pupils (Brett 2003) but also the general classroom processes that promote collaboration, enjoyment and safe opportunities to interact, experiment, create and take risks in learning (Kershner 2000).

The concept of 'pupil voice' is also relevant to *all* pupils. Listening to the experiences of pupils with SEN can have a very powerful impact on anyone who works with children, especially when we hear the life stories of people who have never had much control over the educational decisions made for them (Armstrong 2003). The requirement to listen to pupils and take account of their views is embedded in the SEN Code of Practice (DfES 2001d), with the associated notion of 'partnership with pupils'. However, this focuses mainly on pupils' rights to be involved in assessment, progress reviews, and decision making about future placements and opportunities. When we look more directly at teaching and learning, there are evident benefits of helping pupils of all ages to express their views, although the opportunities to do this at KS2 tend to be limited to involvement in personal target setting and self-monitoring rather than more fundamental decisions about curriculum content and choice, for instance (see Chapter 6). There is a need to find strategies for helping pupils with learning and communication difficulties to tell us what they think, rather than remaining at the level of aspiration (Lewis 2004). When this is done, the impact can be great. For example, Clarke *et al.* (2001) noted the therapeutic value for pupils identified with speech and language difficulties of building on the children's own preferences to develop functional movement and communication, rather than seeking to remediate deficits perceived by others.

The reality of successful teaching: acknowledging different perspectives and using a combination of teaching strategies

In conclusion, if we are to develop even more effective teaching strategies for pupils designated as having SEN, the main research challenges at the moment are to examine the best ways of selecting and combining teaching strategies over time. There is also a need to continue to gather evidence about the degree of precision possible in matching certain 'types' of SEN with certain teaching strategies, bearing in mind the overlap and interrelationship of different needs. In the current policy context we would argue that priority should be given to developing an inclusive pedagogy applying to all learners, making use of the wealth of knowledge about teaching children who experience difficulties in learning available from research on SEN. This depends in part on developing good lines of communication and collaborative working relationships between pupils, parents, families, teachers, researchers and the others involved in supporting pupils' learning in school.

11 Widening the Inclusion Agenda: Policy, Practice and Language Diversity in the Primary Curriculum

Jean Conteh

This chapter explores issues of inclusion for a diverse group of learners who are not always recognized within definitions of the term – those with English as an additional language (EAL). Placing the issues within relevant socio-cultural and political contexts, it traces official responses to the distinctive strengths and needs of EAL learners, and ways in which these are essentially part of a model of good practice, since the introduction of the National Curriculum. It revisits the controversies that have affected the achievements of these learners, particularly in relation to assessment. It reports research that is offering insights to significant ways forward; ways that genuinely play to the strengths of these learners and enhance their success. Two such developments are the 'funds of knowledge' approach to characterizing and shaping home-school links and the 'many pathways' model, which helps to widen our understanding about literacy learning and literacies. Finally, it suggests policy implications and vital areas for future research.

Background: children learning bilingually

It is lunchtime. In a year 3 classroom in a city in the north of England, three eight-year-old children – Yasmin, Nahida and Anwara – are talking to a visitor (JC) about the books they like to read (these are pseudonyms for children who took part in a small-scale, ethnographic study of 'successful' bilingual pupils at key stage two (KS2) in a mainstream school). One child goes to the class library, which is a shelf in the corner of the room. She finds a book, brings it back to the group and opens it. Everyone begins looking carefully at the book and the following conversation ensues:

| 01 | 3 children: | (*spelling out*) khargosh ... khargosh |
| | JC: | the rabbit... |

	Yasmin:	khargosh ... sh ... sh ... em ... gha ... gha
	Nahida:	ghu ... ghu ...
05	Yasmin:	khargosh ... gha ...
	Nahida:	heh ... spell it out ... gha ...
	Yasmin:	what's carrot in Urdu? ... ghajar
	Nahida:	ghajar ...
	Anwar:	ghajar ...
10	Yasmin:	ghajar ...
	Nahida:	ghajar ... sh ... shawk se kah raha hai ...
	Yasmin:	it means ... rabbit is eating ...
	Nahida:	the rabbit is eating happily the carrot
	JC:	the rabbit is happily eating the carrot
15	Nahida:	eating the carrot
	Yasmin:	yeah ... miss

(Conteh 2003: 46–7)

The three children are all bilingual, and indeed multilingual. As well as English, they speak Punjabi and Urdu. There are many definitions of bilingualism and the one I adopt here, developed in Tower Hamlets, captures the important links between language and social practice by defining bilingual pupils as those who:

> live in two languages, who have access to, or need to use, two or more languages at home and at school. It does not mean that they have fluency in both languages or that they are competent and literate in both languages.
>
> (Hall 2001: 5)

The book that Yasmin chose from the library was a dual language text, in Urdu and English, and the children's reading shows evidence of their biliteracy (Datta 2000). Indeed, these children are simultaneously learning to read and write in two scripts in very different ways and for different purposes in the different contexts of community, home and school. In the mainstream classroom, like almost every other KS2 child in England, they are learning to read in English using the approaches embodied in the Literacy Hour, which encourage a range of active, sense-making strategies on the part of the learner. According to their teachers, and their SATs results at key stage one, they are doing this very successfully. At home, or in a relative's house with family members, they are learning to read in Urdu using very formal, repetition and rote-learning approaches. What is interesting about their reading behaviour as shown in the above transcript is the way in which the children are transferring the strategies they have learnt from their lessons in reading in English to their reading of the Urdu text. Their learning to read in one language seems to be supporting their learning in the other. In this way they are demon-strating something of Cummins' theory of 'interdependence', which con-vincingly challenges the commonsense notion that, when learning a second language, the learner's first language will in some way interfere and so should be avoided (Cummins 1984, 1996, and see below).

It is not certain how many children in England experience biliteracy in similar ways to Yasmin, Nahida and Anwar. Official statistics tell us nothing about biliteracy, but normally state the proportion of 'ethnic minority' children in schools in England to be about 10 per cent, or around 650,000 children (DfES 2003a). As yet, we do not have reliable data for the full range of languages spoken in England. In this chapter, I trace the history of official responses in primary education policy in England to supporting the strengths and meeting the needs of bilingual children in mainstream schools. I suggest that such responses to date have been contradictory, un-informed by research and theory and unsupportive of bilingual children's distinctive needs. They also fail to recognize links between learning English as an additional language and learning other languages in school. As such, they have not provided equality of opportunity for bilingual children. I argue that definitions of inclusion in primary policy and practice need to recognize the diversity of ways in which children are learning to talk, read and write in England.

Responding to language diversity – a history of contradiction

The Bullock Report (DES 1975) is, arguably, still the most definitive and comprehensive overview of language teaching and learning in schools in England towards the end of the twentieth century. At the time it was pub-lished, the proportion of 'immigrant children' in schools in England and Wales was estimated as 3.3 per cent, and there was concern about meeting the needs of bilingual learners in mainstream schools. Bourne (2001: 257–8) traces the history of responses to these concerns from that time, showing how the presence in their classes of children whose languages they could not understand often disrupted 'the constructed reality of the classroom' for primary teachers in the post-Plowden days of child-centred education where the teacher's rôle was constructed as 'the monitor of learning' through the 'transparent and unproblematic medium' of language. She describes how, in the 1960s and 1970s, provision for newly arrived bilingual children was often based in special classes and language centres where they were subjected to the intensive teaching of English using audiolingual approaches developed in the US after the Second World War, mainly for military personnel about to be sent on foreign assignments.

The Bullock Report itself had some encouragingly enlightened things to say about bilingualism, schools and society. After a general statement about the value of bilingualism internationally, the report goes on:

> When bilingualism in Britain is discussed it is seldom if ever with reference to the inner city immigrant populations, yet over half the immigrant pupils in our schools have a mother-tongue which is not English, and in some schools this means over 75% of the total number on roll. The language of the home and of a great deal of the central experience of their life is one of the Indian [sic] languages, or Greek, Turkish, Italian or Spanish. These children are genuine bilinguals, but this fact is often ignored or unrecognised by the schools. Their bilingualism is of great importance to the children and their families, and also to society as a whole. In a linguistically conscious nation in the modern world we should see it as an asset, as something to be nurtured, and one of the agencies which should nurture it is the school.
>
> (DES 1975: 293–4)

The far-sighted recommendations for bilingual pupils made by the Bullock committee advocated – among other things – the provision of specialist support for their learning beyond the early stages and across the curriculum, not just in developing proficiency in English. Unfortunately, they did not have much opportunity to be translated into practice. The early 1980s saw a tense period of unrest in cities in different parts of England. One consequence, in the interests of social cohesion, was the construction of the 'Education for All' ideology. The influential Swann Report (DES 1985b) was one of its main manifestations. Swann recommended a move away from the intensive withdrawal approaches to teaching bilingual children that were widely used at the time. This was probably a good thing, pedagogically. But, as part of its *equal access* ideology, Swann also strongly advocated the end of mother tongue teaching in mainstream schools, and of LEA support for supplementary mother tongue classes. This effectively closed down initiatives into researching the potential of mother tongue teaching, such as the national Schools' Council Mother Tongue Project (Tansley and Craft 1984) and the Mother Tongue and English Teaching (MOTET) project in Bradford (Fitzpatrick 1987). Such work had been slowly developing in England and mainland Europe through the 1970s. So, two of the main long-term educational impacts of the Swann Report have been the separation of provision for the teaching of community languages and of English for bilingual children, and the real lack of research into the experiences of bilingual learners in English school settings. Both – arguably – have had negative effects in many ways for such children's attainment in mainstream schools.

The National Curriculum, introduced in 1988, not long after the Swann Report, clearly recognized that all children had an entitlement to learn English (Cox 1991). One of its key aims was that, by the age of 16, all pupils would be able to use spoken and written standard English confidently and accurately. But, it seemed, this aim was to be met at the expense of language diversity, which was only acknowledged in the curriculum in terms of accent and dialect. No specific reference was made to children who may have two or more languages in their repertoire, and of ways in which such children's learning of English in mainstream classrooms may be accomplished in different ways from that of (so-called) monolingual children. Guidance on these issues was disseminated in a circular from the National Curriculum Council (NCC 1991). Its contents epitomize what Safford (2003: 8) calls 'the contradiction at the heart of education policy in England' for bilingual children. The circular recognized positively the presence of bilingual children in schools and welcomed the languages they brought as 'a rich resource'. It went on to offer some guidance and support for teachers working with bilingual pupils. But, essentially, this embodied a transitional model of bilingualism, suggesting that pupils be encouraged to use their first languages for learning only *until* their proficiency in English was strong enough for them to move to the exclusive use of English. Safford (2003: 8) suggests that such ambivalence towards bilingualism leads to two conflicting policy paradigms in the curriculum: 'the celebration of ethnic and linguistic diversity, and the universal model of language development and assessment'. For teachers working with bilingual children, the practical implications of such contradictory messages are complex and have been documented (for example, Conteh 2000; Bourne 2001; Safford 2003). Corson (1993) spells out the negative implications of such policies for children's learning, concluding that ultimately they deny bilingual learners the means to develop cognitively to their full potential, and open the door to educational underachievement at a later stage (Baker 1996).

This failure to activate the positive cognitive implications of bilingualism for learning continued to be reproduced in official documentation throughout the 1990s (see Barwell 2004 for a critical review). In the first version of the National Literacy Strategy Framework for Teaching (DfEE 1998b), matters reached their lowest point; no mention at all was made of bilingualism as a possible factor – either positive or negative – in children learning to read and write. This omission was later corrected by the distribution of an additional section to the files, which included provision for children with English as an additional language, along with those with special educational needs and those in vertically grouped classes in small schools. The harnessing of EAL and SEN in this way continued through early evaluations of the Literacy Hour (for example, OfSTED 1998), with all the ambivalent messages and consequences for inclusion that this entails.

Two recent initiatives indicate that there may be changes in the thinking that is influencing policy about language in the primary curriculum, though the complex links between language and learning suggested by Cummins' interdependence theory remain somewhat undeveloped. The first initiative, the *Languages for All: Languages for Life* strategy, was introduced in 2002 (DfES 2002a). It lays down, clearly with a strong hint of *déjà vu*, long-term objectives aimed towards, among other things, introducing modern foreign languages at KS2 by September 2009. The statutory guidance for this has just been laid out in the *Key Stage 2 Framework for Languages* (DfES 2005a). In the 2002 document it is possible to detect the beginnings of a recognition of the links between modern foreign languages and 'community' languages and the possible ways in which bilingual children – like Anwar, Rehana and Nahida – could be at an advantage compared to monolingual learners in their learning of French, German or Spanish in school. There is also even the hint that speakers of community languages could have a contribution to make to developing England as a nation of 'multilingual and culturally aware citizens' (DfES 2002a: 5). But the second, statutory document, provides virtually no opportunities for teachers to make this happen, leading to the risk of

> schools successfully transforming fluent speakers of foreign languages into monolingual English speakers, at the same time as they struggle, largely unsuccessfully, to transform English monolingual students into foreign language speakers.
>
> (Cummins 2005: 586)

The second initiative focuses more closely on bilingual learners at KS2. This DfES-funded pilot study into provision for 'advanced' EAL learners at KS2 does seem to provide some official recognition of the importance of understanding the ways in which skills in learning may be transferred from the first language to additional languages. It makes explicit in two of its key principles the possible positive outcomes for children's learning of supporting and promoting bilingualism in school:

- Bilingualism is a valuable asset and first language has a continuing and significant rôle in learning
- Language acquisition goes hand in hand with cognitive and academic development.

(NALDIC 2004: 2)

The EAL Pilot Project is the first official partnership between the Primary National Strategy and the Ethnic Minority Achievement Project teams in the DfES. It is currently working in 21 LEAs, most of which cater for large ethnic minority populations. The project document makes clear how its principles relate to the National Curriculum 2000 statement on inclusion (NALDIC

2004: 2). Similarly, its theoretical bases in research into the educational achievement of bilingual learners are clearly indicated, and the work of Cummins and his associates figures strongly. Some of the key features of this are highlighted in the next section.

Bilingualism and educational achievement – what does the research tell us?

Even at the time when the National Curriculum was first introduced, the research evidence from a wide range of contexts around the world for the positive benefits of supporting young learners' bilingualism was already strong (for example, Cummins 1984; Rivera 1984; Skutnabb-Kangas 1984; Fitzpatrick 1987). Gregory (1994: 160) reviews much of this and puts forward key theoretical principles to underpin a notion of bilingual learning. She points out, however, that the 1988 National Curriculum took hardly any account of the research, and suggests that: 'It is beginning to look as if *provision* of the same curriculum might not be adequate to give children equal *access* to it' (my italics).

Providing 'equal access' does not mean treating all children in the same way. Biggs and Edwards (1994) and Bhatti (1999), among others, attest to the unintentional harmful effects of this 'equal means same' model of inclusion. In language learning terms, 'immersion' (Cummins 1996: 100–3) can soon become 'submersion' – and possibly even drowning. It may seem intuitively reasonable to expect that young children will learn a new language if they spend enough time listening to it, that they will somehow 'pick it up' from those around them but this does not take account of the complex interrelationships between first and additional languages that Cummins' work explains.

The insistence that the needs of children with EAL should be kept distinct from those of children with SEN in a chapter that is arguing for language diversity to be part of a definition of inclusion may seem odd and counter-intuitive. Yet it echoes through the literature. Bourne (2001: 262), for example, talks about the dangers of conflating 'bilingual' and 'special needs' in support provision for early stage learners of English. Clearly, the need for the distinction must be explained, and it can be, from the research literature. Cummins (1996), reporting empirical work with French-English bilinguals in Canada, introduced his socio-cognitive theories of 'language thresholds' (pp. 104–8), Basic Interpersonal Communicative Skills (BICS) and Cognitive Academic Language Proficiency (CALP) (pp. 57–8) and 'linguistic interdependence' (pp. 109–12). Together, these provide powerful explanations for many of the distinctive features of bilingualism, showing how learning first and additional languages is linked and how academic language proficiency needs time to develop.

In addition, Cummins demonstrates how the confusion between bilingualism and special educational needs can have social and political as well as linguistic and academic implications, leading, as it has, to many children being assessed as having learning needs and being placed in groups to receive SEN remediation when in fact their needs were for specific support in developing their language competence in order to cope with the demands of the curriculum. His theoretical models, which have been developed over the years (Cummins 2000) permit, in his words, 'a variety of seemingly contradictory data to be integrated' and provide 'a partial basis for prediction and planning with respect to the education of minority students' (Cummins 1984: 6).

Cummins', and his associates', work has had profound effects on the teaching of bilingual children around the world – except in England. Here it remains largely unknown to mainstream teachers and, it seems, to policy makers. Official recommendations for meeting the needs of bilingual children in England are often based on intuitively reasonable pedagogic notions such as 'time on task', which are unsupported by Cummins' empirical research. His work is, however, known widely in England by many of those teachers – ethnic minority achievement (EMA) and others – who, work day by day with bilingual children in mainstream classrooms. Cooke (2004) attests to the almost subversive nature of the dissemination of Cummins' ideas among this community, and to the powerful ways in which, for them, they represent a model of praxis – that 'dynamic relationship' where theory and practice interact (Conteh 2003: 3). One key aspect of Cummins' model is the need to recognize learners' whole experience of language as part of their 'common underlying proficiency' in whichever language they are using, and the ways in which their learning in different languages can work together to provide firm foundations for new learning and cognitive development.

As with all children in the current educational climate, issues of assessment are crucial for bilingual children and are perhaps the area where the interaction of theory and practice is most visible. The implications of bilingualism for assessment and planning have been spelt out by such practitioners as Hall (2001), who emphasize the need for theoretically informed and sensitively executed assessment of individual bilingual pupils' learning needs. Safford (2003) eloquently illustrates the complexity of such work, the subtle and careful judgements that continually need to be made and the lack of support for making such judgements from official policies and assessment criteria. She also points out, incidentally but tellingly, the negative effects of the need to work to crude baseline assessment criteria in order to secure EMA funding for additional support for individual learners. Moreover, she hints at the need to take account of even more complex issues of ideology, identity and cultural diversity in understanding the interplay of language and achievement in any multilingual classroom, which are precisely the focus of Cummins' later work.

Recent research and theorizing into young children's learning, emanating from the work of Street (2003) and Gee (1996) among others, has led to the 'many pathways' model of literacy learning (for example, Gregory *et al.* 2004). Moving beyond Cummins' models, such work draws on theoretical and research paradigms from anthropology, cross-cultural psychology, cultural and literary studies and linguistics, among other academic disciplines. It reconceptualizes literacy, not as a hierarchical set of skills as it is currently embodied in the mainstream curriculum but as different kinds of cultural practices based in, and contributing to, the construction of specific cultural contexts. So, to understand the ways in which children learn we need to know about the places in which they are learning and the people they are learning with. And these are richly diverse, as the research studies reported in their book begin to show. Gregory *et al.* (2004: 4) postulate a *syncretic* model of literacy, which places at its centre the active engagement of participants (both teachers and learners) in learning, and is conceptualized as 'a creative process in which people reinvent culture as they draw on diverse resources, both familiar and new'. Gregory *et al.* argue that this approach has the potential for synthesizing the diverse strands of evidence that help us to understand fully what a sociocultural approach to learning really involves. In this way, we can appreciate the full complexity and power of Vygotsky's ideas for educational practices that are truly inclusive in that they recognize and value the diversity of ways in which children learn. Three key principles are identified as underpinning the sociocultural approach, conceived in this way. They clearly have important implications for policy, practice and future research:

- recognizing that culture and cognition create each other;
- acknowledging that a joint culture creation between teacher and child in classrooms is crucial for learning;
- giving a voice to those whose voices would otherwise not have been heard (Gregory *et al.* 2004: 8, adapted).

Some thoughts about policy, practice and further research

> No child should be expected to cast off the language and culture of the home as he [sic] crosses the school threshold, nor to live and act as though school and home represent two totally separate and different cultures which have to be firmly kept apart.
>
> (DES 1975: 286)

This much-quoted advice from the Bullock Report may have sounded visionary in its time; based on the evidence that is now emerging about children's learning and language diversity it begins to sound like common sense. It indicates our need to know a lot more about how children learn in different contexts, both in and out of school, and to use this knowledge to inform official policies and classroom practices that are truly inclusive. In this concluding section I highlight briefly two possible lines of enquiry from the constellation that surround these questions: parental (or family) involvement, and teacher knowledge and professionalism.

Parental involvement in their children's learning is universally seen as a necessary factor for success. Those charged with improving parental involvement in schools serving large ethnic minority communities regularly interpret the poor attendance of parents at meetings and so on as a lack of concern for their children's education. But, as Crozier (2000) and others have shown, this is perhaps a misreading of the signs on the part of schools – there may be something else going on in these situations. Less well recognized than this 'problem' are the diverse ways in which parents, and indeed whole families, in different cultural contexts are involved in their children's learning. Work in the US is leading the way in understanding this area of education. Moll *et al.* (1992: 134) have developed a 'funds of knowledge' approach to bridging gaps between home and school. This seeks to analyse the 'cultural and cognitive resources of home' which have 'potential utility for classroom instruction'.

One such resource, which repeatedly emerges from studies both in the US and elsewhere, is language. Bilingualism – and indeed biliteracy – is an accepted and uncontroversial feature of life in many minority communities; children are simply expected to participate in family and community life in a range of languages and it would seem odd if they did not. Despite recent government concerns about the languages that the citizens of some parts of the UK speak in their homes (Blunkett 2002), currently we really do not know much about ways in which our second and third generation 'ethnic minority' pupils use the languages they have in their repertoires in the different contexts they mediate. Research into these issues is needed. Another area we need to know more about is the different ways in which all family members, from siblings to grandparents, are involved in a child's learning in different family groups. Such evidence has great potential significance for schools in England who are seeking ways in which they can encourage greater parental involvement. Perhaps, as Bastiani and Wolfendale (1996) suggest, the exclusive focus on parents is not the best way forward. Again, we need to know much more than we do at the moment about these pathways to learning.

A model of learning as joint culture creation between teacher and child inevitably places great emphasis on the relationships between teachers and learners (see Chapter 8) and on the rôle of classroom teachers in enhancing the success of bilingual learners. Teachers need time to consider how issues of language diversity can affect children's learning. Yet teaching about bilingualism, culture and identity still hardly features on initial teacher-training courses. The need for teachers who can identify more dialogically with the cultural and language backgrounds of their pupils is pressing. Yet, despite efforts by the Training and Development Agency for Schools, the teaching workforce in England stubbornly remains predominantly 'white'. We need to know more about the distinctive ways in which teachers can work with bilingual pupils to enhance their learning, to help us move beyond the 'transitional bilingualism' ideology towards a genuinely emancipatory pedagogy for bilingual learners. And 'white teachers' need support too; Gussin Paley (1979) powerfully outlines the ways in which issues of language, culture and identity influence the work of teachers operating in culturally diverse contexts. In so many ways, the need for and the potential of research into all these areas are huge and, as Bourne (2001) suggests, those best placed to do it are the teachers themselves.

12 The Butterfly Effect: Teaching Assistants and Workforce Reform in Primary Schools

Hilary Burgess

Introduction

Government reform of the primary teachers' workforce through the introduction of teaching assistants has major implications for classroom practice and teachers who work in key stage two (KS2). The idea of teaching assistants causing a 'butterfly effect' came from the Primary Strategy document *Excellence and Enjoyment* (DfES 2003b) as the picture that precedes the section on workforce reform in primary schools contains an adult pointing at an information chart titled *A Butterfly is Born*. Smart (2003) in the *Collins English Dictionary*, explains the 'butterfly effect' as

> the idea used in chaos theory, that a very small difference in the initial state of a physical system can make a significant difference to the state at some later time ... (a butterfly flapping its wings in one part of the world might ultimately cause a hurricane in another part of the world).
>
> (Smart 2003: 156)

In the case of teaching assistants and the re-modelling of the workforce what will the 'effect' turn out to be? Will it enhance or compromise educational standards? Will it reduce teacher workload and help prevent teacher stress? Will it have an impact on learning? This chapter will address these questions through reviewing current research on teaching assistants in the period of 'performance culture' identified elsewhere in this book (see, for example, Chapters 2, 3 and 13).

The role of the teaching assistant to support pupil achievement has become increasingly important in an era of international concern about qualified teacher shortages and school improvement. In the UK, Slater and Dean (2001) reported that there were 95,000 teaching assistants working in English schools. The predicted numbers of teaching assistants is set to rise year on year with more than 16,700 full-time equivalent additional support staff recruited since 2003 (Workforce Agreement Monitoring Group Letter, July 2004). By 2004 there were 133,440 full-time equivalent teaching assistants working in mainstream and special schools and Pupil Referral Units in England (Vincett *et al.* 2005). According to the DfES Education statistics, by 2004 there was a ratio of 2.08 teaching assistants to every teacher (DfES 2004g). This dramatic rise confirms that support staff lie at the heart of the government's radical plans for a modernized, remodelled workforce 'to find new ways, for the 21st Century, of helping schools to realise the potential for all our children' (DfES 2003b: para 1).

A major factor behind the increase in teaching assistants is the inclusion in schools of pupils with special educational needs. This defined the type of support these pupils would need and led to new roles for teachers and other adults in schools. Funding was often linked to individual statements for children making contracts for assistants temporary and short-term. It became possible to support a wider range of pupil need when the Code of Practice on the Identification and Assessment of Special Educational Needs was published (DFE 1994). The Code established that children with identifiable learning difficulties, but not requiring the level of support provided for by a statement, should have their needs recognized. This had a significant impact upon the number of teaching assistants employed to work in primary schools and has been perceived to have a positive effect on the work of primary school teachers and pupil learning (Ofsted 1995; Her Majesty's Inspectors 2002).

The Five Year Strategy for Children and Learners (DfES 2004a) claims that the Primary Strategy will bring about a more personalized approach across the whole curriculum. Teachers' skills, it is suggested, will be developed to tailor teaching and learning to the needs of the individual child. The work of the teaching assistant is identified as 'supporting children's individual needs, in helping teachers use and interpret data, in managing behaviour, and in giving teachers time to plan and prepare lessons' (DfES 2004a: 5.42).

This is a short statement but it encompasses a great deal. Teaching assistants are to be involved in personalized learning as they continue to support individual children and their needs. This is to include managing behaviour, interpretation of data and providing teachers with time for preparation. How will this be enacted in practice? In terms of managing behaviour, will it mean in the classroom, at lunch times, in the playground? When helping teachers to use and interpret data will this involve assisting with assessment, testing and recording achievement? Will giving teachers time to plan and prepare lessons involve taking whole classes as suggested in the Primary Strategy document? This chapter attempts to address some of these questions through considering issues in relation to curriculum enrichment, the views of children and issues for teachers.

Curriculum enrichment or a compromise of standards?

The role that teaching assistants might play in curriculum enrichment was emphasized by Ofsted (2002b), which noted that they contributed to both curricular quality and breadth in successful primary schools where they had received training linked to their responsibilities and been deployed to make the best use of their strengths. Ofsted found that, usually, teaching assistants' time was used to support the literacy hours, mathematics or pupils with special needs. Hancock and Eyres (2004) argue that teaching assistants who support children with complex needs have long taken on a pedagogic role which often goes unrecognized. Teaching assistants, they suggest, have been assigned a 'remedial' role in the teaching of literacy and numeracy as children in the lowest achievement quartile are often withdrawn from their classes or taught in small groups by the teaching assistant. They comment that the essential work teaching assistants do is barely visible in reports such as the evaluation of the implementation of the literacy and numeracy strategies (Earl *et al.* 2000, 2001, 2003).

Where teaching assistants regularly work with the same lower ability groups of children this can lead to a situation in which SEN children rarely receive teaching and support from their class teacher (Ofsted 2002b; Webb and Vulliamy 2006). However, as Webb and Vulliamy's research indicates, where teachers have developed a heightened awareness of this issue the needs and progress of all pupils can be monitored through regular exchange of groups with the teaching assistants.

Teaching assistants are seen as key in providing curriculum enrichment in the Primary Strategy. As well as freeing up time for teachers it is considered that they have a wealth of expertise that will help to keep the curriculum alive. Of the schools surveyed for the Primary Strategy document it is claimed that 96 per cent of schools use teaching assistants to work with individual pupils, 99 per cent to work with small groups and that 1 in 10 of the schools surveyed (600 primary headteachers and deputy headteachers were polled) used teaching assistants to lead whole classes. Examples of creative use of teaching assistants include leading a knitting club and providing non-contact for the music coordinator to train an 80-piece orchestra. The case study states:

> At Key stage 2, teaching assistants work with half the class whilst the teacher works with the rest of the class in the ICT suite. Those in-volved with the early years also take half classes for practical work in partnership with the teacher. The school also uses one member of support staff to do all the photocopying to reduce the administrative burdens of the teachers. The teaching assistants contribute to

assessment procedures and deliver tests. They have also developed their own handbook which explains their role to parents.

(DfES 2003b: 69)

The roles described above are all, no doubt, both valuable and helpful to the teachers in that particular school. The fact that the teaching assistants have developed their own handbook bears testimony to the ownership and confidence those teaching assistants felt about their jobs. However, there are more diverse and dynamic ways of using teaching assistants to personalize the curriculum alongside considering the implications for change in practice.

When discussing teaching assistant support in the mathematics curriculum, Cronin and Bold (2005) argue that assistants should be perceived as partners in teaching mathematics to children. They suggest that confidence and enthusiasm for helping with mathematics support may vary among teaching assistants and this is the first key issue to address if the partnership is to be effective and productive in terms of children's learning. Attitudes of the teaching assistants towards mathematics may have been affected by their early learning experiences in the subject if they were taught through rote learning rather than understanding (Skemp 1989) and suffer from 'sum stress' (Fraser and Honeyford 2000). To help overcome the negative impact of such attitudes to the subject, Cronin and Bold (2005) argue that encouraging teaching assistants to discuss their own learning experiences and the ways they were taught mathematics results in a greater level of confidence when working with children in classrooms. They suggest that the best way to do this is through shared planning and feedback.

Competence, or lack of it, in teaching mathematics and particularly some of the methods of calculation in the National Numeracy Strategy, may also prevent teachers and assistants from working together effectively as partners in this curriculum area. This is a difficult area to resolve but it can begin to be addressed, argue Cronin and Bold (2005), by sharing with teaching assistants the importance of making mathematical connections with children. Making explicit links between different aspects of mathematics and connections with other subject areas when planning work with teaching assistants can be a valuable aid towards developing competence. This does mean, though, that teachers have to be willing to share knowledge, expertise and new developments in teaching and learning with teaching assistants. Such a shared and collaborative way of working in the curriculum relies on good levels of communication supported by strong relationships among all levels of teaching staff in a primary school.

The involvement of teaching assistants in the Literacy Hour has provoked much discussion around the importance of their role in this key curriculum area. The third evaluation report of the strategies (Earl *et al.* 2003) identifies teaching assistants as playing an essential role through targeted interventions with children who are making slower progress than their peers. Ofsted (2002b) report that teaching assistants have a major role in intervention and catch-up programmes while Webb and Vulliamy (2006) suggest that teaching assistants are more confident and competent in teaching and supporting literacy because they have had much more training and have built up experience through taking booster classes. Hancock and Eyres (2004) argue that the value of teaching assistants in terms of improving children's performance has been greatly underrated and claim that the success of teaching assistants, particularly in booster classes, has contributed significantly to the numbers of children achieving the expected standards of literacy at the ages of 7 and 11.

Information and communication technology has a unique place in the primary curriculum, linked as it is to all subject areas, and as such, provides a key opportunity for imaginative ways of working in primary classrooms with children and teaching assistants (see Chapter 7). The interactive nature of ICT makes it a key tool in achieving the agenda for personalized learning. A study by Wegerif and Scrimshaw (1997) on the quality of children's talk when using ICT software revealed that talk and input from a teacher (or teaching assistant) would have greatly enhanced pupil understanding and use of the materials and their subsequent development in knowledge. As Ralston (2004) acknowledges, just because when using ICT children appear to be performing technologically complex tasks it does not necessarily mean that they are learning anything important. Information and communication technology cannot in itself transform teaching and learning but the way that teachers collaborate with teaching assistants to plan stimulating and exciting use of technologies can.

How teachers work with teaching assistants across the range of curriculum subjects will have a considerable impact upon the way they are perceived by children. Even very young children will have views or opinions about the adults who work with them in their classrooms and yet despite a professional rhetoric on the importance of consulting children this rarely happens in practice (Hancock and Mansfield 2002). This is quite extraordinary as how enriched or 'alive' a curriculum might be is often best judged by children.

Views of children

Views of children on the perceptions of adults in their classroom (Eyres *et al.* 2004: 155) show that children easily differentiate between their own class teacher and other adults and the roles and tasks they perform:

> Barbara isn't a proper teacher: she helps us, she doesn't actually teach us. (Mark, Y6)

> Well, Selma is just a helper and Krystel (class teacher) does more stuff. (Veronica, Y1)

> He used to normally work in the lowest group because he just helps. (Sadia, Y4)

The views of these children indicate that teaching assistants are perceived in a variety of different ways both in terms of status and the different type of activities that they undertake. When planning for ways in which teaching assistants will be used in classrooms the views and perceptions of children have an important role to play. Taking children's views into account on a range of issues linked to their schooling has been explored by a number of researchers and writers (see Chapters 5 and 6). Children's views can inform teachers about their teaching (Abdullah and Scaife 1997), give teachers feedback on how school is being experienced (Cullingford 1991) and help children to act as partners in planning (Fajerman *et al.* 2000). The case for listening to children to bring meaning to the teaching of the literacy hour is cogently argued by Hancock and Mansfield (2002) who suggest that there is a growing tendency for teachers, and teaching assistants, to see themselves simply as 'deliverers' of a centrally organized curriculum. In a small-scale study a number of children were interviewed about the literacy hour and they also had opinions on the teaching styles of their teachers and teaching assistants. One eight-year-old girl had the following conversation.

> *Interviewer: So, you were saying that your teacher is different in the Literacy Hour?*
> Jackie: Yeah, she's sort of different. She speaks different and moves around a lot – a bit like she's worried or something.
> *Interviewer: Worried?*
> Jackie: It's like she's cross if we don't do it right and don't concentrate. She makes us concentrate, especially on the carpet, and kids muck around a lot. She talks too much and goes over the same things too much.
>
> (Hancock and Mansfield 2002: 193–4)

Hancock and Mansfield go on to explore how the plenary in the literacy hour could be used to invite children to comment on how successful the lesson has been and whether it could have been better. They suggest that teaching assistants are in a good position to facilitate feedback as they are usually assigned to a small group during this time.

The management of working patterns in a classroom is clearly evident to children and they are often well aware of the group to which they have been assigned (Doddington *et al.* 2002). Eyres *et al.* (2004) argue that children welcome the additional support they receive although they may be rather fuzzy about the different activities a teacher and a teaching assistant do and often regard teachers and assistants as doing very similar things:

> Well, Miss McAngel is the actual teacher, teacher, teacher. She actually teaches us everything because she's just a teacher and teaches us everything. But, if you like, you've got another teacher, they teach us – pretty much they'd teach us everything but Miss McAngel would do different things with us – d'you know what I mean? – sort of, I can't put it into words really – but – can you help? [looking towards Tim, her friend]. (Lisette, Y6).
>
> (Eyres *et al.* 2004: 157–8)

Eyres' research concluded that where teaching assistants took on more teaching related activities children found it difficult to support the view that people with different job titles must be doing different things. They suggest that the introduction of the literacy hour and the numeracy strategy have led to blurring of the teacher/teaching assistant boundary. This blurring at the boundaries was not perceived as problematic by the children but what are the issues it raises for teachers?

Teacher issues

While there is no doubt that teaching assistants are welcomed as classroom support, some of the future roles outlined in the Primary Strategy (DfES 2003b) such as whole-class teaching, even if carried out by those newly qualified as higher-level teaching assistants (DfES 2002b), have caused concern amongst teachers. The National Union of Teachers (2003) is quite clear that a move to use support staff for whole-class teaching would both compromise standards and the quality of education experienced by pupils. It is argued that teachers who have undergone rigorous inspection for a number of years would be 'outraged' at the suggestion that unqualified adults could do the job equally well. There is evidence in Webb and Vulliamy's (2006) research that most headteachers and teachers would not wish teaching assistants to teach whole classes and they also identify some confusion around what 'whole-class' teaching actually implies. For example, up to 50 per cent of teaching assistants claimed to provide whole-class cover but most of these instances related to unplanned teacher absence or when a teacher was dealing with an incident elsewhere. Webb and Vulliamy provide an example of a teaching assistant who took a year 5/6 for art while the class teacher withdrew small groups to work on the computer. The head of the school was full of praise for the work of the teaching assistants but adamant that they should not take classes to release teachers. It would appear that the teaching assistant who taught art was not seen as fulfilling a whole-class teaching role as the teacher was regarded as still in charge of the class even though teaching another subject. The class teacher had also planned the art lesson that was 'delivered' by the teaching assistant and headteachers and teachers clearly distinguished between teaching a lesson and delivering a lesson to whole classes. Many teachers disagreed entirely with teaching assistants teaching whole classes as they thought it devalued their profession:

> When it comes to asking classroom assistants to teach – I do not agree. I think that devalues me as a teacher if a classroom assistant can come in and take my class without any training ... We're not being fair to the kids. These people do not have the skills and experience to teach in the way they should be taught, so we're short-changing children when staff are off. It's teaching on the cheap and we're not being fair to them – they're doing a teaching job, for half my salary and no, I can't agree with that. It's happening and it will happen more and more, but no, I can't agree with that. (Y3 teacher, July 2005).
>
> (Webb and Vulliamy 2006: 89)

Other factors that constrain or promote collaborative working between teachers and teaching assistants can also be identified. For example, Jackson and Bedford (2005) identified a number of key themes in relation to workforce remodelling, which included lack of training for teachers and teaching assistants when working with other adults in a learning situation, lack of time for planning, teachers fearing a threat to their professional integrity, and the unclear nature of the terms of partnership and pay differential between teachers and teaching assistants. There appears to be little evidence, as yet, that using teaching assistants to assist with teaching tasks would reduce teacher workload and teacher stress. As Troman and Woods (2001) argue, teacher stress is often about feeling out of control in their personal and professional lives and that stress prevention is best achieved by handing control back and providing 'buddy' or mentoring support. Teachers, in this study, found that classroom assistants helped to relieve stress not because they took over some of the teaching tasks but because they became friends to share things with. As one of the teachers in their study explained:

> I've got two classroom assistants (LSAs) who work with me but they've actually ended up being my closest friends as well. So we've got a good team there. And they're the people that actually see me, and know when I've been overdoing things or when work is infringing on my social life.
>
> (Troman and Woods 2001: 105)

This teacher did not say that her stress was reduced because her workload was lessened and indeed there is evidence to suggest that having additional adults in the classroom actually increases workload as they have to manage and plan for several adults to work with children in different ways. Indeed, the areas that teachers have identified as creating excessive workload are bureaucracy and paperwork, planning, government initiatives, unrealistic targets and discipline (Butt and Lance 2005).

Another issue was identified in Moran and Abbott's (2002) study in learning support encountered by teachers in Northern Ireland. One primary unit head stated:

> Sometimes in the past, I must admit, I have felt, not threatened, but that she's overstepping the mark slightly. I had to deal with that at the time and it was very difficult to do. Without a doubt, she's inclined to do a thing for the child which I find very frustrating. I know that when I go back to the classroom (after the interview) that the maths I've set for the children will all be correct. I think she feels that I'm keeping an eye on her as opposed to the children, and that when she's left in charge, everything must be done perfectly. I would much rather she left the children to try themselves, and then I'd help them fix whatever mistakes they've made so they would understand better. It's always a problem when this happens because the children must have challenges.
>
> (Moran and Abbott 2002: 168)

Different understandings about how children learn caused this teacher concern as she worried that the children would not fully understand if they were spoonfed the answers. There is a need for much stronger evidence about the impact of other adults on teaching and learning and reduction in teacher workload (NUT 2003). Given the variety of roles and tasks that teaching assistants have undertaken in the past (Hancock *et al.* 2001) it is not surprising that much research has concentrated on changes in classroom roles and the move from domestic help to providing curriculum support (Clayton 1993; Farrell *et al.* 1999; Eyres *et al.* 2004). More in-depth research into teaching assistants and the impact of increased numbers of adults in classrooms on children's attainment continues to be required, as the paucity of available work that addresses these issues reveals (Welch *et al.* 1995; Roberts and Dyson 2002; Wilson *et al.* 2002; Vincett *et al.* 2005).

Research into how adults can be best utilized in classrooms has been addressed by Cremin *et al.* (2005) and Vincett *et al.* (2005) who evaluated three models of team organization and planning for working with teaching assistants in relation to 'room management', 'zoning' and 'reflective team-work'. Room management is about ensuring that every adult has a clear role to occupy and function to perform. Zoning is a system that works by organizing a class into learning zones, usually structured by the placement of groups in the class. Reflective teamwork aims to improve planning and organization through teamwork games and exercises and by implementing a regime of planning and reflection meetings. They worked with six primary and secondary schools, not to find out which was the most effective method, as each has its own strengths, but to encourage the participating schools to adapt the models to their own contexts. They consider that their research provides a case for effective work with teaching assistants but they are cautious at this stage in drawing more generalizable conclusions from their research.

As the range and variety of classroom roles and tasks that teaching assistants undertake increases, the question of training and further professional development for teaching assistants needs to be addressed urgently.

Conclusion

A number of key issues have emerged in this chapter that need further research and consideration by policy makers. The first centres around the ways in which teaching assistants are employed in classrooms to provide an enriched curriculum. The changing roles of teaching assistants may provide opportunities for developing stimulating and exciting activities in classrooms where teachers work in partnership in terms of both planning and teaching. Shared responsibilities imply shared knowledge and skills and the ways in which schools might support this have not yet been fully explored. A second consideration is the impact teaching assistants may have upon children's learning and achievement at KS2. Outcomes of the new workforce reforms and the impact upon children urgently require investigation. The third consideration is the changes to primary teacher practice and curriculum pedagogy that the workforce remodelling will bring and this will only emerge over a period of time. In all of these areas the views of children should be an important feature in both research and decision making.

The butterfly effect brought about by the employment and deployment of large numbers of teaching assistants in primary schools is far reaching as can be seen from the research and issues discussed in this chapter. Just how positive that butterfly effect will be for teaching assistants, primary school teachers and children's learning and achievement in the future remains to be seen.

13 What a Performance! The Impact of Performance Management and Threshold Assessment on the Work and Lives of Primary Teachers

Ian Menter, Pat Mahony and Ian Hextall

Introduction

Concluding her classic study of primary teachers in 1970s and 80s England, Jennifer Nias (1989: 214) expressed concern about the possible impact of the Education Reform Act, which had been passed in 1988:

> ... if they [primary teachers] cannot satisfy their needs which they are daily made aware of in their work in classrooms and schools (ie if they are not rewarded), then the effort that they make through their heavy investment of self in work will eventually decline.
> Can we afford to take that risk?

In the years which have elapsed since Nias wrote these words perhaps even greater risks have been taken that have very fundamentally challenged the nature of primary teachers' work and professional identity. Nias's intensive study of primary teachers as professionals whose personal identity was deeply embedded in their work and in their commitment to children – especially those children within their own classroom – makes an important backdrop against which to consider, on the basis of a range of research evidence, how primary teaching has changed over this period.

What we offer in this chapter is, firstly, a reminder of how the 'reforms' of the 1980s appeared to change the nature of primary teaching. We then examine the impact of the range of policies brought in during the second half of the 1990s, especially by the New Labour government (we thus emphasize the third of Campbell's three phases discussed in Chapter 2). In particular we focus on some elements of the 1998 Green Paper (DfEE 1998c) and draw on a study we carried out into the *Impact of Performance Threshold Assessment on*

Teachers' Work (ESRC R000239286) in 2001–3. This then enables us to make an overall assessment of the nature of primary teaching in England in the early twenty-first century and to make some suggestions about what has been gained and what has been lost through the range of changes.

1988 and all that

The introduction of the National Curriculum and national assessment following the 1988 Education Reform Act initially presented what turned out to be impossible demands in terms of curriculum coverage and assessment against attainment targets. Following major adjustments brought in from 1993, in the wake of the Dearing Review, primary teachers began to find that they could at least more-or-less deliver what was required. However, the lasting impact of those five years should not be underestimated. Teachers' trust in politicians and civil servants was severely undermined, which may partially account for the extremely cynical responses that later policy initiatives were to receive from primary teachers.

The effects of these changes in curriculum and assessment were most fully documented by the Bristol-based PACE team. The volume edited by Croll (1996), which focuses on KS2, concludes that schools, teachers and pupils were 'embedded in a dynamic network of personal identity, values and understandings that are constantly developing in the light of internal and external interaction, pressure and constraint' (Croll 1996: 156). More recently Osborn *et al.* (2000) not only show the impact of curricular reforms but also assess the likely effects of the reforms to teachers' work that were emerging in the late 1990s. Invoking the work of Bernstein on pedagogic codes, they suggest that primary teaching was moving from a competence-based approach to a performance-based approach. This movement, they argue, mirrors what has also been happening to pupils in the primary school. For teachers, the performance model implies managerialism rather than autonomous professionalism, technical rationality rather than creative interaction, and 'contractual' rather than moral accountability (see also Chapters 3, 14 and 15). Our own study of performance assessment, reported below, confirms these tendencies.

It was clearly not only the curricular reforms of 1988 that affected teachers' work. The impact of the 'marketization' elements of the Education Reform Act can also be detected. A study of primary schools in an English market town during the early 1990s showed how the perceived challenges of 'open enrolment' and devolved financial management influenced the lives in teachers in classrooms and staffrooms. Menter *et al.* (1997) found that there was a growing sense of alienation and a loss of control among primary teachers, very much of the kind that was worrying Nias in 1989. They concluded:

The gap between the model of the responsible, accountable professional on public display, and their private experience of bitterness, anxiety and overload is also indicative of the covert coercion of the new management ... Re-professionalization as an effective team member, a good organizer and coordinator, and a skilled facilitator does not seem to be sufficient to meet the absence of traditional child-centred and teaching-oriented professional identity for these particular teachers.

(Menter *et al.* 1997: 115)

If this implies a sense of 'them and us' between teachers and head-teachers, the study also revealed much disquiet among school managers at the requirements being placed upon them. Several headteachers were eagerly looking forward to retirement as the only practical way of resolving these dilemmas.

Lest the account so far appears negative and pessimistic, by invoking Acker's ethnography of one primary school during the 1980s and into the 1990s (Acker 1999) we can find plenty of evidence of teachers continuing to be creative and effective in their work with children and with each other. However these facets of a predominantly female workforce are frequently ignored by policy makers:

The conditions under which teachers work are full of contradictions. Teachers are charged with improving society through preparing the next generation, yet treated as if they are little more than children themselves and expected to spin gold from straw. Their jobs are hard in so many ways, yet socially defined as easy and natural, for women at least.

(Acker 1999: 197)

Two further key aspects of policy were inspection and standards. Much has been written about the emotional and personal impact of the schools' inspection regime that developed following the creation of Ofsted in 1992. There is no doubt that many teachers experienced deep stress through the inspection process. Workers who are already experiencing deep-seated conflict in their work are likely to be vulnerable during such external regulation processes. Woods, Jeffrey and Troman have provided graphic, qualitative evidence of the emotional impact of many of these changes on primary teachers (Woods *et al.* 1997; Jeffrey and Woods 1998; Troman and Woods 2001). Cuckle and Broadhead (1999: 186) surveyed 124 primary headteachers and one of their conclusions was that the extent to which the inspection was judged to be valuable depended in part on 'the residual effect on the morale or sense of professionalism of the school staff'.

The imposition of standards as a means of defining teaching started as an initiative from the Teacher Training Agency, itself only established in 1994. From 1992 however, the underlying notion of competences for beginning teachers was being promoted in government circulars. The translation of these into standards for beginning teachers, to be mirrored by a whole series of standards for headteachers, SEN coordinators and subject specialist teachers was a rapid development. Mahony and Hextall (2000: Ch. 2) trace this process and suggest that standards may either be constructed as a developmental or regulatory framework. Tracing through the process by which the TTA constructed the standards in England, they reach the conclusion both that the process was not a genuinely consultative one and that the outcome was much more of a regulatory structure than a professionally developmental one.

Primary teachers and performance management

In one of its first major education initiatives following electoral success in 1997, the Labour government produced *Teachers: Meeting the Challenge of Change* (DfEE 1998c). The overall intention behind this document was the modernization of the teaching profession. Located within a performance management model, the policy aimed to transform the management of schools, career progression and the basis of remuneration.

As part of the overall aim of raising standards, and assuming that 'we can only realise the full potential of our education system if we attract and motivate teachers and other staff with the ambition, incentives, training and support ...' (DfEE 1998c: 6, para. 2), the model of performance management outlined in the Green Paper aimed to bring together a tighter system of annually assessing individual teacher's performance, in order to set targets for improvement, and a new pay policy that rewards good performance. From induction to Threshold, teachers progress by yearly increment. Threshold is highly significant as the point at which, normally after five years, teachers submit themselves to an assessment process that involves providing evidence that they have met eight performance standards. Their applications are assessed by their headteacher and, until recently, were verified by an external Threshold assessor (TA). If teachers meet the Threshold standards, they receive, in the form of a performance related promotion, an additional £2000 per annum and transfer to an upper pay spine (UPS) where further promotions are possible to the grades of 'excellent teacher', 'advanced skills teacher' and so on. What was a national pay system has in effect been transformed into one that is locally determined and managed.

In order to explore the Threshold policy from its sources, through development and implementation, to its impact on teachers, teaching and the profession, our study adopted a three-strand methodological approach consisting of: documentary analysis (including an audit of surveys commissioned by teacher unions and DfES); semi-structured, tape-recorded interviews with a range of key actors, and indicative case studies. Our study spanned three successive Threshold application cycles (Rounds 1–3), and included the first point of assessment for progression post-Threshold. Of the 13 case studies, selected to take account of location, size, demography and age phase, nine were located in schools (four secondary, three primary, one nursery and one special) and four in LEAs, to access the experiences of teachers employed in 'non-standard settings'. In this chapter we draw mainly on the material gained from the primary school case studies. Previously published papers that draw on the full range of data include an examination of the policy development process (Mahony *et al.* 2002), the failure to instigate adequate equal opportunities monitoring (Menter *et al.* 2003), the emotional impact of the process (Mahony *et al.* 2004c), the gendered nature of the process (Mahony *et al.* 2004b) and the significant involvement of the private sector in administering the procedures (Mahony *et al.* 2004a).

Teachers' responses to Threshold

The study revealed that a range of strategies had been adopted by teachers and by heads around the implementation of the Threshold. There was widespread cynicism about the overall approach and few teachers believed that there had been a positive impact on their own teaching. In addition there were some very negative emotional impacts on individuals and groups of teachers.

Only four teachers out of the 46 interviewed reported feeling initially positive about Threshold. Three of these were in one primary school, Forestglade, which was an atypical setting because it had a long history of performance management. The emphasis here was on a supportive, developmental model of performance management with pay added later and relegated to 'a very small part'. It is therefore not surprising that three female teachers from Forestglade Primary emphasized the potential of Threshold to 'recognize achievement', provide 'a lot more opportunities for teachers' and to make 'good teachers feel more valued, especially after the bad press that we've had over the years'.

The remaining 42 teachers all reported negative feelings towards the initial announcement of Threshold. These were expressed with varying degrees of strength ranging from weariness – 'here we go again', through: caution – 'I was a bit suspicious about it'; resentment – 'why do I need to do that to get more money?'; contempt – 'what a load of old rubbish'; anger – 'I just felt angry' and fury – 'furious ... how can they make teachers jump through hundreds of hoops'. From her broader perspective, a Threshold assessor both confirmed the overall feelings of negativity and began to identify some reasons for it that clearly connect with the wider context within which teachers' professional identities are framed:

> I can't think of many [better] ways of introducing an initiative and putting people's backs up. It came with all that New Labour macho stuff, which came as a surprise, I hadn't expected them to be so anti teachers . . . a lot of teachers were angry. There was an awful lot of bad feeling in school . . . a large number of teachers saw it as a rod to beat them with.

It could be argued that requiring experienced teachers (who had already been inspected by Ofsted) to undergo a further process of 'proof' to access a pay rise was a misconceived way of motivating teachers. Certainly there is evidence that the strength of opposition had been underestimated:

> I just don't think it's fair, [that] we actually have to apply for our own pay rise. It would be nice if somebody came to me and said, 'I think you've done a jolly good job for the last five years, I think you deserve the extra £2,000'. (Teacher 2/f Riverton Primary) [In this chapter, each teacher in the study is identified by the fictional name of their school, a number (for classteachers) or HT for the head-teacher, and by an indication of their gender]

Refusing to 'justify her existence', a teacher described by the deputy head at Clearview as 'brilliant' and 'absolutely fantastic' felt so strongly that she left teaching. A number of teachers expressed considerable cynicism about what they perceived to be their own position as pawns in a wider context of political motivation behind the policy. Finally, deep resistance was expressed by teachers who objected to being judged through what they perceived as a bureaucratic, 'paper exercise' introduced 'by somebody who doesn't understand education'.

The extent to which financial enhancement operated as a motivator was far from straightforward. There is a sense in which, of course, people are motivated by money:

> I think you're lying if you say that pay isn't a motivator. Why do I come to work? I come to work because I get paid for it. (HT/f Forestglade Primary)

It is also probably safe to claim that most of us would prefer our financial circumstances to improve rather than deteriorate. But beyond these commonsense comments, few primary teachers define level of pay as a motivator or incentive.

Working in the context of the nursery class, close working relationships made for even more uncomfortable comparisons for another teacher, even though she had previously acknowledged that she could 'do with the money'. These, combined with the 'pressure to perform' made for a negative view of the future. These attitudes come as no surprise. To this extent the policy seems not to have pressed the right buttons in terms of the professional cultures and identities of teachers. As one primary teacher put it:

> ...the sheer vulgarity of the system that can ... have the arrogance to suggest that good performance needs more money ... I will do it for this but I won't do it for that. The idea that that is money, is appalling. Vulgar and crass and just crude. (Acting HT/m Haymead Primary)

The impact of Threshold

The surveys show that in the early days of Threshold the process was fraught with difficulties mainly related to the technology of the application form, although many also found the standards to be repetitive and unclear. Negativity towards yet more change is one accumulated effect of years of 'initiative overload', although we did not find that teachers were resistant to demands for accountability *per se*, merely to this form of it. In addition to Ofsted inspection, invoked as demonstrating that external accountability measures were already in place, there were mechanisms of 'work scrutiny' internal to the school:

> ...we're talking about people's emotions, people's feelings here, you can be professional and still have feelings. You know, if you've got effective methods for observing, work scrutiny, positive feedback methods for people growth, you don't need this business about targets linked with pay. (Teacher 1/f Clearview Primary)

For women teachers in particular, the sense of exposure and vulnerability that the process triggered was a further source of negativity:

> I don't think I've ever felt so stressed in my entire teaching career, as the time when I was trying to fill out that application ... you kind of doubt yourself really ... it's that constant worry that, you know, will I get through it? And, it's not so much, I'm not going to get through it, so therefore I'm not going to get my money. It's more the fact,

that I'm not going to get through so I might as well give up teaching. That's how I felt. (Teacher 4/f Clearview Primary)

A number of teachers also felt discomfort at 'selling' themselves. Whilst some explained their aversion to the commodification of self in terms of professional culture and not being accustomed to 'blowing our own trumpets', one cited nationality – 'I'm British. I'm English. And the English don't like selling themselves' (Teacher 2/f Riverton Primary).

We have argued elsewhere (Mahony *et al.* 2004b) that a more convincing explanation is to be found within the gendered response to the policy, in which women (the majority in our sample) tend both to underrate their achievements and to proclaim them less than men (Collinson and Hearn 1996). The gender bias inherent in the requirement to 'sell oneself' is rendered invisible when its structurally gendered impacts remain buried under a welter of individual, personal experiences (that just happen to be predominantly female):

> I'm not very good at saying, 'yes, I'm good at doing this' and 'yes, I'm good at doing that'. I never really think I've done a very good job on anything and I find it incredibly difficult to say, 'yes, I did a really good job there'. Because, I can always see, that there are bits that, you know, I should have done and I didn't ... I found it incredibly difficult to sell myself. (Teacher 2/f Riverton Primary)

Although the process sometimes had a very divisive effect among staff, this was not always the case. Teachers who supported each other found the experience rather more positive than those who carried out the task in isolation. Feelings about the process were also influenced by how it was dealt with by their headteachers, all of whom had been to similar training courses but had come to quite different conclusions about how to manage implementation in their schools.

The evidence we gathered demonstrated that heads' judgements about teachers' performance may be profoundly influenced by management priorities and by their responsibility for managing the whole institution, rather than by the 'objective' assessment of individual performance implied by Threshold procedures. The head at Riverton, would have been:

> ... happier with the impression that I got from the first training where ... if you're doing an unsatisfactory job then the competency models kicks in ... satisfactory, you get your pay. Good and above, then the *Threshold*. That's what I would have liked to have seen. I'm very comfortable with performance related pay. (HT/m, Riverton Primary)

Headteachers' stances became translated into a range of very different approaches. At Forestglade Primary the head:

> ... had taken the forms in and glanced at them. And made, perhaps one or two suggestions. She didn't change it but she just made maybe one suggestion on mine. (Teacher 5/f)

This gave the teacher confidence that she would be successful.

Variation is bound to occur in implementing an innovation of this scale. However, given the claims of fair and purposeful assessment that were made by the government (not least in their assurances to the unions), variation that raises issues of fairness and probity is likely to provoke strong feelings. The whole raft of technologies surrounding the policy, whilst giving the appearance of creating 'a level playing field', in reality masked the extent to which opportunities were unequal, were perceived to be unequal and hence became a further source of negativity. Echoing an issue that was raised in relation to Black teachers' confidence in their headteachers, two female teachers at Haymead Primary believed that the male head was not supportive of them. One said:

> I didn't feel hugely confident that it was something that I should do ... I felt that as my line manager, [the Head] rarely supported me in anything that I did ... So, I had no confidence in actually submitting paperwork to him. (Teacher 1/f Haymead Primary)

The head of Riverton Primary, a school that had been through a very difficult phase, appeared, by contrast, to have felt compromised when it came to making the judgement as to whether or not to support some teachers' applications. As he explained:

> ... how can any teachers in this school be good enough to be paid extra money when they are the teachers who are part of the problem. And [they] are also the teachers who have refused to accept any responsibility for the problem ... In terms of their ability to move the school forward, they are likely to be resistant to change, negative and not have the capacity to help the school improve. In fact they are against it, to stop it improving ... There was an Ofsted ... they got through with a lot of propping up.

But, he added 'if we'd gone into special measures I would have been very happy to say "no" to three of them.'

Cases such as these capture the way in which judgements about teachers' performance may be profoundly influenced by management priorities and heads' responsibilities in managing the whole institution, rather than by the 'objective' assessment of individual performance implied by Threshold procedures. We can be far from confident that 'passing the Threshold' means the same thing in different contexts or to different people. However, despite this variation in approach, the vast majority (97 per cent) of teachers who applied in the Round 1 of Threshold were judged to have met the standards (Hutchings *et al.* 2002). The strength of feeling for those who 'failed' is discussed by Wragg *et al.* (2004). In one case reported in the press, a 'failed' teacher was so incensed that she made a physical threat to her headteacher, which led to a finding of serious professional misconduct by the General Teaching Council (Fawcett 2005).

Changes in teachers' practice?

Asked about the impact of Threshold on their practice, teachers' usual immediate response was 'none'. They were, they said, already working as hard as they could because of their commitments to the children, their 'love' of teaching and their efforts to 'do my job fully and professionally'. However, our evidence suggests, that if 'practice' is interpreted as referring more broadly to wider aspects of teachers' work, then Threshold has had a marked impact. First, collection of evidence, especially data on children's progress, has assumed a much greater importance. Second, there was some concern about whether the current vogue for 'target setting' would lead to people 'playing safe'. In terms of the impact on their professional identities, teachers at Riverton reported being 'given a boost after our difficult patch'. For others, however, Threshold represented 'a looming factor', a reminder that 'it begins performance management'. Being 'constantly under scrutiny', being ready to 'prove yourself' were not responses confined to those who wanted to progress up the UPS. Many commented on the tightening of the managerial culture and one rationalized this as serving demands for accountability in a commercialized context where, 'schools are run as a business now, and you have to be accountable to the consumer' (Teacher 5/f Forestglade Primary).

Another major study of incentive pay was carried out by Wragg *et al.* (2004). This included large-scale surveys. Some interesting differences between primary and secondary schools emerged. Seventy-one per cent of primary heads made negative comments about the merits of performance-related pay, compared with only 50 per cent of secondary heads (Wragg *et al.* 2004: 60). A third of primary heads expressed concerns about the divisive nature of the performance pay. They quote one primary head as saying:

> I have no problem in setting targets and objectives, these are vital for development and improvement. I object to the role I had to play. I feel it drove a wedge between myself and staff – which was

unnecessary and unproductive. Fortunately all applicants were successful. I dread to think of the consequences if any had been unsuccessful.

(Wragg et al. 2004: 60)

Wragg et al. (2004: 60) suggest that such differences reflect:

> ...the sometimes different cultures of primary and secondary
> schools. Primary school staff see themselves more as a single team,
> while secondary schools, with their different subject departments
> and faculties, appear more fragmented.

The reshaping of primary teaching in England

There is no doubt that primary teachers' work has changed drastically in
England since the early 1990s. It has often been suggested that the influence
and extent of child centredness in the 1960s and 1970s has been grossly
exaggerated, but there can be no argument that primary teachers' work in the
1990s was dominated initially by curriculum and standardized assessment
and then by performance management, targets and standardized pedagogy.
League tables, inspections, assessment of teachers have all had a major impact
on the working lives of primary teachers (see also Chapters 3, 4 and 15).

There have been gains, certainly. Notwithstanding the reservations stated
above, improvements in literacy and numeracy have been made and have
helped England to move up the tables of international comparisons. However
these, like other developments, appear to have been at some cost to the
professional identity of the English primary teacher. Another aspect of 'loss'
which is frequently referred to is that of creativity and imagination in the
profession and this is often linked to the lack of inspiration for primary
children in their contemporary experience of schooling. This was a major
factor cited by teachers leaving the profession in London during the late
1990s (Hutchings et al. 2002).

The particular 'Englishness' of these primary teachers' work experience
has been highlighted by international comparisons (Alexander 2000). For
example, the approach to the modernization of teaching has taken a very
different form north of the border. As we have discussed elsewhere (Menter et
al. 2004), in the wake of a national agreement on the reform of the teaching
profession in Scotland, teachers can now pursue a developmental and ac-
credited programme towards the award of chartered teacher status and gain a
considerable salary enhancement. This is a fundamentally different approach
to the one-off assessment process that constitutes the Threshold in England.
However, such a positive view of Scottish developments should be tempered

by some evidence that the traditional influences of hierarchy on primary teachers there may not have been significantly influenced by the new structures (MacDonald 2004).

Primary teaching in England in the early twenty-first century is very different from primary teaching in the 1970s and 1980s. Processes of change continue. In addition to the introduction of performance management, national strategies, national curriculum and assessment, we have seen the creation of a 'workload agreement' and the 'remodelling of the workforce'. Again these policies apply across the age phases of schooling, but do have a particular impact on primary teachers. The deployment of significant numbers of classroom assistants, including 'high-level teaching assistants', the entitlement to non-contact time for all teachers, and the removal of some 25 routine tasks previously carried out by teachers, would all appear to affect significantly the work of primary staff, most of whom were previously unsupported, had little or no non-contact time and were especially likely to carry out routine bureaucratic tasks (see also Chapters 12 and 15). These new steps are designed to enable teachers to concentrate on those aspects of their work that require particular professional skill, such as planning, teaching and assessment. However, merely creating better conditions for teachers to do 'what they are best at' and 'what they have been trained for' does not necessarily lead to increased professionalism (see Chapter 15 for further discussion of teacher professionalism). That will also depend on how the core tasks of teaching are defined, on who defines them and on how teachers' work is managed.

It is our view that the majority of people entering primary teaching still do so because they believe they have some personal qualities and commitments that will contribute to children's development and learning. On the basis of the research we have carried out, our judgement is that, at present, the ways in which primary teachers' work is defined and managed provides little scope for teachers to build upon these qualities and commitments, and therefore, to use Nias's phrase quoted at the beginning of this chapter, for many primary teachers there has been a decline of their 'heavy investment of self' in their work.

14 Leading and Managing Teaching and Learning

Linda Hammersley-Fletcher and Rosemary Webb

Introduction

Leading and managing teaching and learning has traditionally been the core of the professional role of primary school headteachers. However, distributed leadership by teacher leaders is advocated increasingly as the way forward for school improvement and raising pupil attainment. This chapter examines the changing nature of management and leadership in primary schools, the interrelationship between headteacher and teacher leadership and the school context factors necessary for teacher leadership to flourish. Management and leadership are often viewed as inseparable concepts. However, management tends to be defined as 'ensuring that tasks are completed through effective planning, organisation, supervision and the deployment of human and other resources' whereas leadership is about 'developing and sustaining a shared vision and set of values in an organisation, providing clear direction, and most crucially motivating others and releasing their energies, commitment, ideas and skills' (Lawlor and Sills 1999: 53).

This chapter begins by briefly considering those roles in the primary school that have evolved to enable headteachers to delegate managerial responsibilities. In the next section the possibilities and constraints on teacher leadership are identified through discussion of a research project into the role of subject leaders because increasing their influence is viewed as 'at the heart of developing distributed leadership' (Southworth 2004: 156). Following this the ways in which distributed leadership is enabled by, and contributes to, the development of primary schools as professional learning communities is explored. It is argued that, owing to their hierarchical management and leadership structures and the highly prescriptive controlling nature of government reform, schools generally do not display the key characteristics of such communities as portrayed in the literature. However, supported and empowered by headteachers with a commitment to develop their schools in that direction, teacher leaders could introduce innovative approaches to teaching and learning and challenge, as well as implement, the diktats of government.

Headteacher leadership

National policy is underpinned by a belief that headteachers are of central importance to continuous improvement in the quality of teaching and learning (DfEE 1997b). Prior to the Education Reform Act 1988 (ERA) primary headteachers, as 'educative leaders' (Grace 1995), were routinely involved in teaching and direct working relations with children and classteachers and generally sought to promote improvements in teaching predominantly through their own exemplary practice. However, in the current educational climate given the diversification of the headteacher's role and the intensification of their work (Southworth 1995; Webb and Vulliamy 1996; Osborn *et al.* 2000), while some headteachers continue to aspire to the ideals of 'educative leadership' it appears unsustainable and likely to lead to stress and burnout as illustrated in Woods *et al.* (1997) and Webb (2005).

The climate of performativity generated by national testing, target setting and league tables has meant that educative leadership has necessarily given way to 'instructional leadership' geared to 'the raising of student achievement through focusing on the teaching-learning process and the conditions that support it' (Hopkins 2003: 68). The driving force and contemporary moral purpose underpinning such leadership is 'closing the gap between our highest and lowest achieving students and to raise standards of learning and achievement for all' (Hopkins 2003: 60). Through incentives such as increased pay and promotion, fear of reprisals as a result of unfavourable Ofsted inspections and critical performance reviews and through adherence to headteachers' visions and school improvement plans (SIPs) teachers are persuaded to adjust their practice to achieve school targets determined by those set nationally and within LEAs. However, although this model of leadership appears effective for producing compliance with government reforms and achieving New Labour's narrow standards agenda, it is argued that it minimizes the central importance of headteachers' professional values in the process of school leadership, stifles teachers' creativity and constrains school innovation (Bottery 2001; Webb 2005).

Delegating management responsibilities

As post-ERA headteachers spend increasing amounts of time acting as financial directors, entrepreneurs, site managers and personnel officers, they delegate more roles and responsibilities in relation to the curriculum and pedagogy to teachers in order to cope with the demands for new knowledge and skills created by continuous curriculum and assessment reform.

Deputy heads

In England, medium and large primary schools have traditionally had deputy headteachers who, because of their class teaching commitments and the lack of availability of non-contact time, have assumed few management and/or leadership roles and served mainly as a confidante for the head and a two-way channel of communication between the head and classteachers (Webb and Vulliamy 1996). As headteachers became more distanced from the curriculum and teaching, deputy heads assumed the role of leading professionals and exemplary teachers. From the findings of Southworth's (2004: 142) study of primary school leadership in small, medium and large primary schools, this situation appears to have changed little with deputy headship often remaining 'an underpowered role in primary schools'.

Senior management teams

In response to the pace of change and expansion of management tasks in a high-risk context of ever increasing external accountability, medium and large schools in England introduced senior management teams (SMTs). The York-Finnish Project (YFP) (1994–5), which involved in-depth case-study research in six schools in England and six schools in Finland, documented the setting up of SMTs in three of the English schools. Membership included the head, deputy and up to three other senior teachers. Drawing particularly on an analysis of the way in which the SMT operated in one school and its impact on staff, it was argued that the existence of an SMT manufactured the consent of participants to changes advocated by the head and denied classteachers, who were not involved, opportunities to influence school policies and practice (Webb and Vulliamy 1999). The study of Meadowfield by Woods *et al.* (1997: 40), where the head, acting unilaterally, introduced the SMT, also reported that 'although the discourse of the SMT was about shared decision-making, teamwork and flattened hierarchy, they were perceived by other colleagues as "the elite", "the cherries on the cake", "those that do" and "the chiefs"' (the other teachers referring to themselves as 'the Indians'). Thus Woods *et al.* (1997: 40) conclude that 'the pyramid organisation had been replaced by merely another form of hierarchy' – 'the manipulative mosaic', which controlled with whom teachers worked and the group tasks tackled. Relationships between the SMT and other staff, and the SMT and the head, also emerged as an important theme in Wallace and Huckman's (1999) research into SMTs in large schools. They found that team members and other staff were critical of headteachers operating hierarchically and that teachers favoured more egalitarian and participative approaches to decision making. Interestingly in the York-Jyväskylä Teacher Professionalism Project (Webb *et al.* 2004a) – a follow-up study to the YFP – some municipalities in Finland required schools to have managerial teams to deal with the escalation of management tasks and to distribute leadership. The strategies, such as changing the membership every two years, that the Finnish principals adopted to make teams democratic is in stark contrast with the hierarchical management structures of English primary schools (Webb *et al.* forthcoming).

Subject coordinators/leaders

Webb and Vulliamy (1996) chart the growth in the role of subject co-ordinators as a result of the ERA and the contribution they made to planning and policy making, resource management, INSET provision and raising the collective confidence of staff in their subjects. Three major constraints on their influence on classroom practice were identified: inadequate coordinator subject expertise; lack of time for coordination tasks; and the nature of power relationships in a school culture still characterized by teacher autonomy and privacy in the classroom. The YFP found that the majority of teachers still appeared reluctant to seek coordinator advice because this went against the traditional culture of individualism and they were sceptical about the depth of knowledge of coordinators who often had little background in their subjects (Webb and Vulliamy 1999). However, interview data in the follow-up study suggested that such posts had become accepted and indeed appreciated by teachers. Also, while initially the introduction of subject monitoring was resisted by staff, especially when it involved classroom observation, by the second project it had become accepted practice. However, there was a feeling among the teachers that the greater accessibility of classrooms reinforced adherence to government advice and discouraged taking risks, such as experimenting with alternative teaching approaches, and so discouraged creativity.

Hammersley-Fletcher carried out research for her PhD in 1997/8 (Hammersley-Fletcher, 2000). She discovered the following differences between the findings of her research for the National College of School leadership (NCSL) (Hammersley-Fletcher *et al.* 2004) and those of her earlier study:

- Greater emphasis was given to curriculum knowledge and it was believed that this was what commanded respect from colleagues. In acknowledgement of the expertise located within key stages, leaders of specific subjects sometimes worked in key stage pairs.
- Literacy and numeracy leaders and the SENCO had greater status, more release time, more of an overview of whole-school developments than other subject leaders and were often part of the SMT,

whereas foundation subject leaders tended to be marginalized and operated within a rotational subject focus in the SIP.

- A particular format for introducing change had developed during the period between the two research projects – that is, the subject leader drew up plans which went to the headteacher and probably the SMT for approval and then to the whole staff and maybe the governors for comment. Then, in the light of the discussion, the plans were reworked, represented and agreed upon.
- Increasingly pupil attainment was monitored through tests, book scans and classroom observation, although skills in such monitoring processes were variable.
- Subject leaders were increasingly involved in networking to share experience and were less likely to be constrained in sharing ideas by concerns over competition between schools.

Distributed leadership

Since the 1990s there has been an increasing recognition that 'traditional leadership approaches have had little, if any, direct or sustained impact on organisational effectiveness' and that 'the notion of the leader as visionary champion who is able to drive through change and improvement is one that has been shown to be fundamentally flawed' (Harris 2003: 76). Furthermore, establishing a direct link between headteachers' leadership and pupil achievement is problematic which is of particular concern given the government's standards agenda (see Chapter 3). Bell *et al.* (2003: 3) report that 'the evidence relating to the effect of headteachers on student outcomes indicates that such an effect is largely indirect' and is 'mediated through key intermediate factors, these being the work of teachers, the organisation of the school, and relationship with parents and the wider community.' They therefore tentatively conclude that 'leadership that is distributed among the wider school staff might be more likely to have an effect on the positive achievement of student outcomes than that which is largely, or exclusively, "top-down".'

Thus approaches to leadership, variously referred to as teacher leadership (Katzenmeyer and Moller 2001) and distributed leadership (Gronn 2000), are viewed as the way forward for improving teaching and learning (Ofsted 2003). Research evidence from school improvement projects internationally is cited as evidence of the success of teacher leaders in improving school and classroom practice (Harris 2002) and raising student performance (Silns and Mulford 2002). However, as pointed out by Leithwood (2003), three major studies conducted at the University of Toronto that inquired about teacher leadership effects on selected aspects of school organization and on students found little to support such advocacy and as yet there is little evidence available on such effects from other large-scale quantitative studies. Consequently, he questions the usefulness of the notion of teacher leadership considering the marriage of concepts could devalue both the status of teaching and the distinctive nature of leadership.

As illustrated by a review of the literature on teacher leadership (Harris and Muijs 2004), endorsement for such leadership comes from Canada, Australia and particularly the US, where over the last decade there have been a growing number of teacher leadership programmes concerned to promote teachers' contribution to school development and decision making without taking them out of the classroom (Smylie 1995). Leadership within this approach is perceived to be 'fluid and emergent rather than as a fixed phenomenon' (Gronn 2000: 324) and involves teachers at various times as both leaders and followers working together to solve problems and accomplish tasks. As observed by Harris and Muijs (2004: 7) most writers on this issue view 'teacher leaders as collaborators with senior management in decision making on specific aspects of school policy rather than replacing them'. In the context of English primary schools this is likely to mean taking on management responsibilities to realize the vision of the school set by the head and SMT rather than substantially influencing it. However, an alternative conceptualization as offered, for example, by Barth (1990) emphasizes the leadership rather than the management dimension of their brief and envisages teacher leaders as playing a major role in running the school and setting its agenda.

The evidence on the changing roles and responsibilities of subject coordinators (first renamed managers and then leaders) over the last decade provides insights into the tensions and dilemmas characterizing the practice of distributed leadership. Hammersley-Fletcher *et al.* (2004) interviewed the headteacher, one 'core' subject leader and one 'foundation' subject leader in each of 22 schools – 12 selected on the basis of LEA recommendations of 'forward looking' practice in subject leadership and 10 schools in the NCSL network that had leadership practices that they wished to share. Given the nature of the sample it is unsurprising that at a rhetorical level all the headteachers in this study wholeheartedly subscribed to various 'shared' and 'distributed' leadership ideals stressing the importance of such leadership in giving teachers ownership of school developments. However, although the discourse was one of distributed leadership, the actual practices to which it gave rise varied considerably across the schools. The headteachers' actions could be viewed as on a continuum with those at one end being exceedingly directive and delegating responsibility within a clearly agreed framework and those at the other end encouraging staff to take risks and trusting in their professional judgement to make decisions on what needed to be done and how to do it. Hammersley-Fletcher *et al.* (2004) concluded that, in almost half the schools visited, distributed leadership was being practised to some extent by the subject leaders interviewed. Nevertheless, in all the schools 'the head was still the driving force, albeit in the background and the final line of command and responsibility' (Hammersley-Fletcher *et al.* 2004: 75). The following comments typify the perceptions expressed:

> ... leadership is getting ... people to do what you think is the correct thing to do, through co-operation, sharing of an idea or a vision with everyone being involved, but you as leader are leading, driving them forward, but also empowering them ... so at the end of the day whatever vision or idea you had will materialize. (Headteacher)

> the Head is very positive and supportive and manages to get you to do what the head wants you to do by using strategies rather than criticism. 'Wouldn't it be brilliant if we did this?' ... the Head is very enthusiastic and although the Head delegates quite a lot ... the Head always keeps on top ... to make sure that you're doing the job you should be doing without being intrusive. (Foundation subject leader)

The headteachers recognized the need to support subject leaders through the provision of time, access to training and working alongside them but they did this within the context of specified expectations, goals and targets. Maintaining overall control was deemed necessary as accountability for all aspects of the school ultimately lies with the head. However, Hammersley-Fletcher *et al.* (2004) found that in the schools where not only the head but also subject leaders interviewed considered that they practised distributive leadership the head placed considerable emphasis on having a transformatory role and developing a culture of professional learning. Unlike instructional leadership, transformational leadership does not focus predominantly on performance goals but also prioritizes wider social, moral and intellectual goals and accomplishments. According to Leithwood *et al.* (1999), it is concerned with modelling best practices and important organizational values, the continuous professional development of teachers, shared decision making and leadership, experimentation, teacher reflection and building relationships with the school community. Through these processes change is brought about in the cultural context in which people work and 'the capacity of an organisation to continuously improve is increased' (Leithwood *et al.* 1999: 117). Where heads were perceived to promote such processes, Hammersley-Fletcher *et al.* (2004) found that teachers considered themselves to be informing the direction of the school, felt valued, were confident about their status and were ambitious.

In Hammersley-Fletcher *et al.*'s study, although headteachers held philosophies of leadership within which vision creation was central, subject leaders viewed leadership predominantly in terms of the practicalities of their role in motivating, supporting and gently coercing staff to implement externally determined subject requirements rather than providing ideas to guide policy formation. Subject leaders also operated within the vision, agreed systems and procedures of the school and the priorities identified in the SIP that determined whether and when their subject might be the focus of whole-school attention. Consequently, there was little that was uniquely generated by them for which they could claim ownership. However, Hammersley-Fletcher *et al.* (2004) found that teachers assuming new leadership roles in their schools, which reflected current interests in learning and thematic approaches to the curriculum, were in a position to own both the substance and the process of change. Consequently, they had greater freedom to be creative and to generate their own initiatives. The following typology serves to illustrate the ways in which a teacher assuming a new leadership role might act differently from teachers operating in a subject manager role:

Teacher manager	**Teacher leader**
delegated tasks	distributed role
headteacher's vision	own vision
reactive	proactive
implements decisions	influences decisions
complies	innovates

MacBeath (2005) also conducted research into the practice of distributed leadership in 11 schools including five in the primary sector. He depicts distributed leadership as a developing process that can be characterized under six headings (MacBeath 2005: 356–7): distribution formally (through designated roles); pragmatically (through necessity); strategically (based on planned staff appointments); incrementally (as staff demonstrate capacity to lead); opportunistically (where capable staff take the initiative) and culturally (reflecting a school's ethos and traditions). Each of these forms of distribution represents 'a different way of thinking about leadership and exemplifies differing processes of distribution' that are 'neither fixed nor mutually exclusive' (MacBeath 2005: 356). As MacBeath (2005) points out, the first three imply a process of delegation from the top down. They can be viewed as the managerial roles discussed in the previous section. However, incremental distribution is not simply an instrumental process to raise standards but is essentially about staff professional development. Distributed leadership that is opportunistic is assumed rather than 'distributed' but in order to flourish requires headteacher encouragement, a supportive school environment and to be congruent with the school's mission. In the final category distribution culturally reflects an established way of working where 'people exercise initiative spontaneously and collaboratively, with no necessary identification of

leaders and followers' (MacBeath 2005: 362). This form of distributed leadership is enabled by, and contributes towards, the development of a school
as one that has variously been termed and conceptualized as a learning organization (Senge 1990) a community of practice (Wenger 1998) and a professional learning community (Hargreaves 2003), all of which are
underpinned by similar beliefs and values.

Schools as Professional Learning Communities

For Senge (1990: 3) a learning community is one 'where people continually
expand their capacity to create the results they truly desire, where new and
expansive patterns of thinking are nurtured, where collective aspiration is set
free, and where people are continually learning how to learn together.' The
emphasis he places on the need for a climate of cooperative sharing echoes
Rosenholtz's (1989) findings that collegiality was an important element that
differentiated 'learning enriched' from 'learning impoverished' schools.
Hargreaves (2003: 184) also emphasizes that such communities 'put a pre-
mium on teachers working together' but states that they 'also insist that this
joint work consistently focuses on improving teaching and learning, and uses
evidence and data as a basis for informing classroom improvement efforts and
solving whole-school problems'.

From the literature (Harris and Muijs 2004) the realization of distributed
leadership within professional learning communities appears particularly
dependent on the following factors, which will be briefly reviewed in turn:

- the development of a collaborative climate fostering mutual trust in
  which teachers feel able to take risks;
- the redistribution of power within schools from hierarchical to democratic control; and
- high levels of teacher capacity.

Collaborative climate

Research has documented the increase in teacher interaction and collaborative working as a result of government reform. In the PACE study Pollard *et al.*
(1994: 93) found that as a result of collaboration over the implementation of
the National Curriculum 'most of the teachers welcomed the increase in
collaboration and partnership with colleagues, and felt that it added a new
dimension to their professionalism'. Working together in the face of the
threat of Ofsted inspections, LEA monitoring, DfES requirements, parental
expectations and media derision also encouraged social bonding and provided a sense of security. However, as revealed by the YFP (Webb *et al.* 1998;

Webb and Vulliamy 1999), as the pace of change accelerated and account-ability measures grew generating escalating paperwork, increasingly teachers in the case-study schools were 'collaborating under constraint' (Woods *et al.* 1997) and forced into 'contrived collegiality' (Hargreaves 1994). They became critical of the escalating numbers of meetings with colleagues, governors and parents, which reduced opportunities to exercise professional choice and di-minished the time they had to prepare and resource their individual lessons, build relationships with children and engage in informal unplanned ex-changes with colleagues (see also Woods *et al.* 1997; Osborn *et al.* 2000). The dominance and prescription of the Literacy and Numeracy Strategies, the narrowing of the curriculum as a result and the use of government-approved schemes of work further reduced teacher initiated collaboration (Webb *et al.* 2004a). However, initial interpretations of, and responses to, the Primary National Strategy (DfES 2003b) by teachers suggest that the opportunities to innovate that it encourages, such as the teaching and learning initiatives found by Hammersley-Fletcher *et al.* (2004), are enabling such teacher-in-itiated collaboration to resurface.

Redistribution of power

As stated by Southworth (1998: 319), 'one consistent finding from research into primary school headship shows them to be pivotal, proprietal, and powerful in their schools', which makes them 'predominant and controlling figures'; they 'enjoy the power because it is for them truly empowering'. On the one hand, the continual expansion and diversification of headteachers' work since 1988 has brought about the increasing delegation to teachers of management responsibilities, particularly in relation to the curriculum and its assessment. Distributed leadership is now also viewed as the way forward for school improvement. On the other hand, the government's standards agenda with its emphasis on performativity and accountability has further strengthened the power of headteachers by giving them additional me-chanisms for controlling teachers and their work. As a result primary school management has become more hierarchical, and the roles of headteachers and teacher leaders have been predominantly interpreted as ensuring com-pliance with government reforms. This situation makes it extremely difficult for headteachers to relinquish the role of ultimate decision makers in any key area affecting teaching and learning and to place their trust in others to make the best decisions.

Teacher capacity

Hopkins (2003) considers that establishing a school as a professional learning community should be one of the main priorities of instructional leadership.

However, in this model of leadership the learning community is structured according to the government's policy for continuing professional development (CPD) based on a framework of professional standards (DfEE 2001a) and teacher capacity is increased predominantly through teachers assimilating knowledge and skills developed externally in order to deliver competently prescribed best practice. As illustrated in Chapter 3 in relation to teachers' perceptions of the NLS and NNS, such performance training can challenge teachers' beliefs and stimulate professional learning. Nevertheless, Hargreaves (2003: 189) warns that over time teachers who have become dependent on 'the external authority of bureaucrats, on scripted texts, or on "incontrovertible" results of research' will 'lose the capacity or desire to make professional judgements and become more reflective'. In the follow-up study to the YFP teachers complained of the increasing narrowness of in-service opportunities reflecting government priorities and the tensions that sometimes existed between their own perceived needs and interests and the training needs of the school as a whole (Webb 2005). However, in two schools where headteachers practised transformative leadership, while they maintained an emphasis on capacity building to meet school improvement needs, they nevertheless enabled teachers to pursue a range of professional development activities, such as participation with pupils in local events, workshops by school visitors, exchanges with teachers overseas and action-research projects, which enhanced their own learning and contributed to the learning of the school as a whole (Webb 2005). These activities encouraged 'choice', 'trust' and 'risk' in teaching and learning, regarded as essential ingredients in building teacher capacity (Day *et al.* 2002: 20).

An extended interpretation of a professional learning community is one incorporating not only members of the school staff but also pupils, parents and the local community who all work together to identify for themselves shared aims, values and an agenda for action for their school, which, although it is likely to be influenced by national concerns, is not dictated by them. In such a learning community professional knowledge is created in the pursuit of problem solving and by critical reflection on action. MacBeath's (2005) research on distributed leadership suggests that in many schools there appears to be a considerable gap between these aspirations and reality and that a major turn around in teacher attitudes will be required if parents and pupils are to become accepted contributors to school learning communities. A questionnaire requiring respondents to express agreement/disagreement with 54 items, found that 'parents are encouraged to take on leadership roles' came 54th and also received the least wholehearted support of any item on the importance scale thus revealing 'not only some scepticism as to parents as leaders but also parents as sources of learning' (MacBeath 2005: 352). Pupils' contribution to leadership fared little better in that the next two lowest ranked items related to pupil involvement in decision making and pupil leadership. However, there are schools to point the way forward. Jeffrey and Woods (2003: 123) in their in-depth study of Coombes Infant and Nursery school describe the involvement of the whole community in the school and argue that 'Coombes is a paradigm case of a learning community' and 'the heart of its success lies in that concept.'

Conclusion

As the work of headteachers has intensified and their role diversified, so the whole-school roles and responsibilities of teachers have grown. However, research in English primary schools on the roles of those dubbed as teacher leaders suggests that according to the definition of management and leadership offered at the outset of this chapter the majority are fulfilling a management rather than a leadership function. The expectation that all teachers should be exercising leadership as part of their role as teachers appears unnecessary and unrealistic. Also, if the notion of teacher leadership becomes regarded as routine and therefore mundane, the impact of teacher leaders will surely be lessened. However, for teaching and learning to be enhanced by creativity and innovation, teachers with ideas and enthusiasm to take the lead in developing school and/or classroom practice need to be provided with the necessary opportunities, resources and support.

The notion of professional learning communities seems a particularly appropriate one for schools and, although likely to be very variously interpreted, it embodies intentions and processes that most teachers value. As shown by Jeffrey and Woods (2003), the ethos of such communities can both sustain and develop individuals and provide a collective power base enabling government reforms to be evaluated and incorporated into schools without sacrificing fundamental beliefs and preferred practices. As argued by Groundwater-Smith and Sachs (2002: 353), such school-based learning communities could also enable teachers to take on an 'activist identity', which is 'negotiated, collaborative, socially critical, future orientated, strategic and tactical', and so develop and disseminate a constructive critique of government requirements and suggestions of alternative ways forward. Activist professionals as headteachers and 'distributed leaders' could revitalize primary education and counter the negative effects on morale and creativity of so many years of centralized reform. However, as acknowledged by some headteachers in Hammersley-Fletcher et al.'s (2004) study, this takes courage, foresight and openness.

15 Primary Teacher Professionalism

Graham Vulliamy

There have been longstanding debates within sociology about the nature of professionalism and within education about the status of teaching as a profession (Lawn 1989). Recent sociological conceptualizations of professionalism follow Johnson (1972) in viewing the concept as a social construction that has been used at different times, and in different ways, as a mechanism of political and ideological control. Thus, for example, Hanlon (1998: 45) suggests that 'professionalism is a shifting rather than a concrete phenomenon' and defines professionals simply in terms of 'those groups commonly thought of as professional by the lay public, academics, the professionals themselves and so on.' In doing so, he argues that such groups, far from being homogeneous as characterized in classical trait theory, are beset by internal conflicts – most notably between those espousing a traditional 'social service' view of professionalism and those adopting a newer 'commercialized professionalism' with its emphasis upon managerial and financial skills. These latter skills are needed, it is argued, for the conduct of professional life in a postmodern era where accountability is required following a widespread breakdown in trust in professionals.

From this sociological perspective one would expect considerable contestation over the meaning of the term 'teacher professionalism' and this is well exemplified by current debates both in education policy circles and amongst academics. On the one hand, the New Labour government is promoting a particular conception of teacher professionalism that is prefaced on the manner in which teachers accommodate themselves to agendas associated with the drive to raise standards and 'commercialized professionalism' (see Chapter 1). This 'new professionalism' is based upon a discourse of instructional leadership, school-based accountability, New Public Management and the measurement of performance indicators in an attempt to raise quality that has already been witnessed in other countries such as the US (Apple 1996) and Australia (Smyth *et al.* 2000).

On the other hand, a number of academics advocate alternative conceptions of teacher professionalism that they see as more suited to the changing nature of education as a response to the pressures of globalization in the twenty-first century. Examples of this include Nixon *et al.*'s (1997) deli-neation of 'emergent professionalism', which emphasizes both the need for teachers' continuous reflection and learning and the building of alliances by teachers with pupils and parents, Hargreaves' (2000) advocacy of partnerships between teachers and the wider public, and the promotion of various forms of professionalism based upon democratic collaboration and teacher activism (Quicke 2000; Sachs 2003). At the same time, many academics have looked critically at the effects of the government-imposed conception of teacher professionalism (for example, Richards 1999; Dadds 2001; Hayes 2002). It has been argued that the associated intensification of teachers' work, together with increased prescription in both curriculum and pedagogy, is resulting in the deskilling of the teacher profession and a loss of professional autonomy, which are in turn having deleterious consequences on teacher morale, tea-cher retention and teacher recruitment. This is perhaps reflected in the fact that in 2001 the Office of National Statistics scale used for sociological re-search in England downgraded the occupational role of teachers from the top category of 'higher managerial and professional' to the one below 'lower managerial and professional' (Woodward 2001).

Day (2000: 110–11) has suggested that 'teachers' voices are an important and under-represented part of the macro debate which focuses on whether educational reforms in England and elsewhere are resulting in the "depro-fessionalization" or "technicization" of teachers' work or whether they result in "reprofessionalization".' Such a neglect has been remedied by the pub-lication of Osborn *et al.*'s (2000) book, which provides the culmination of analysis of teacher perspectives from the Primary Assessment, Curriculum and Experience (PACE) project. This large-scale project, conducted in three pha-ses, provides extensive evidence on changing teacher perspectives – particu-larly on the introduction of the National Curriculum and its associated assessment procedures – between 1989 and 1997. However, the fieldwork for the PACE project was completed before the implementation of the New La-bour 'new professionalism' agenda of reforms – such as prescriptions on pedagogy in the Literacy and Numeracy Strategies, performance management and workforce remodelling. This chapter will discuss the findings of three research projects on teacher professionalism that explicitly address these themes.

The first two – the York-Jyväskylä Teacher Professionalism Project, to-gether with the inter-linked York-Waikato Teacher Professionalism Project – explored changing discourses of primary teacher professionalism in the context of globalized educational reforms in England, Finland and New Zealand (Vulliamy *et al.* 2004; Webb *et al.* 2004a,b; Locke *et al.* 2005). The English component of these involved an analysis of tape-recorded in-depth interviews with 24 primary school teachers in 2001, 23 of whom had been researched six years previously in ethnographic case studies for the York-

Finnish Project. The third is an ongoing four-year (2003–6) Association of Teachers and Lecturers (ATL) project, which in its first phase has involved 188 tape-recorded in-depth interviews with primary teachers from a national sample of 50 schools throughout England, supplemented with classroom observation of 51 lessons in these schools (Webb and Vulliamy 2006).

Evidence from these three projects will be used here to provide a teacher's voice on the polarized debate between the government's espousal of a 'new professionalism' and the critique by many academics of this for the loss of teacher professional autonomy that they believe it embodies. Three key themes will be addressed: curriculum, assessment and pedagogy; account-ability and the new managerialism; and workforce remodelling.

Curriculum, assessment and pedagogy

Our findings on teachers' responses to curriculum and assessment changes and how they affected their sense of professionalism can be summarized briefly because they very much accord with the previous research in the 1990s for the PACE project (Osborn *et al.* 2000).

There was widespread regret amongst primary teachers at the manner in which a content-heavy curriculum, together with the pressures derived from league tables of school assessment results in the core subjects, resulted in a loss of opportunities to be flexible and creative in their teaching. They also mourned the loss of spontaneity to teach to the children's interests or to build teaching around an unanticipated local or national event. Younger teachers who had been trained since the 1988 Education Reform Act tended not to perceive this negatively in terms of their professionalism, but some older teachers expressed concern that a prescribed curriculum, backed by resources provided by the Qualifications and Curriculum Authority (QCA), would result in a permanent loss to the profession of the ability for creative teaching of the kind documented by Woods (1995). While the ATL project interviewees, in-terviewed between 2003 and 2005, had various interpretations of the gov-ernment's Primary National Strategy (DfES 2003b), many viewed this as a welcome opportunity for teachers to take a more flexible approach to the curriculum and put back elements – such as cross-curricular work and creative arts subjects – that had been lost in the focus on the 'effective' at the expense of the 'affective' (McNess *et al.* 2003).

In relation to assessment, we found much evidence that teachers had developed more confidence and increased skills in the ways in which they assessed pupils (see also Chapter 4). Teachers felt that the greater knowledge of individual children's attainment derived from more formal and focused teacher assessment contributed to better planning and helped children's learning. However, such potential benefits in teacher assessment were more than offset by teachers' very negative view of the impact of national testing and the associated league tables, including the newer value-added ones, which, they argued, had major deficiencies (Webb and Vulliamy 2006; see also Chapter 3). SATs were seen seriously to distort both the balance of the curriculum and the process of teaching, especially in year 6 classes, and to cause many children considerable stress and anxiety. Teaching to the tests went against teachers' sense of professionalism but was nevertheless deemed necessary in order to reduce the stress involved for the children by thorough preparation and to enable them to do as well as possible.

Contrary to the expressed fears of many academics (for example, Dadds 2001; Davies and Edwards 2001; Hayes 2002) that centralized prescription of pedagogy would result in deprofessionalization and deskilling, this is not generally the way in which teachers perceived it (see also Chapter 3). The evidence from our comparative research projects and from the much larger scale ATL national study found that the Strategies were seen as contributing to teachers' professionalism by increasing their effectiveness and giving them the confidence and awareness to explain precisely what they were doing and why. Interestingly, Silcock (2002), in his survey of members of the Association for the Study of Primary Education (ASPE), which investigated the effects of legislated changes on teacher professionalism, found that 'central prescription of literacy and numeracy' was the item with the most conflicting responses as between academics in higher education, who were overwhelmingly negative, and practitioners (teachers and LEA advisers), who were very positive. He also found that practitioners' perspectives on professionalism were strongly filtered through core values of putting the child first. This contrasted with the academics from higher education in his sample who typically explained their views 'by reference to abstract principle (the nature of teaching and professionalism, historical trends etc.)' where 'legislation is judged in a somewhat sceptical manner, with legislators blamed for a decline in teacher professionalism' (Silcock 2002: 144).

Much research on the implementation of the National Curriculum in England has illustrated the manner in which policies are mediated in practice by teachers (Vulliamy et al. 1997; Osborn et al. 2000). Teachers' reactions to the Literacy and Numeracy Strategies provide an interesting exception to this theme of teachers' values mediating policy by suggesting an inverse relationship whereby policy implementation can mediate teachers' values. Thus, through compliance with the imposed changes in pedagogy, which were generally regarded by interviewees as having been implemented begrudgingly, teachers' experiences led them to change some of their professional values concerning desirable pedagogy:

> I think that the Literacy strategy and the Numeracy Strategy changed everybody's views ... I am saying 'everybody's', but it certainly

changed mine, it really did change mine. In my views as a teacher and how to teach the subjects because I think that if we are all honest we weren't teaching literacy as it should have been taught. (ATL project)

The more focused and structured nature of teaching required by the strategies and the sharing of learning objectives with the pupils were generally felt to have led to much improved learning experiences for the children:

> Going back a few years I didn't know what I was teaching, the kids didn't know what they were learning and at the end of the lesson we didn't know whether we'd learnt it and nobody bothered to find out whether we'd learnt it. Now I know what I'm teaching, they know what they're learning and at the end of the lesson I'm going to know whether they've learnt it and what's more important they're going to know whether they've learnt it – and that's what's improved teaching. (ATL project)

Teachers viewed the core of primary teaching that was at the very heart of their conception of professionalism as the ability to motivate and develop children's learning and to boost their confidence and self-image. Consequently, as they perceived the changes in their practice as bringing identifiable benefits for children (see also Chapter 3), they experienced these pedagogical reforms as empowering and as enhancing their professionalism.

The possible reasons for primary teacher interviewees' positive reactions to similar pedagogical reforms in both England and New Zealand are explored in Vulliamy *et al.* (2004). Some researchers might interpret such responses to the prescribed changes in pedagogy as examples of 'false consciousness' (Robertson 1996) or the product of new managerial discourses that '"manufacture" consent to reform, making it increasingly difficult for those in schools to talk about loss of control over teaching' (Menter *et al.* 1997: 223). However, the data from 24 in-depth interviews in 2001 in the York comparative projects and 188 in-depth interviews between 2003 and 2005 from the ATL project (supplemented by classroom observations of 26 literacy and numeracy lessons) do not support such an interpretation. This is because not only did our teachers mount a very forceful critique of many other aspects of the 'new professionalism' – such as target setting, national testing and league tables, performance management and the tyranny of escalating paperwork – but they also approached their discussions of teaching methods in a very considered and reflexive manner. Moreover, as seen in Chapter 3, some teachers were very critical of the Literacy Strategy whilst being full of praise for the Numeracy Strategy.

I should note here that this very favourable response by teachers to the Numeracy Strategy is not what I would have predicted before researching teachers' voices on this theme. As suggested elsewhere (Vulliamy 2004), such findings might be viewed as an illustration of Becker's (1970) argument that, contrary to much received opinion, qualitative research methods are less susceptible to the prior bias of the researcher than either surveys or experiments. Part of the rationale for the Numeracy Strategy was David Reynolds' now infamous *Worlds Apart?* survey for Ofsted, which suggested that it was the greater use of whole-class teaching in countries such as Taiwan that helped explain their school children's supposedly better results in international league tables of mathematics test scores (Reynolds and Farrell 1996). In common with some other academics and comparativists, I wrote an article that was highly critical of this (Vulliamy 1998). The article drew upon a combination of brief observations in five Taiwanese primary schools and the research literature on the international transfer of educational innovations that demonstrates that what works in one culture is unlikely to work in another, unless very careful attention is paid to contextual factors. The fact that the Numeracy Strategy did not meet with the strong resistance from primary teachers that I would have anticipated leads me now to consider some other possible reasons for this.

Research suggests that secondary teachers' perspectives on the curriculum and pedagogic reforms are much more critical than those of primary teachers (Helsby and McCulloch 1996). A key difference here is that secondary teachers have a strong subject identity derived from their degree and in postgraduate teacher training 'pedagogical content knowledge' (Shulman 1986) is welded to this to give an interrelated pedagogical identity. As argued by Locke (2001: 8), this strong preexisting body of professional knowledge 'may well sit awkwardly or in conflict with the curriculum they are expected to teach'.

Primary teachers, on the other hand, are expected to teach a wide range of subjects and research indicates that, especially after the introduction of a broad-based national curriculum, they lacked confidence in their knowledge of, and ability to teach, many of the subjects embodied within it (Bennett *et al.* 1994). Moreover, prior to the curriculum reforms, there was little attempt in teacher training to give specific guidance on primary teaching pedagogy. As one of our English headteacher interviewees put it:

> You were actually told that it was up to you how you taught ... I had no guidance from college at all about how to teach ... The students [student teachers] who are coming in now seem very confident and very capable. When I look back, I think 'gosh, I wish I had been like that'. I felt really naïve and dropped in at the deep end. (York-Waikato project)

This might be compared with the experience of Strong (quoted in Earl *et al.* 2003: 26, as an illustration of what has been called an era of 'uninformed professionalism'):

> I started teaching [in England] in 1972. There was no curriculum. You could do what you liked ... I hadn't the faintest idea of what I was doing but I went out there and did what I could ... Nobody should have been expected to do what I was expected to do.

Given this context, primary teachers' perspectives that the curriculum and pedagogic guidance that they have received has made them better teachers and has improved their children's learning need to be taken seriously. Many of our interviewees freely admitted that major deficiencies in their prior teaching had been remedied by such guidance (see Webb and Vulliamy 2006: chs. 2 and 7) and welcomed the clearer structure to their teaching that ensued. Other researchers have found likewise; Stronach *et al.* (2002: 127), for example, in a study based on interviews with 24 primary teachers implementing the Numeracy Strategy found that 'coerced change can be welcomed' and argue that a reason for the positive reception of the Numeracy Strategy is teachers' prior weaknesses in maths and what they call 'the sub-professional ecology of some maths teaching' (Stronach *et al.* 2002: 124).

Accountability and the new managerialism

A central finding of both the comparative research projects and the ATL one is teachers' increasing resentment at the escalating pressures of external accountability over the last decade and their consequent loss of professional autonomy. A national survey of nearly 2400 teachers, conducted in 2003 as the first phase of the four-year Teacher Status Project (TSP), also found that teachers felt that they were under very strong external control and primary teachers felt this significantly more than their secondary teacher counterparts (Hargreaves *et al.* 2004). The New Labour government's standards agenda has intensified a 'performativity discourse' (Jeffrey 2002) where primary teachers' work is subjected to a variety of controls and is measured by performance indicators through Ofsted ratings, national testing and league tables (see also Chapters 3 and 13).

There are several ways in which the intensifying pressures of external accountability and the surveillance culture of 'low-trust' schooling (Troman 2000) impact negatively on teachers' conceptions of their professionalism. They direct teachers' energies away from their core role of teaching children towards the escalating paperwork required to provide evidence to external bodies that such teaching is effective: policies and plans for Ofsted, analysis of target setting for LEAs, a continual demand for written responses to national and LEA initiatives, and reports to parents and governors. They are also perceived by teachers as symptomatic of the low regard in which they are held by the government, the media and the public (Webb *et al.* 2004b). Thus, for example, the TSP survey found that teachers strongly identified public respect as a key component of a profession but felt that teaching did not currently have such public respect; it also found that teachers perceived that there had been a progressive decline in their status since the late 1960s and that one of the main ways in which this decline might be reversed would be if the public and policy makers had a better understanding of the nature of teachers' work (Hargreaves *et al.* 2004).

One response to the pressures of external accountability has been the growth of the 'new managerialism' (Mahony and Hextall 2000). The increased emphases on top-down management styles at the expense of more collegial and democratic ones identified in 1990s research in primary schools (Webb and Vulliamy 1996; Osborn *et al.* 2000) have intensified further. They have been further exacerbated by the introduction of performance management in 2000. Here the findings of both our comparative and ATL projects are very much in accord with those discussed in Chapter 13 by Ian Menter, Pat Mahony and Ian Hextall. Thus, for example, responses to the Threshold assessment, whereby teachers had to apply for a performance-related pay increase and transfer to an upper pay spine, were generally highly critical with comments such as 'a major insult', 'an absolute nightmare' and 'an expensive farce' being commonplace. The rhetorical 'why do you feel that you constantly have to justify yourself?' response of one interviewee exemplified a pervasive feeling that such accountability measures implied an unwarranted questioning of teachers' professionalism.

The performance review system of annual teacher interviews and target setting had a more varied response from our interviewees. On the one hand, many teachers, and especially headteachers, felt that it was beneficial, particularly if it could be harnessed towards specific whole-school concerns for a particular year and allied to professional development activities. On the other hand, many other teachers were cynical about the usefulness of yet another 'bureaucratic' chore, together with a suspicion that it is 'based on the premise that we are not doing our jobs properly'.

The external accountability pressures referred to in this section are those associated with the 'new managerialism' dimension of the new professionalism, but the establishment in 1999 of a General Teaching Council by the government might be viewed as a throwback to the classical trait theory of professionalism with its emphasis on professional self-regulation (Hoyle and John 1995). However, our comparative project interviewees were highly sceptical that it would have any positive benefits – so much so that they resented being forced to subscribe to it – and to date its main function seems to have been disciplinary.

Workforce remodelling

Fieldwork for our ATL project coincided with the early stages of implementation of the National Agreement on *Raising Standards and Tackling Workload*. As discussed in Chapter 1, this agreement contained proposals for a major expansion of classroom support assistants, the allocation of 10% of teachers' time for preparation, planning and pupil assessment (PPA time), redesigned patterns of progression through the career structure – coupled with a new performance management system – and the introduction of a 'fast-track' to allow speedy progress through the restructured levels of the teaching force (Menter *et al.* 2004). In this section some teacher reactions to these changes will be reviewed, with particular reference to potential consequences, as they see it, for teacher professionalism.

The first phase of the National Agreement required that from September 2003 24 administrative tasks should be delegated from teachers to support staff. Whilst in some of our 50 schools such delegation was welcomed, the most common response was that the changes had had minimal effects. The suggestion that teaching assistants (TAs) should mount teachers' displays proved to be particularly contentious because most teachers preferred to do their own, as they took considerable professional pride from the quality of their wall displays and also enjoyed putting them up.

The large increase in the number of TAs in schools was strongly welcomed by almost all our interviewees. The reasons for this were, not so much that it reduced teacher workload – planning for, and sharing plans with, TAs could in some cases increase teachers' workload – but that it markedly improved the quality of teaching and learning through the provision of an extra adult to help with group and individual work in the classroom (see also Chapter 12). This accords with the findings of other research studies into the use of teaching assistants in schools (P. Smith *et al.* 2004). Brehony and Deem (2005: 402) suggest that this aspect of workforce remodelling has similarities with the restructuring of the National Health Service workforce where 'the periphery is now composed of healthcare assistants and "associate professionals"' with such remodelling in schools further 'enhancing the trend to transform teachers into managers of teams of support staff'. While there is some suggestion of this in our research – one fast-track teacher we interviewed, for example, said that 'teachers are going to become less and less of teachers and more and more of managers, but not managers of children' – classteachers generally did not view the increased use of teaching assistants as in any way detracting from their teaching or their contact with children.

Teachers valued the help of teaching assistants highly, but their use to teach whole classes to enable Phase 3 of the National Agreement to be implemented by September 2005, whereby all classteachers could have 10 per cent PPA time was generally strongly resisted, with comments such as 'if you were a parent, would you want your child's education being taught by someone that is not a professional?' and 'a teaching assistant cannot take the place of a teacher and teach whole classes ... that is taking away the professionalism of the teacher.' There were a few exceptions to this – one school, for example, had already implemented Phase 3 a year ahead of schedule and each class had both a teacher and a full-time teaching assistant in it. The headteacher told the reseacher that 'the classteacher manages the curriculum side and co-ordinates what's happening but, as you go around, you'll find it difficult to pick up who's the classteacher and who's the assistant in all the classrooms'. However, by far the most common plans for releasing the full PPA time in Phase 3 involved the appointment of part-time specialist subject teachers – particularly in PE, music and art – to release classteachers. There were widespread complaints that the funding to release this 10 per cent of contact time was totally inadequate and large schools, in particular, were anticipating major problems in its implementation.

Teachers who had already been given their full PPA time appreciated this change, especially if it could be scheduled in blocks, but there was widespread cynicism as to whether the government's declared intention of trying to reduce teachers' workloads would be achieved. The escalating paperwork about which they complained was generally identified as being a product of what Jeffrey (2002: 542) calls 'the "audit explosion" in which trust has been replaced by audit accountability'. There were frequent references to the theme that 'primary teachers now, or teachers in general, don't seem to be trusted' and the debilitating consequences of this lack of trust are captured in the following comment:

> Not only do you have to do a job now, you have to prove that you have done it. So you are spending your time getting evidence and back up to prove that you had a good lesson. You can't just have good lessons now as you have to prove it all the time. So that is ridiculous – it is like Big Brother watching and it has gone over the top now and then the people who are conscientious, we are worn out now, you see. I am thinking of retiring early now, I am fifty-five and I think that is it. I want a life as well outside school, as it can't all be work.

In the face of a continuation of such external accountability audit pressures, it would seem that attempts to reduce teacher workloads by strategies such as PPA time are merely chipping away at the surface of the problem. As argued by Stronach *et al.* (2002: 131–2):

Professionalism, then, cannot thrive on performance indicators. It has to rely, in the end, on positive trust rather than be driven by performance ranking ... Excellence can only be motivated, it cannot be coerced.

Conclusion

We are witnessing profound shifts in the discourses of teacher professionalism as a result of New Labour's policy reforms. Traditional hallmarks of a profession, such as altruism (Hoyle and John 1995), which our teacher interview data suggest are central to teachers' identities and motivation, become redefined. Thus a holistic child-centred concern to benefit children's lives shifts in the 'new professionalism' discourse to a 'making a difference' that is viewed in terms of raising standards, measured by test results, of all children and closing the gap between high and low achievers (for other examples of such discursive shifts, see Locke *et al.* 2005).

Other traditional hallmarks of a profession, such as autonomy, become severely constrained when teachers are increasingly accountable to mandated change from the government. Academics have generally been highly critical of such government control and the limitations on teacher autonomy that it implies. Moreover, Osborn *et al.* (1992: 150) conclude, following the early stages of the PACE research, that:

> educational change cannot be brought about simply by manipulating institutional structures or by issuing policy directives. To be successful it must involve teachers from the outset and take into account the real influences on teachers' professional motivation and practice.

Our own research for the York-Finnish Project concurs with this, suggesting that English teachers' responses to the pre-New Labour reforms of the 1990s resulted in a 'change without commitment' (Webb and Vulliamy, 1999). However, the analysis of teachers' responses to the implementation of the Literacy and Numeracy Strategies discussed here suggests that, for this aspect of New Labour's reforms, Barber's justification for mandated change (see Chapter 1, p. 10) may, at least to some extent, be warranted. We have extensive evidence from the 188 ATL interviews that, in relation to aspects of pedagogy, primary teachers have been shown, in Barber's words, 'a new world from which they do not want to return' and that consequent changes are likely to be enduring ones because teachers have become committed to them. Thus a comparison with major longitudinal research projects in primary schools in previous decades, such as the ORACLE studies (Galton *et al.* 1980,

1999) and the PACE research between 1989 and 1997 (Osborn *et al.* 2000), suggest that patterns of primary classroom practice that survived the impact of the Education Reform Act 1988 and the introduction of the National Curriculum have been transformed in the last few years. As documented in the ATL project's comparisons of observations and interviews in the 1992–4 and 2003–5 periods (Webb and Vulliamy 2006), such major changes in primary classroom practice relate to teaching approaches (such as the sharing of learning objectives with children and the use of more whole-class teaching), curricular organization (such as the elimination of the integrated day) and seating patterns (moves towards pupils seated in rows rather than grouped around tables), as well as to the greatly increased use of ICT, especially whiteboards, and of classroom assistants.

However, it has been argued here that teachers view most other aspects of the New Labour government's reforms – notably the emphasis upon testing and league tables, performance management, the increased paperwork associated with accountability measures, and parts of the workforce remodelling programme – as impacting negatively on their conception of professionalism. The apparent lack of trust shown in the teaching profession by the government can be profoundly demotivating and, unless remedied, is likely further to affect adversely both teacher recruitment and retention.

In response to government intervention, notions of primary teacher professionalism are undergoing review and reconstruction by primary teachers (Woods and Jeffrey 2002). Such notions are shaped by past and present ideology, policy and practice and display multiple and situational dimensions. It is too early to predict what the longer term impact of the government's attempts to raise the status of teaching through redefining the notion of professionalism are likely to be. However, whatever composite new professionalism ultimately prevails, the evidence from research suggests that a concern for children and their learning will remain constant and central in it.

References

Abbott, C. (2001) *ICT: Changing Education*. London: RoutledgeFalmer.

Abdullah, A. and Scaife, J. (1997) Using interviews to assess children's understanding of science concepts, *School Science Review*, 78: 79–83.

ACCAC (2004) *Review of the School Curriculum and Assessment Arrangements 5–16. A Report to the Welsh Assembly Government* [the Daughtery Report]. Cardiff: ACCAC.

Acker, S. (1999) *The Realities of Teachers' Work – Never a Dull Moment*. London: Cassell.

Adey, P. and Shayer, M. (1994) *Really Raising Standards*. London: Routledge.

Ainscow, M. (1995) Education for all: making it happen, *Support for Learning*, 10(4): 147–54.

Ainscow, M., Farrell, P. and Tweddle, D. (2000) Developing policies for inclusive education: a study of the role of local education authorities, *International Journal of Inclusive Education*, 4(3): 211–29.

Alexander, R. (1984) *Primary Teaching*. London: Cassell.

Alexander, R. (1995) *Versions of Primary Education*. London: Routledge.

Alexander, R. (1997) *Policy and Practice in Primary Education*, 2nd edn. London: Routledge.

Alexander, R. (2000) *Culture and Pedagogy – International Comparisons in Primary Education*. Oxford: Blackwell.

Alexander, R. (2004) Still no pedagogy? Principle, pragmatism and compliance in primary education, *Cambridge Journal of Education*, 34(1): 7–33.

Alexander, R., Rose, J. and Woodhead, C. (1992) *Curriculum Organisation and Classroom Practice in Primary Schools: A Discussion Paper*. London: DES.

Allan, J. (2003) Productive pedagogies and the challenge of inclusion, *British Journal of Special Education*, 30(4): 175–9.

Ames, C. (1992) Classrooms: Goals, structures and student motivation, *Journal of Educational Psychology*, 84(3): 261–71.

Ames, C. and Ames, R. (1984) Systems of student and teacher motivation: toward a qualitative definition, *Journal of Education Psychology*, 76: 535–56.

Anning, A., Cullen, J. and Fleer, M. (2003) *Early Childhood Education: Society and Culture*. London: Sage.

Apple, M. (1996) *Cultural Politics and Education*. Buckingham: Open University Press.

Armstrong, D. (2003) *Experiences of Special Education: Re-evaluating Policy and Practice through Life Stories*. London: RoutledgeFalmer.

Assessment Reform Group (ARG) (1999) *Assessment for Learning: Beyond the Black Box*. Cambridge: University of Cambridge, School of Education.

Assessment Reform Group (ARG) (2002) *Assessment for Learning: 10 Principles.* Cambridge: University of Cambridge, School of Education.

Avramidis, E., (2001) Mainstream teachers' attitudes towards the inclusion of children with special educational needs in the ordinary school. Unpublished PhD thesis, School of Education, University of Exeter.

Avramidis, E., Bayliss, P. and Burden, R. (2000a) Student teachers' attitudes towards the inclusion of children with special educational needs in the ordinary school, *Teaching and Teacher Education*, 16(3): 277–93.

Avramidis, E., Bayliss, P. and Burden, R. (2000b) A survey into mainstream teachers' attitudes towards the inclusion of children with special educational needs in the ordinary school in one Local Educational Authority, *Educational Psychology*, 20(2): 193–213.

Avramidis, E. Bayliss, P. and Burden, R. (2002) Inclusion in action: an in-depth case study of an effective inclusive secondary school in the Southwest of England, *International Journal of Inclusive Education*, 6(2): 143–63.

Avramidis, E. and Norwich, B. (2002) Mainstream teachers' attitudes towards inclusion/integration: a review of the literature, *European Journal of Special Needs Education*, 17(2): 1–19.

Baker, C. (1996) *Foundations of Bilingual Education and Bilingualism*, 2nd edn. Clevedon: Multilingual Matters.

Baker, K. (1993) *Turbulent Times*. London: Faber & Faber.

Ball, S. J. (1990) *Politics and Policy Making in Education*. London: Routledge.

Ball, S. J. (1999) Labour, learning and the economy, a 'policy sociology' perspective, *Cambridge Journal of Education*, 29(2): 195–206.

Ball, S. J. (2003) The teacher's soul and the terrors of performativity, *Journal of Education Policy*, 18(2): 215–28.

Barber, M. (1996) How to Do the Impossible: A Guide for politicians with a passion for education, Inaugural Lecture, Institute of Education, London University, December 11.

Barber, M. (2001) High expectations and standards for all, no matter what: creating a world class education service in England, in M. Fielding (ed.) *Taking Education Really Seriously: Four Years' Hard Labour*. London: RoutledgeFalmer.

Barnes, D. (1976) *From Communication to Curriculum*. Penguin: Harmondsworth.

Barth, R. (1990) *Improving Schools from Within*. San Francisco: Jossey-Bass.

Barwell, R. (2004) *Teaching Learners of English as an Additional Language: A Review of Official Language*. Watford: National Association for Language Development in the Curriculum (NALDIC).

Bass, A. and Hoskins, D. (1999) *Let's not Talk about it for a Change*. Birmingham: Aston University Business School Research Papers.

Bastiani, J. and Wolfendale, S. (ed.) (1996) *Home-school Work in Britain: Review, Reflection and Development*. London: David Fulton.

Bayliss, P. D. (1998) Theorising special education: Models of complexity: theory driven intervention practices, in C. Clark, A. Dyson and A. Millward (eds) *Theorising Special Education*. London: Routledge.

Beauchamp, G. (2004) Teacher use of the interactive whiteboard in primary schools: towards an effective transition framework, *Technology, Pedagogy and Education*, 13(3): 327–48.

Beauchamp, G. and Bicknell, C. (2005) Interactivity in the primary school: primary teachers' perceptions in mathematics, science and second language teaching. Paper presented at the British Educational Research Association annual conference, University of Glamorgan, 14–17 September.

Beauchamp, G. and Parkinson, J. (2005) Beyond the 'wow' factor: developing interactivity with the interactive whiteboard, *School Science Review*, 86: 97–103.

Becker, H. S. (1970) Field work evidence, in H. S. Becker (ed.) *Sociological Work: Method and Substance*. Chicago: Aldine.

BECTA (2001) *Primary Schools of the Future: Achieving Today*. Coventry: BECTA.

BECTA (2002) *Impact2: Final Report*. Coventry: BECTA.

BECTA (2003) *What Research Says About Interactive Whiteboards*. Coventry: BECTA.

Beebe, B. and Lachmann, F. (2003) *Infant Research and Adult Treatment: Co-constructing Interactions*. London: The Analytic Press.

Bell, L., Bolam, R. and Cubillo, L. (2003) A systematic review of the impact of school leadership and management on student outcomes; in *Research Evidence in Education Library*. London: EPPI-Centre, Social Science Research Unit, Institute of Education.

Bennett, N. (1976) *Teaching Styles and Pupil Progress*. London: Open Books.

Bennett, N., Desforges, C., Cockburn, A. and Wilkinson, B. (1984) *The Quality of Pupil Learning Experiences*. New York: Lawrence Erlbaum Associates.

Bennett, N., Summers, M. and Askew, M. (1994) Knowledge for teaching and teaching performance, in A. Pollard (ed.) *Look Before You Leap? Research Evidence for the Curriculum at Key Stage Two*. London: Tufnell Press.

Bhatti, G. (1999) *Asian Children at Home and at School: An Ethnographic Study*. London: Routledge.

Bichard, M. (1999) Modernising the policy process. http://ntweb1/Gen Bef Speeches/Michael%20Bichard/pmp/ahtm.

Biggs, A. P. and Edwards, V. (1994) I treat them all the same: Teacher-pupil talk in multi-ethnic classrooms, in D. Graddol, J. Maybin and B. Steier (eds) *Researching Language and Literacy in Social Context*. Clevedon: Multilingual Matters.

Black, P. (1993) The shifting scenery of the National Curriculum, in C. Chitty and B. Simon (eds) *Education Answers Back*. London: Lawrence & Wishart.

Black, P., Harrison, C., Marshall, B. and Wiliam, D. (2003) *Assessment for Learning: Putting it into Practice*. Buckingham: Open University Press.

Black, P. and Wiliam, D. (1998) Assessment and Classroom Learning, *Assessment in Education*, 5(1): 7–74.

Blair, T. (1999) Quality is key to progress. *Times Educational Supplement*, 4 June.

Blatchford, P. (2003) *The Class Size Debate: Is Small Better?* Buckingham: Open University Press.

Blunkett, D. (2002) Integration with diversity: globalisation and the renewal of democracy and civil society, in P. Griffith and M. Leonard (eds) *Reclaiming Britishness*. London: The Foreign Policy Centre.

Blyth, A. (1990) *Making the Grade for the Primary Humanities*. Milton Keynes: Open University Press.

Blythe, T. and Associates (1998) *The Teaching for Understanding Guide*. San Francisco: Jossey Bass Inc.

Bottery, M. (2001) Globalization and the UK competition state: no room for transformational leadership in education, *School Leadership and Management*, 21(2): 199–218.

Boulton, M. (1997) Teachers' views on bullying: definitions, attitudes and ability to cope, *British Journal of Educational Psychology*, 67(2): 223–33.

Bourne, J. (2001) Doing 'what comes naturally': How the discourses and routines of teachers' practice constrain opportunities for bilingual support in UK primary schools, *Language and Education*, 15(4), 250–68.

Brehony, K. J. (2005) Primary schooling under New Labour: the irresolvable contradiction of excellence and enjoyment, *Oxford Review of Education*, 31(1): 29–46.

Brehony, K. J. and Deem, R. (2005) Challenging the post-Fordist/flexible organisation thesis: the case of reformed educational organisations, *British Journal of Sociology of Education*, 26(3): 395–414.

Brett, R. (2003) *Assessing the Benefits of Classroom Amplification Systems on Educational Achievement*. Manchester: Faculty of Education, University of Manchester.

Broadfoot, P. and Pollard, A. (1996) Continuity and change in English Primary Education, in P. Croll (ed.) *Teachers, Pupils and Primary Schooling: Continuity and Change*. London: Cassell.

Broadfoot, P. and Pollard, A. (1998) Categories, standards and instrumentalism: theorizing the changing discourse of assessment policy in English primary education. Paper given to AERA Conference, San Diego, April.

Brooks, G. (1998) Trends in standards of literacy in the UK, 1948–1996, *Topic*. Slough: NFER.

Brown, M. (1996) FIMS and SIMS: the first two IEA international mathematics surveys, *Assessment in Education*, 3(2): 193–212.

Brown, M., Askew, M., Millett, A. and Rhodes, V. (2003) The key role of educational research in the development and evaluation of the National Numeracy Strategy, *British Educational Research Journal*, 29(5), 655–72.

Brundrett, M. (2002) Mission, faith and management: co-constructing leadership in a Beacon Lower School, *Education 3–13*, 30(3): 42–7.

Brundrett, M. and Silcock, P. J. (2002) *Achieving Competence, Success and Excellence in Teaching*. London: RoutledgeFalmer.

Bruner, J. (1966) *The Growth of Mind*. Cambridge MA: Educational Services Incorporated.

Bullock, K., Bishop, K., Martin, S. and Reid, A. (2002) Learning from coursework in English and Geography, *Cambridge Journal of Education*, 32(3): 325–40.

Bullock, K. and Muschamp, Y. (2006) Learning about learning in the primary school, *Cambridge Journal of Education*, 36(1): 49–62.

Burns, C. and Myhill, D. (2004) Interactive or inactive? A consideration of the nature of interaction in whole class teaching, *Cambridge Journal of Education*, 34(1): 35–49.

Butt, G. and Lance, A. (2005) Modernizing the roles of support staff in primary schools: changing focus, changing function, *Educational Review*, 57(2): 139–49.

Campbell, R. J. (1985) *Developing the Primary School Curriculum*. Cassell: London.

Campbell, R. J. (1989) HMI and aspects of public policy for the primary school curriculum, in A. Hargreaves and D. Reynolds (eds) *Education Policies: Controversies and Critiques*. London: Falmer.

Campbell, R. J. (1996) Standards of literacy and numeracy in English primary schools: a real or imaginary crisis? Presidential Address to the Education Section of the British Association for the Advancment of Science, Birmingham University.

Campbell, R. J. (1998) Broader thinking about the primary curriculum, in S. Dainton (ed.) *Take Care Mr Blunkett*. London: ATL.

Campbell, J. and Emery, H. (1994) Curriculum policy for Key Stage 2: Possibilities, contradictions and constraints, in A. Pollard (ed.) *Look Before You Leap*. London: Tufnell Press.

Campbell, R. J., Kyriakides, L., Muijs, R. D. and Robinson, W. (2003) Differential teacher effectiveness: a model for research and teacher appraisal, *Oxford Review of Education*, 29(3): 347–62.

Campbell, R. J., Kyriakides, L., Muijs, R. D. and Robinson, W. (2004) Effective teaching and values: some implications for research and teacher appraisal, *Oxford Review of Education*, 30(4): 451–65.

Campbell, R. J. and Neill, S. R. St. J. (1994a) *Curriculum Reform at Key Stage 1: Teacher Commitment and Policy Failure*. London: Longman.

Campbell, R. J and Neill, S. R. St. J. (1994b) *Primary Teachers at Work*. London: Routledge.

Carr, W. (1994) Wise men and clever tricks, *Cambridge Journal of Education*, 24(1): 89–112.

Central Advisory Council for Education (1967) *Children and their Primary Schools*. London: HMSO.

Chaplain, R. (2000) Helping children to perservere and be well-motivated, in D. Whitebread (ed.) *The Psychology of Teaching and Learning in the Primary School*. London: RoutledgeFalmer.

Chitty, C. (2004) *Education Policy in Britain*. London: Palgrave-Macmillan.

Clarke, C. (2003) Pupil centred learning: using data to improve performance. Specialist Schools Trust annual lecture.

Clarke, M., McConachie, H., Price, K. and Wood, P. (2001) Speech and language therapy provision for children using augmentative and alternative communication systems, *European Journal of Special Needs Education*, 16(1): 41–54.

Claxton, G. (1999) *Wise Up: The Challenge of Lifelong Learning*. London: Bloomsbury.

Clayton, T. (1993) From domestic helper to 'assistant teacher' – the changing role of the British classroom assistant, *European Journal of Special Needs Education*, 8(1): 32–44.

Coffield, F., Moseley, D., Hall, E. and Ecclestone, K. (2004) *Learning Styles and Pedagogy in Post-16 Learning: A Systematic and Critical Review*. London: Learning and Skills Research Centre.

Collinson, D. and Hearn, J. (eds) (1996) *Men as Managers, Managers as Men*. London: Sage.

Connor, C. (1991) *Assessment and Testing in the Primary School*. London: Falmer Press.

Conteh, J. (2000) Multilingual classrooms, standards and quality: three children and a lot of bouncing balls, *Language and Education*, 14(1): 1–17.

Conteh, J. (2003) *Succeeding in Diversity: Culture, Language and Learning in Primary Classrooms*. Stoke-on-Trent: Trentham Books.

Cooke, S. (2004) Building a library, *National Association for Language Development in the Curriculum (NALDIC) Quarterly*, 1(3): 33–4.

Corson, D. (1993) *Language, Minority Education and Gender: Linking Social Justice and Power*. Clevedon: Multilingual Matters / Toronto: Ontario Institute for Studies in Education.

Cowie, H., Smith, P., Boulton, M. and Laver, R. (1994) *Cooperation in the Multi-Ethnic Classroom*. London: David Fulton.

Cox, B. (1991) *Cox on Cox: an English Curriculum for the 1990s*. London: Hodder & Stoughton.

Cox, M. (1997) *The Effects of Information Technology on Students' Motivation*. London: National Council for Education Technology.

Cox, M. and Abbott, C. (2004) *ICT and Attainment – A Review of the Research Literature*. London: DfES/BECTA.

Cox, M. and Webb, M. (2004) *ICT and Pedagogy – A Review of the Research Literature*. London: DfES/BECTA.

Creemers, B. P. M. (1994) Effective instruction: an empirical basis for a theory of educational effectiveness, in D. Reynolds, B. P. M. Creemers, P. S. Nesselrdt, E. C. Schaffer, S. Stringfield and C. Teddlie (eds) *Advances in School Effectiveness Research and Practice*. Oxford: Pergamon.

Cremin, H., Thomas, G. and Vincett, K. (2005) Working with teaching assistants: three models evaluated, *Research Papers in Education*, 20(4): 413–32.

Croll, P. (ed.) (1996) *Teachers, Pupils and Primary Schools: Continuity and Change*. London: Cassell.

Croll, P. and Moses, D. (2000a) Continuity and change in special school provision: some perspectives on local education authority policy making, *British Educational Research Journal*, 26(2): 177–90.

Croll, P. and Moses, D. (2000b) Ideologies and utopias: education professionals' views of inclusion, *European Journal of Special Needs Education*, 15(1): 1–12.

Cronin, S. and Bold, C. (2005) Partners in mathematical learning, in A. Campbell and G. Fairbairn (eds) *Working with Support in the Classroom*. London: Paul Chapman.

Crozier, G. (2000) *Parents and Schools: Partners or Protagonists*. Stoke-on-Trent: Trentham Books.

Cuckle, P. and Broadhead, P. (1999) Effects of Ofsted inspection on school development and staff morale, in C. Cullingford (ed.) *An Inspector Calls – Ofsted and its Effects on School Standards*. London: Kogan Page.

Cullen, J. (1998) What do teachers need to know about learning in the early years? Keynote address to Early Childhood Development Unit Seminar, 'Promoting Positive Partnerships', Auckland, 23 April.

Cullen, J. and St George, A. (1996) Scripts for learning: reflecting dynamics of classroom Life, *Journal for Australian Research in Early Childhood Education*, 1: 10–19.

Cullingford, C. (1991) *The Finer World of the School*. London: Cassell.

Cullingford, C. (1999) *The Human Experience: the Early Years*. Aldershot: Ashgate.

Cullingford, C. (2000) *Prejudice: From Individual Identity to Nationalism*. London: Kogan Page.

Cullingford, C. (2002) *The Best Years of Their Lives? Pupils' Experience of School*. London: Kogan Page.

Cummins, J. (1984) *Bilingualism and Special Education: Issues in Assessment and Pedagogy*. Clevedon: Multilingual Matters.

Cummins, J. (1996) *Negotiating Identities: Education for Empowerment in a Diverse Society*. Ontario CA: California Association for Bilingual Education.

Cummins, J. (2000) *Language, Power and Pedagogy: Bilingual Children in the Crossfire*. Clevedon: Multilingual Matters.

Cummins, J. (2005) A proposal for action: strategies for recognizing heritage language competence as a learning resource within the mainstream classroom, *The Modern Language Journal*, 89(4): 585–92.

Cuthell, J. (2002) *Virtual Learning; The Impact of ICT on the Way Young People Work and Learn*. Aldershot: Ashgate.

Dadds, M. (1992) Monty Python and the Three Wise Men, *Cambridge Journal of Education*, 22(2): 129–41.

Dadds, M. (2001) The politics of pedagogy, *Teachers and Teaching: Theory and Practice*, 7: 43–58.

Datta, M. (ed.) (2001) *Bilinguality and Literacy*. London: Continuum.

Davies, M. and Edwards, G. (2001) Will the curriculum caterpillar ever learn to fly? In M. Fielding (ed.) *Taking Education Really Seriously: Four Years' Hard Labour*. London: RoutledgeFalmer.

Davis, A. (1995) Criterion-referenced assessment and the development of knowledge and understanding, *Journal of the Philosophy of Education*, 29(1): 3–21.

Davis, A. (1999) Prescribing teaching methods, *Journal of the Philosophy of Education*, 33(3): 387–401.

Davis, P. and Florian, L. (2004) *Teaching Strategies and Approaches for Pupils with Special Educational Needs: A Scoping Study*, Research Report 516. London: DfES.

Davis, P. and Hopwood, V. (2002) Including children with a visual impairment in the mainstream primary school classroom, *Journal of Research in Special Educational Needs*, 2(3): 1–11.

Dawes, L. (2001) What stops teachers using new technology? In M. Leask (ed.) *Issues in Teaching Using ICT*. London: RoutledgeFalmer.

Day, C. (2000) Stories of change and professional development: the costs of commitment, in C. Day, A. Fernandez, T. E. Hauge and J. Moller (eds) *The Life and Work of Teachers*. London: Falmer Press.

Day, C. (2002) School reform and transitions in teacher professionalism and identity. *International Journal of Educational Research*, 37, 677–92.

Day, C., Hadfield, M. and Kellow, M. (2002) Schools as learning communities: building capacity through network learning, *Education 3–13*, 30(3): 19–22.

Day, C., Harris, A., Hadfield, M., Tolley, H. and Beresford, J. (2000) *Leading Schools in Times of Change*. Buckingham: Open University Press.

Dearing, R. (1993) *The National Curriculum and its Assessment, Final Report*. London: SCAA.

Department for Education (DFE) (1994) *The Code of Practice on the Identification and Assessment of Special Educational Needs*. London: DfE.

Department for Education (DFEE) (1997a) *Excellence for All Children: Meeting Special Educational Needs*. London: HMSO.

Department for Education and Employment (DfEE) (1997b) *Excellence in Schools*, cmd 3681. London: HMSO.

Department for Education and Employment (DfEE) (1997c) *The Implementation of the National Literacy Strategy*. London: DfEE.

Department for Education and Employment (DFEE) (1998a) *Meeting Special Educational Needs: A Programme of Action*. London: HMSO.

Department for Education and Employment (DfEE) (1998b) *The National Literacy Strategy: Framework for Teaching*. London: HMSO.

Department for Education and Employment (DfEE) (1998c) *Teachers: Meeting the Challenge of Change*. London: Stationery Office.

Department for Education and Employment (DfEE) (2001a) *Learning and Teaching: A Strategy for Professional Development*. London: DfEE.

Department for Education and Employment (DfEE) (2001b) *Schools: Building on Success*. London: HMSO.

Department for Education and Employment (DfEE) / Qualifications and Curriculum Authority (QCA) (1999) *The National Curriculum: Handbook for Primary Teachers in England*. London: Department for Education and Employment/ Qualifications and Curriculum Authority.

Department for Education and Skills (DfES) (2001a) *Inclusive Schooling: Children with Special Educational Needs*. London: DfES.

Department for Education and Skills (DfES) (2001b) *Professionalism and Trust: The Future of Teachers and Teaching*. London: Social Market Foundation/DfES.

Department for Education and Skills (DfES) (2001c) *Schools Achieving Success*. London: DfES.

Department for Education and Skills (DfES) (2001d) *Special Educational Needs Code of Practice*. London: DfES.

Department for Education and Skills (DfES) (2002a) *Languages for All: Languages for Life*. http://www.standards.dfes.gov.uk/primary/publications/languages/framework/introduction/languagesstrategy/ (consulted 20 December 2005).

Department for Education and Skills (DfES) (2002b) *Time for Standards: Reforming the School Workforce*. London: DfES.

Department for Education and Skills (DfES) (2003a) *Aiming High: Raising the Achievement of Minority Ethnic Pupils* (consultation document). London: DfES.

Department for Education and Skills (DfES) (2003b) *Excellence and Enjoyment: A Strategy for Primary Schools*. London: HMSO.

Department for Education and Skills (DfES) (2003c) *Fulfilling the Potential: Transforming Teaching and Learning through ICT and Schools*. London: DfES.

Department for Education and Skills (DfES) (2003d) *Raising Standards and Tackling Workload: A National Agreement*. London: DfES.

Department for Education and Skills (DfES) (2003e) *Report of Special Schools Working Group*. London: HMSO.

Department for Education and Skills (DfES) (2004a) *Department for Education and Skills: Five Year Strategy for Children and Learners*. London: DfES.

Department for Education and Skills (DfES) (2004b) *Every Child Matters: Next Steps*. London: DfES.

Department for Education and Skills (DfES) (2004c) *Excellence and Enjoyment: Learning and Teaching in the Primary Years. Professional Development Materials – Creating a Learning Culture: Classroom Community, Collaborative and Personalised Learning*. London: DfES.

Department for Education and Skills (DfES) (2004d) *Permanent Exclusions from Maintained Schools in England 2002/2003*. http://www.dfes.gov.uk/rsgateway/ DB/SFR/s000535/SFR42-2004.pdf

Department for Education and Skills (DfES) (2004e) *Primary National Strategy. Excellence and Enjoyment: Learning and Teaching in the Primary Years. Professional Development Materials: Planning and Assessment for Learning*. London: HMSO.

Department for Education and Skills (DfES) (2004f) *Removing Barriers to Achievement: The Government's Strategy for SEN*. London: DfES.

Department for Education and Skills (DfES) (2004g) *Statistics of Education, Schools in England*. London: DfES.

Department for Education and Skills (DfES) (2005a) *The Key Stage 2 Framework for Languages*. http://www.standards.dfes.gov.uk/primary/features/languages/ (consulted, 20 December 2005).

Department for Education and Skills (DfES) (2005b) *Special Educational Needs in England, January 2005*. National Statistics First Release (SFR 24/2005). http://www.dfes.gov.uk/rsgateway/DB/SFR (accessed July 2005).

Department of Education and Science (DES) (1975) *A Language for Life* (The Bullock Report). London: HMSO.

Department of Education and Science (DES) (1978) *Primary Education in England: A Survey by HMI*. London: HMSO.

Department of Education and Science (DES) (1981) *The School Curriculum*. London: HMSO.

Department of Education and Science (DES) (1985a) *Better Schools*. London: HMSO.

Department of Education and Science (DES) (1985b) *Education for All – The Report of the Committee of Inquiry into the Education of Children from Ethnic Minority Groups* (The Swann Report). London: HMSO.

Department of Education and Science (DES) (1985c) *The School Curriculum 5–16*. London: HMSO.

Department of Education and Science (DES) (1987) *The National Curriculum 5–16, A Consultation Document*. London: HMSO.

Department of Education and Science (DES) (1988) *National Curriculum Task Group on Assessment and Testing. A Report*. London: HMSO.

Dewey, J. (1900) *The Child and Society*. Chicago: University of Chicago Press.

Dewey, J. (1902) *The Child and the Curriculum*. Chicago: University of Chicago Press.

Dewey, J. (1976) *The School and Society*. Carbondale IL: Arcturus Books – a facsimile of the first edition published in 1899.

Doddington, C. and Flutter, J., with Bearne, E. and Demetriou, H. (2001) *Sustaining Pupils' Progress at Year 3: A Report on the Research Project Supported by Ofsted*. Cambridge: University of Cambridge Faculty of Education.

Doddington, C., Bearne, E., Demetriou, H. and Flutter, J. (2002) *Sustaining Children's Progress in Learning at Year 3*. Cambridge: Homerton College.

Driver, R., Asoko, J., Turner, E. and Morris, B. (2000) Constructing scientific knowledge in the classroom, *Educational Researcher*, 23(7): 5–12.

Dunn, J. (1988) *The Beginnings of Social Understanding*. Oxford: Blackwell.

Dweck, C. S. (1986) Motivational processes affecting learning, *American Psychologist*, October: 1040–6.

Dweck, C. S. (1999) *Self-Theories: Their Role in Motivation, Personality and Development*. Philadelphia PA: Psychology Press.

Dyson, A., Gallannaugh, F. and Millward, A. (2003) Making space in the standards agenda: developing inclusive practices in schools, *European Educational Research Journal*, 2(2): 228–44.

Earl, L., Levin, B., Leithwood, K., Fullan, M. and Watson, N. (2000) *Watching and Learning: OISE/UT Evaluation of the Implementation of the National Literacy and Numeracy Strategies*, Summary: First Annual Report. Toronto: Ontario Institute for Studies in Education, University of Toronto, DfES Publications.

Earl, L., Levin, B., Leithwood, K., Fullan, M. and Watson, N. (2001) *Watching and Learning 2: OISE/UT Evaluation of the Implementation of the National Literacy and Numeracy Strategies*. Toronto: Ontario Institute for Studies in Education, University of Toronto, DfES Publications.

Earl, L., Watson, N., Levin, B. *et al.* (2003) *Watching and Learning 3: Final Report of the External Evaluation of England's National Literacy and Numeracy Strategies*. Toronto: Ontario Institute for Studies in Education, University of Toronto, DfES Publications.

Easen, P. and Bolden, D. (2005) Location, location, location: What do league tables really tell us about primary schools? *Education 3–13*, 33(3), 49–56.

Edwards, A. (2001) Researching pedagogy: a sociocultural agenda, *Pedagogy, Culture and Society*, 9(2): 161–86.

Edwards, T. (2003) Report of the Colloquium, in BERA, *Educational Policy and Research across the UK*. Southwell: British Educational Research Association.

Egan, K. (1997) *The Educated Mind: How Cognitive Tools Shape our Understanding*. Chicago: University of Chicago Press.

Elliott, J. G. (2000) The psychological assessment of children with learning difficulties, *British Journal of Special Education*, 27(2): 59–66.

Eraut, M. (1991) *The Information Society – A Challenge for Education Policies? Policy Options and Implementations Strategies*. London: Cassell.

Evans, J. and Lunt, I. (2002) Inclusive education: are there limits? *European Journal of Special Needs Education*, 17(1): 1–14.

Evans, J., Harden, A. and Thomas, J. (2004) What are effective strategies to support pupils with emotional and behavioural difficulties (EBD) in mainstream primary schools? Findings from a systematic review of research, *Journal of Research in Special Educational Needs*, 4(1): 2–16.

Eyres, I., Cable, C., Hancock, R. and Turner, J. (2004) 'Whoops, I forgot David': children's perceptions of the adults who work in their classrooms, *Early Years*, 24(2): 149–62.

Fajerman, L., Jarrett, M. and Sutton, F. (2000) *Children as Partners in Planning*. London: Save the Children.

Farrell, P. (2001) Special Education in the last twenty years: have things really got better? *British Journal of Special Education*, 28(1): 3–9.

Farrell, P., Balshaw, M. and Polat, F. (1999) *The Management, Role and Training of Learning Support Assistants.* London: DfEE.

Fawcett, T. (2005) Reprimand for stab threat, *Times Educational Supplement,* 21 January.

Fielding, M. (2001) Target setting, policy pathology and student perspectives: learning to labour in new times, in M. Fielding (ed.) *Taking Education Really Seriously: Four Years' Hard Labour.* London: RoutledgeFalmer.

Fitz, J. (2003) The politics of accountability: A perspective from England and Wales, *Peabody Journal of Education,* 78(4): 230–41.

Fitzpatrick, F. (1987) *The Open Door: The Bradford Bilingual Project.* Clevedon: Multilingual Matters.

Florian, L. and Rouse, M. (2001) Inclusive practice in English secondary schools: lessons learned, *Cambridge Journal of Education,* 31(3): 399–412.

Flutter, J. and Ruddock, J. (2004) *Consulting Pupils: What's in it for Schools?* London: RoutledgeFalmer.

Foxman, D. (1998) Monitoring trends in numeracy in the UK, 1953–1995, *Topic.* Slough: NFER.

Fraser, H. and Honeyford, G. (2000) *Children, Parents and Teachers Enjoying Numeracy: Numeracy Hour Success through Collaboration.* London: David Fulton.

Gallagher, D. (2001) Neutrality as a moral standpoint, conceptual confusion and the full inclusion debate, *Disability and Society,* 16(5): 637–54.

Galton, M. (1989) *Teaching in the Primary School.* London: David Fulton.

Galton, M. (2000) The National Curriculum: a balance sheet for Key Stage 2: a researcher's view, *The Curriculum Journal,* 11(3): 323–41.

Galton, M. and Hargreaves, L. (2002) Transfer: a future agenda, in L. Hargreaves and M. Galton (eds) *Transfer from the Primary Classroom: 20 Years On.* London: RoutledgeFalmer.

Galton, M., Hargreaves, L., Comber, C., Wall, D. with Pell, A. (1999) *Inside the Primary Classroom: 20 Years On.* London: Routledge.

Galton, M., MacBeath, J. with Page, C. and Steward, S. (2002) *A Life in Teaching? The Impact of Change on Primary Teachers' Working Lives.* London: NUT.

Galton, M. and Simon, B. (eds) (1980) *Progress and Performance in the Primary Classroom.* London: Routledge & Kegan Paul.

Galton, M., Simon, B. and Croll, P. (1980) *Inside the Primary Classroom.* London: Routledge & Kegan Paul.

Garner, P. (1996) Students' views on special educational needs courses in Initial Teacher Education, *British Journal of Special Education,* 23: 176–9.

Gee, J. P. (1996) *Social Linguistics and Literacies.* London: Routledge.

Gewirtz, S., Dickson, M., Power, S., Halpin, D. and Whitty, G. (2005) The deployment of social capital theory in educational policy and provision: the case of education action zones in England, *British Educational Research Journal,* 31(6): 651–73.

Giddens, A. (1998) *The Third Way: the Renewal of Social Democracy.* Cambridge: Polity Press.

Gipps, C. (1992) *What We Know about Effective Primary Teaching*. London: Tufnell Press.

Gipps, C., Brown, M., McCallum, B. and McAlister, S. (1995) *Intuition or Evidence? Teachers and National Assessment of Seven Year Olds*. Milton Keynes: Open University Press.

Gipps, C., McCallum, B. and Brown, M. (1996) Models of teacher assessment among primary school teachers in England, *Curriculum Journal*, 7(2): 167–83.

Gipps, C., McCallum, B. and Brown, M. (1999) Primary teachers' beliefs about teaching and learning, *The Curriculum Journal*, 10(1): 123–34.

Gipps, C., McCallum, B. and Hargreaves, E. (2000) *What Makes a Good Primary School Teacher? Expert Classroom Strategies*. London: RoutledgeFalmer.

Gipps, C., Steadman, S., Blackstone, T. and Stierer, B. (1983) *Testing Children: Standardised Testing in Local Education Authorities and Schools*. London: Heinemann Educational Books.

Goldstein, H. (2001) Using pupil performance data for judging schools and teachers: scope and limitations, *British Educational Research Journal*, 27(4): 433–42.

Goodison, T. A. (2002) Learning with ICT at primary level: pupils' perceptions, *Journal of Computer Assisted Learning*, 18: 282–95.

Goodson, I. F. (2003) *Professional Knowledge. Professional Lives*. Maidenhead: Open University Press.

Gorwood, B. (1994) Primary-secondary transfer after the national curriculum, in A. Pollard and J. Bourne (eds) *Teaching and Learning in the Primary School*. London: Routledge.

Grace, G. (1995) *School Leadership: Beyond Education Management*. London: Falmer Press.

Graham, D. and Tytler, D. (1993) *A Lesson For Us All*. London: Routledge.

Greenberg, M. and Kusche, C. (1998) Preventive intervention for school age deaf children: The PATHS curriculum, *Journal of Deaf Studies and Deaf Education*, 3(1): 50–63.

Gregory, E. (1994) The National Curriculum and non-native speakers of English, in G. V. Blenkin and A. V. Kelly (eds) *The National Curriculum and Early Learning*. London: Paul Chapman.

Gregory, E., Long, S. and Volk, D. (eds) (2004) *Many Pathways to Literacy: Young Children Learning with Siblings, Grandparents, Peers and Communities*. London: RoutledgeFalmer.

Gronn, P. (2000) Distributed properties: a new architecture for leadership, *Educational Management and Administration*, 28(93): 317–38.

Groundwater-Smith, S. and Sachs, J. (2002) The activist professional and the reinstatement of trust, *Cambridge Journal of Education*, 32(3): 341–57.

Gussin Paley, V. (1979) *White Teacher*. Cambridge MA and London: Harvard University Press.

Hall, D. (2001) *Assessing the Needs of Bilingual Pupils: Living in Two Languages*, 2nd edn. London: David Fulton.

Hall, I. and Higgins, S. (2005) Primary school students' perceptions of interactive whiteboards, *Journal of Computer Assisted Learning*, 21: 102–17.

Hallam, S., Ireson, J. and Davies, J. (2004) Grouping practices in the primary school: what influences change? *British Educational Research Journal*, 30(1): 117–40.

Hammersley-Fletcher, L. (2000) Co-ordinating subjects in the primary school: perceptions of subject leaders, their implementation of the role and the influence of external factors. Unpublished PhD thesis, University of Liverpool.

Hammersley-Fletcher, L. with Colwell, H. and Croft, L. (2004) *Primary School Middle Leaders: Subject Leaders, their Headteachers and the Influence of Distributed Leadership Ideals*. Report to the National College of School Leadership. Staffordshire University: Institute for Education Policy Research.

Hancock, R. and Eyres, I. (2004) Implementing a required curriculum reform: teachers at the core, teaching assistants on the periphery? *Westminster Studies in Education*, 27(2): 223–35.

Hancock, R. and Mansfield, M. (2002) The Literacy Hour: a case for listening to children, *The Curriculum Journal*, 13(2): 183–200.

Hancock, R., Swann, W., Marr, A. and Turner, J. (2001) *Classroom Assistants in the Primary School: Employment and Deployment*. Milton Keynes: Open University, Faculty of Education and Language Studies.

Hanlon, G. (1998) Professionalism as enterprise: service class politics and the redefinition of professionalism, *Sociology*, 32: 43–63.

Hargreaves, A. (1994) *Changing Teachers, Changing Times: Teachers' Work and Culture in the Postmodern Age*. London: Cassell.

Hargreaves, A. (2000) Four ages of professionalism and professional learning, *Teachers and Teaching: History and Practice*, 6: 151–82.

Hargreaves, A. (2003) Professional learning communities and performance training sects, in A. Harris, C. Day, D. Hopkins, M. Hadfield, A. Hargreaves and C. Chapman (2003) *Effective Leadership for School Improvement*. London: RoutledgeFalmer.

Hargreaves, L., Moyles, J., Merry, R. *et al.* (2003) How do primary school teachers define and implement 'interactive teaching' in the National Literacy Strategy in England? *Research Papers in Education*, 18(3), 217–36.

Hargreaves, L., Pell, T. and Hopper, B. (2004) Teachers' perceptions of their status: in what ways is teaching a high status profession? Paper presented at the British Educational Research Association annual conference, UMIST, Manchester, 16–18 September.

Harlen. W. (1985) *Teaching and Learning Primary Science*. London: Harper & Row.

Harris, A. (2002) *School Improvement: What's in it for Schools?* London: Falmer Press.

Harris, A. (2003) Teacher leadership and school improvement, in A. Harris, C. Day, D. Hopkins, M. Hadfield, A. Hargreaves and C. Chapman (2003) *Effective Leadership for School Improvement*. London: RoutledgeFalmer.

Harris, A. and Muijs, D. (2004) *Teacher Leadership: A Review of Research*. Nottingham: NCSL.

Harris, A. and Ranson, S. (2005) The contradictions of education policy: disadvantage and achievement, *British Educational Research Journal*, 31(5): 571–87.

Harris, J. (1998) *The Nurture Assumption*. London: Bloomsbury.

Harris, S. (2002) Innovative pedagogical practices using ICT in schools in England, *Journal of Computer Assisted Learning*, 18: 449–58.

Hartley, D. (2003) The instrumentalisation of the expressive in education, *British Journal of Educational Studies*, 51(1): 6–19.

Haviland, J. (1988) *Take Care, Mr Baker!* London: Fourth Estate.

Hayes, D. (2002) Purpose, power and constraint in the primary curriculum: the Taylor Report, *Education 3–13*, 30: 5–11.

Helsby, G. and McCulloch, G. (1996) Teacher professionalism and curriculum control, in I. Goodson and A. Hargreaves (eds) *Teachers' Professional Lives*. London: Falmer Press.

Herbert, M. (2005) *Development Problems of Childhood and Adolescence*. Oxford: BPS Blackwell.

Her Majesty's Inspectors (HMI) (2002) *Teaching Assistants in Primary Schools: An Evaluation of the Quality and Impact of their Work: A Report by HMI*. London: Ofsted.

Hildebrand, G. M. (1999) Contesting learning models. Paper presented at the AARE and NZARE Conference, Melbourne.

Hogan, P. (2003) Teaching and learning as a way of life, *Journal of the Philosophy of Education*, 37(2): 207–23.

Holt, J. (1982) *How Children Fail*. Harmondsworth: Penguin.

Hopkins, D. (2003) Instructional leadership and school improvement, in A. Harris, C. Day, D. Hopkins *et al*. (2003) *Effective Leadership for School Improvement*. London: RoutledgeFalmer.

Hopkins, D. and Reynolds, D. (2001) The past, present and future of school improvement: towards the Third Age, *British Educational Research Journal*, 27(4): 459–75.

Hornby, G. (1999) Inclusion or delusion? Can one size fit all? *Support for Learning*, 14(4): 152–7.

House of Commons (1986) *Third Report of the Education Science and Arts Committee, Achievement in Primary School*, Vol 1. London: HMSO.

Hoyle, E. and John, P. D. (1995) The idea of a profession, in E. Hoyle and P. D. John (eds) *Professional Knowledge and Professional Practice*. London: Cassell.

Hutchings, M., Menter, I. and Ross, A. (2000) *Teacher Supply and Retention in Six London Boroughs*. London: Teacher Training Agency.

Hutchings, M., Menter, I., Ross, A. and Thomson, D. (2002) Teacher supply and retention in London – Key findings and implications from a study carried out in six boroughs in 1998/9, in I. Menter, M. Hutchings and A. Ross (eds) *The Crisis in Teacher Supply: Research and Strategies for Retention*. Stoke-on-Trent: Trentham.

Jackson, C. R. and Bedford, D. (2005) Unlocking the potential: the enhanced role of support staff for schools in England. Paper presented at the British Educational Research Association annual conference, University of Glamorgan, 14–17 September.

Jackson, D. (2000) The school improvement journey: Perspectives on leadership, *School Leadership and Management*, 20(1): 61–79.

Jedeskog, G. and Nissen, J. (2004) ICT in the classroom: is doing more important than knowing? *Education and Information Technologies*, 9(1): 37–45.

Jeffrey, B. (2002) Performativity and primary teacher relations, *Journal of Education Policy*, 17(5): 531–46.

Jeffrey, B. (2003) Countering learner 'instrumentalism' through creative mediation, *British Educational Research Journal*, 29(4): 489–503.

Jeffrey, B. and Woods, P. (1998) *Testing Teachers: The Effects of School Inspections on Primary Teachers*. London: Falmer Press.

Jeffrey, B. and Woods, P. (2003) *The Creative School*. London: RoutledgeFalmer.

Johnson, T. J. (1972) *Professions and Power*. London: Macmillan.

Kalechstein, A. and Nowicki, S. (1987) A meta-analytic examination of the relationships between control and expectancies and academic achievement, *Genetic, Social and General Psychology Monographs*, 123: 27–57.

Katz, S. (2000) Competence, epistemology and pedagogy, *The Curriculum Journal*, 11(2): 133–44.

Katz, S. (2002) Reconnecting the child and the curriculum: places of paradox, *The Curriculum Journal*, 17(1): 5–20.

Katzenmeyer, M. and Moller, G. (2001) *Awakening the Sleeping Giant. Helping Teachers Develop as Leaders*. Thousand Oaks, California: Corwin Press.

Kennewell, S. (2001) Using affordances and constraints to evaluate the use of information and communication technology in teaching and learning, *Journal of Information Technology for Teacher Education*, 10(1&2): 101–16.

Kennewell, S. (2004) Researching the influence of interactive presentation tools on teachers' pedagogy. Paper presented at the British Educational Research Association annual conference, University of Manchester, September.

Kennewell, S. and Beauchamp, G. (2003) The influence of a technology-rich classroom environment on elementary teachers' pedagogy and children's learning, in J. Wright, A. McDougall, J. Murnane and J. Lowe (eds) *International Federation for Information Processing Working Group 3.5 Open Conference*. Sydney: Australian Computer Society Inc.

Kershner, R. (2000) Organising the physical environment of the classroom to support children's learning, in D. Whitebread (ed.) *The Psychology of Teaching and Learning in the Primary School*. London: RoutledgeFalmer.

Kogan, M. (1975) *Educational Policy Making: A Study of Interest Groups and Parliament*. London: Allen & Unwin.

Kutnick, P., Blatchford, P. and Baines, E. (2002) Pupil groupings in primary school classrooms: sites for learning and social pedagogy, *British Educational Research Journal*, 28(2): 187–206.

Kyriacou, C. and Goulding, M. (2004) *A Systematic Review of the Impact of the Daily Mathematics Lesson in Enhancing Pupil Confidence and Competence in Early Mathematics*. Review conducted by the Mathematics Education Review Group. London: EPPI-Centre, Institute of Education, University of London.

Labour Party (1996) *New Labour, New Life for Britain*. London: Labour Party.

Lave, J. and Wenger, E. (1991) *Situated Learning: Legitimate Peripheral Participation*. Cambridge: Cambridge University Press.

Law, N., Lee, Y. and Chow, A. (2002) Practice characteristics that lead to 21st century learning outcomes, *Journal of Computer Assisted Learning*, 18: 415–26.

Lawlor, H. and Sills, P. (1999) Successful leadership – evidence from highly effective headteachers, *Improving Schools* 2(2): 53–60.

Lawn, M. (1989) Being caught in schoolwork: the possibilities of research in teachers' work, in W. Carr (ed.) *Quality in Teaching: Arguments for a Reflective Profession*. Lewes: Falmer Press.

Lawton, D. (1992) Whatever happened to the TGAT Report?, in C. Gipps (ed.) *Developing Assessment for National Curriculum*. London: Kogan Page.

Lee, B. (2002) *Teaching Assistants in Schools: The Current State of Play*. Slough: NFER.

Leithwood, K. (2003) Teacher leadership: its nature, development, and impact on schools and students, in M. Brundrett, N. Burton and R. Smith (eds) *Leadership in Education*. London: Sage Publications.

Leithwood, K., Jantzi, D. and Seinbach, R. (1999) *Changing Leadership for Changing Times*. Buckingham: Open University Press.

Letwin, O. (1988) *A Core Curriculum*. London: Centre for Policy Studies.

Levine, J. (1996) Pedagogy: the case of the missing concept, in M. Meek (ed.) *Developing Pedagogies in the Multilingual Classroom: The Writings of Josie Levine*. Stoke-on-Trent: Trentham Books.

Lewis, A. (2004) 'And when did you last see your father?' Exploring the views of children with learning difficulties/disabilities, *British Journal of Special Education*, 31(1): 3–9.

Lewis, A. and Norwich, B. (eds) (2005) *Special Teaching for Special Children? Pedagogies for Inclusion*. Maidenhead: Open University Press.

Lindsay, J. (2003) Inclusive education: a critical perspective, *British Journal of Special Education*, 30(1): 3–12.

Lingard, B., Hayes, D. and Mills, M. (2003) Teaching and productive pedagogies: contextualising, conceptualising, utilising, *Pedagogy, Culture and Society*, 11(3): 399–424.

Lipsky, D. K. and Gartner, A. (1998) Factors for successful inclusion: learning from the past, looking forward to the future, in S. V. Vitello and D. E. Mithaug (eds) *Inclusive Schooling: National and International Perspectives*. Mahurah NJ: Lawrence Erlbaum.

Lloyd, C. (2000) Excellence for all children – false promises! The failure of current policy for inclusive education and implications for schooling in the 21st century, *International Journal of Inclusive Education*, 4(2): 133–51.

Locke, T. (2001) Curriculum, assessment and the erosion of professionalism, *New Zealand Journal of Educational Studies*, 36: 5–23.

Locke, T., Vulliamy, G., Webb, R. and Hill, M. (2005) Being a 'professional' primary school teacher at the beginning of the 21st century: a comparative analysis of primary teacher professionalism in New Zealand and England, *Journal of Education Policy*, 20(5): 555–81.

Loveless, A. (2002) ICT in the primary curriculum, in A. Loveless and B. Dore (eds) *ICT in the Primary School*. Buckingham: Open University Press.

Loveless, A. (2003) The interaction between primary teachers' perceptions of ICT and their pedagogy, *Education and Information Technologies*, 8(4): 313–26.

Loxley, A. and Thomas, G. (2001) Neo-conservatives, neo-liberals, the New Left and inclusion: stirring the pot, *Cambridge Journal of Education*, 31(3): 291–301.

Luckner, J. L. and Muir, S. (2001) Successful students who are deaf in general education settings, *American Annals of the Deaf*, 146(5): 450–61.

Luke, A., Ladwig, J., Lingard, B., Hayes, D. and Mills, M. (1999) *Queensland School Reform Longitudinal Study*. St Lucia: University of Queensland.

MacBeath, J. (1999) *Schools Must Speak for Themsleves: The Case for School Self-evaluation*. London: Routledge.

MacBeath, J. (2005) Leadership as distributed: a matter of practice, *School Leadership and Management*, 25(4): 349–66.

MacBeath, J., Demetrious, H., Ruddock, J. and Myers, K. (2003) *Consulting Pupils: A Toolkit for Teachers*. Cambridge: Pearson.

MacDonald, A. (2004) Collegiate or compliant? Primary teachers in post-McCrone Scotland, *British Educational Research Journal*, 30(3): 413–33.

MacDonald, D. (2003) Curriculum change and the post-modern world: is the school curriculum-reform movement an anachromism? *Journal of Curriculum Studies*, 35(2): 139–49.

MacGilchrist, B. and Buttress, M. (2005) *Transforming Learning and Teaching*. London: Paul Chapman Publishing.

Mahony, P. and Hextall, I. (2000) *Reconstructing Teaching: Standards, Performance and Accountability*. London: RoutledgeFalmer.

Mahony, P., Hextall, I. and Menter, I. (2004a) Building dams in Jordan, assessing teachers in England: a case-study in edu-business, *Globalisation, Societies and Education*, 2(2): 277–96.

Mahony, P., Hextall, I. and Menter, I. (2004b) Threshold assessment and performance management: modernising or masculinising teaching? *Gender and Education*, 16(2): 131–49.

Mahony, P., Menter, I. and Hextall, I. (2002) Threshold assessment of teachers – more Macdonaldization or another peculiarity of the English? *International Studies in the Sociology of Education*, 12(2): 145–68.

Mahony, P., Menter, I. and Hextall, I. (2004c) The emotional impact of performance-related pay on teachers in England, *British Educational Research Journal*, 30(3): 435–56.

Mansell, W., Shaw, M. and Ward, H. (2005) Tony's second-term report, *Times Educational Supplement*, 22 April.

McCarney, J. (2004) Effective models of staff development in ICT, *European Journal of Teacher Education*, 27(1): 61–72.

McCulloch, G., Helsby, G. and Knight, P. (2000) *The Politics of Professionalism*. London: Continuum.

McEvoy, J. and Walker, R. (2000) Antisocial behaviour, academic failure, and school climate: a critical review, *Journal of Emotional and Behavioural Disorders*, 8(3): 130–46.

McFarlane, A. and Sakellariou, A. (2002) The role of ICT in science education, *Cambridge Journal of Education*, 32(2): 219–32.

McMaster, K. and Fuchs, D. (2002) Effects of co-operative learning on the academic achievement of students with learning disabilities: an update of Tateyama-Sniezek's review, *Learning Disabilities Research and Practice*, 17(2): 107–17.

McNamara, D. and Waugh, D. (1993) Classroom organisation: a discussion of grouping strategies in the light of the '3 Wise Men's Report', *School Organisation*, 13(1): 41–50.

McNess, E., Broadfoot, P. and Osborn, M. (2003) Is the effective compromising the affective? *British Educational Research Journal*, 29(2): 243–57.

Measor, L. and Woods, P. (1984) *Changing Schools: Pupils' Perspectives on Transfer to a Comprehensive School*. Milton Keynes: Open University Press.

Menter, I., Hextall, I. and Mahony, P. (2003) Rhetoric or reality?: Ethnic monitoring in the *Threshold Assessment* of teachers in England and Wales, *Race, Ethnicity and Education*, 6(4): 308–30.

Menter, I., Mahony, P. and Hextall, I. (2004) Ne'er the twain shall meet? Modernizing the teaching profession in Scotland and England, *Journal of Education Policy*, 19(2): 195–214.

Menter, I., Muschamp, Y., Nicholls, P. and Ozga, J. with Pollard, A. (1997) *Work and Identity in the Primary School: A Post-Fordist Analysis*. Buckingham: Open University Press.

Meyer, J. W., Kamens, D. H. and Benavot, A. (1992) *School Knowledge for the Masses: World Models and National Primary Curricular Categories in the Twentieth Century*. London: Falmer.

Miliband, D. (2004) Personalised learning: building a new relationship with schools. Speech to the North of England Education Conference, Belfast, 8 January.

Moll, L. C., Amanti, C., Neff, D. and Gonzalez, N. (1992) Funds of knowledge for teaching: Using a qualitative approach to connect homes and classrooms, *Theory into Practice*, 31(2): 132–41.

Moran, A. and Abbott, L. (2002) Developing inclusive schools: the pivotal role of teaching assistants in promoting inclusion in special and mainstream schools in Northern Ireland, *European Journal of Special Needs in Education*, 17(2): 161–73.

Moyles, J., Hargreaves, L., Merry, R., Paterson, F. and Esarte-Sarries, V. (2003) *Interactive Teaching in the Primary School: Digging Deeper into Meanings*. Maidenhead: Open University Press.

Murphy, P. and Ivinson, G. (2003) Pedagogy and cultural knowledge: a sociocultural perspective, *Pedagogy, Culture and Society*, 11(1): 2–5.

Muschamp, Y., Pollard, A. and Sharpe, R. (1992) Curriculum management in primary schools, *The Curriculum Journal*, 3(1): 21–39.

National Association for Language Development in the Curriculum (NALDIC) (2004) http://www.naldic.org.uk/docs/members/documents/EALPilotDiscussionPaper.pdf (consulted 20 December 2005).

National College for School Leadership (2003) *Sustaining Improvement in the Primary School, Leadership Programme for Primary School Leaders*. Nottingham: NCSL.

National Curriculum Council (NCC) (1990) *Curriculum Guidance Three: The Whole Curriculum*. York: NCC.

National Curriculum Council (NCC) (1991) *Linguistic Diversity and the National Curriculum*, circular number 11. York: NCC.

National Curriculum Council (NCC) (1993) *The National Curriculum at Key Stages 1 and 2: Advice to the Secretary of State for Education*. York: NCC.

National Union of Teachers (NUT) (2003) *The Response of the National Union of Teachers to the DfES Document 'Excellence and Enjoyment – A Strategy for Primary Schools'*. London: NUT.

Nelson, K. and Cammarata, S. (1996) Improving English literacy and speech acquisition learning conditions for children with severe to profound hearing impairments, *Volta Review*, 98: 17–42.

Nias, J. (1989) *Primary Teachers Talking – A Study of Teaching as Work*. London: Routledge.

Nias, J. (2000) Preface, in A. Pollard and P. Triggs with P. Broadfoot, E. McNess and M. Osborn (2000) *What Pupils Say: Changing Policy and Practice in Primary Education*. London: Continuum.

Nicholls, G. and Gardner, J. (1999) *Pupils in Transition: Moving Between Key Stages*. London: Routledge.

Nisbett, J. and Entwistle, N. (1969) *The Transition to Secondary Education*. London: University of London Press.

Nixon, J., Martin, J., McKeown, P. and Ranson, S. (1997) Towards a learning profession: changing codes of occupational practice within the new management of education, *British Journal of Sociology of Education*, 18: 5–28.

Norwich, B. (1997) *A Trend Towards Inclusion: Statistics on Special School Placements and Pupils with Statements in Ordinary Schools, England 1992–1996*. Bristol: CSIE.

Norwich, B. (2002a) Education, inclusion and individual differences: recognising and resolving dilemmas, *British Journal of Educational Studies*, 50(4): 482–502.

Norwich, B. (2002b) *LEA Inclusion Trends in England 1997–2001. Statistics on Special School Placements and Pupils with Statements in Special Schools*. Bristol: CSIE.

Norwich, B. and Kelly, N. (2005) *Moderate Learning Difficulties and the Future of Inclusion*. London: RoutledgeFalmer.

Norwich, B. and Lewis, A. (2001) A critical review of evidence concerning teaching strategies for pupils with special educational needs, *British Educational Research Journal*, 27(3): 313–29.

Noyes, A. (2004) Learning landscapes, *British Educational Research Journal*, 30(1): 27–41.

Ofsted (1993a) *Curriculum Organisation and Classroom Practice in Primary Schools: a Follow-up Report*. London: HMSO.

Ofsted (1993b) *Standards and Quality in Schools 1991/92* (Annual Report of the Chief Inspector of Schools). London: HMSO.

Ofsted (1995) *Class Size and the Quality of Education*. London: Ofsted.

Ofsted (1996) *Annual Report of HMCI*. London: HMSO.

Ofsted (1998) *The National Literacy Project: an HMI Evaluation*. London: The Stationery Office.

Ofsted (1999a) *Annual Report of HMCI*. London: The Stationery Office.

Ofsted (1999b) *Primary Education 1994–98, A Review of Primary Schools in England*. London: The Stationery Office.

Ofsted (2002a) *The Curriculum in Successful Primary Schools*. London: Ofsted.

Ofsted (2002b) *Teaching Assistants in Primary Schools: an Evaluation by Ofsted 2001–2002*. London: Ofsted.

Ofsted (2003) *Leadership and Management, What Inspection Tells Us*. London: Ofsted.

Olson, M. R. and Craig, C. J. (2001) Opportunities and challenges in the development of teachers' knowledge: the development of narrative authority through knowledge communities, *Teaching and Teacher Education*, 17(6): 667–84.

Osborn, M. and Broadfoot, P. with Abbott, D., Croll, P. and Pollard, A. (1992) The impact of current changes in English primary schools on teacher professionalism, *Teachers College Record*, 94(1): 138–51.

Osborn, M., Broadfoot, P., McNess, E. *et al.* (2003) *A World of Difference: Comparing Learners Across Europe*. Buckingham: Open University Press.

Osborn, M., McNess, E. and Broadfoot, P. with Pollard, A. and Triggs, P. (2000) *What Teachers Do: Changing Policy and Practice in Primary Education*. London: Continuum.

Pinker, S. (1997) *How the Mind Works*. London: Allen Lane.

Pollard, A. (1994) *Look Before You Leap: Research Evidence for the Curriculum at Key Stage Two*. London: Tufnell Press.

Pollard, A., Broadfoot, P., Croll, P., Osborn, M. and Abbott, D. (1994) *Changing*

English Primary Schools? The Impact of the Education Reform Act at Key Stage One. London: Cassell.

Pollard, A. and Filer, A. (1999) *The Social World of Pupil Career.* London: Cassell.

Pollard, A. with Filer, A. (2000) *The Social World of Pupil Assessment.* London: Continuum.

Pollard, A., Thiessen, D. and Filer, A. (eds) (1997) *Children and their Curriculum: The Perspectives of Primary and Elementary School Children.* London: Falmer Press.

Pollard, A. and Triggs, P. with Broadfoot, P., McNess, E. and Osborn, M. (2000) *What Pupils Say: Changing Policy and Practice in Primary Education.* London: Continuum.

Ponting, C. (1986) *Whitehall: Tragedy or Farce?* London: Hamish Hamilton.

Poulson, L. (1998) Accountability, teacher professionalism and education reform in England, *Teacher Development*, 2(3): 419–31.

Poulson, L. and Avramidis, E. (2003) Pathways and possibilities in professional development: case studies of effective teachers of literacy, *British Educational Research Journal*, 29(4): 543–60.

Power, S. and Whitty, G. (1999) New Labour's education policy: first, second or third way? *Journal of Education Policy*, 14(5): 535–46.

Prawat, R. S. (1989) Teaching for understanding: three attributes, *Teaching and Teacher Education*, 5(4): 315–28.

Pugh, G. (1997) Early childhood education finds its voice: but is anyone listening? In C. Cullingford (ed.) *The Politics of Primary Education.* Buckingham: Open University Press.

Pye, J. (1989) *Invisible Children: Who Are the Real Losers at School?* Oxford: Oxford University Press.

Qualifications and Curriculum Authority (QCA) (2004) *The 10 Principles.* http://qca.org.uk/ages 3–14/afl/907.html

Qualifications and Curriculum Authority (QCA)/Department for Education and Employment (DfEE) (1999) *The Review of the National Curriculum: The Consultation Materials.* London: QCA.

Quicke, J. (2000) A new professionalism for a collaborative culture of organizational learning in contemporary society, *Educational Management and Administration*, 28: 299–315.

Ralston, J. (2004) ICT, learning and primary Mathematics, *Education 3–13*, 32(2): 60–4.

Resnick, L. B., Bill, V. and Lesgold, S. (1992) Developing thinking abilities in arithmetic class, in A. Demitriou, M. Shayer and A. E. Efklides (eds) *Neo-Piagetian Theories of Cognitive Development: Implications and Applications for Education.* London: Routledge.

Reynolds, D. and Farrell, S. (1996) *Worlds Apart? A Review of International Surveys of Educational Achievement Involving England.* London: HMSO.

Richards, C. (1998) The primary school curriculum: Changes, challenges, questions, in C. Richards and P. Taylor (eds) *How Shall We School Our Children?* London: Falmer.

Richards, C. (1999) *Primary Education: At a Hinge of History*. London: Falmer Press.

Richards, C. (2005) *Standards in English Primary Schools: Are They Rising?* London: Association of Teachers and Lecturers.

Rivera, C. (ed.) (1984) *Language Proficiency and Academic Achievement*. Clevedon: Multilingual Matters.

Roberts, B. and Dyson, A. (2002) *Final Evaluation Report of the Learning Support Assistants Project*. Newcastle upon Tyne: Special Needs Research Centre, School of Education, Communication and Language Skills, University of Newcastle-upon-Tyne.

Robertson, J. (2002) The ambiguous embrace: twenty years of IT (ICT) in UK primary schools, *British Journal of Educational Technology*, 33(4): 403–9.

Robertson, R. (1995) Glocalization: time-space and homogeneity-heterogeneity, in M. Featherstone, S. Lash and R. Robertson (eds) *Global Modernities*. London: Sage.

Robertson, S. (1996) Teachers' work, restructuring and postfordism: constructing the New 'Professionalism', in I. Goodson and A. Hargreaves (eds) *Teachers' Professional Lives*. London: Falmer Press.

Rogoff, B. (1995) Observing sociocultural activity on three planes: participatory appropriation, guided participation and apprenticeship, in J. V. Wertsch, P. Delrio and A. Alvarez (eds) *Sociocultural Studies of Mind*. Cambridge: Cambridge University Press.

Rose, R. (2001) Primary school teacher perceptions of the conditions required to include pupils with special educational needs, *Educational Review*, 53(2): 147–56.

Rosenholtz, S. J. (1989) *Teachers' Workplace: The Social Organisation of Schools*. White Plains NY: Longman.

Rudduck, J. (1996) Going to the big school: the turbulence of transition, in G. Wallance (ed.) *School Improvement: What Can Pupils Tell Us?* London: David Fulton.

Rustemier, S. and Vaughan, M. (2005) *Segregation Trends – LEAs in England 2002–2004. Placements of Pupils with Statements in Special Schools and Other Segregated Settings*. Bristol: CSIE.

Sachs, J. (2003) *The Activist Teaching Profession*. Buckingham: Open University Press.

Sadler, R. (1998) Formative assessment: revisiting the territory, *Assessment in Education*, 5(1): 77–84.

Safford, K. (2003) *Teachers and Pupils in the Big Picture: Seeing Real Children in Routinised Assessment*. Watford: National Association for Language Development in the Curriculum (NALDIC).

Sammons, P., Elliot, K., Sylva, K. *et al.* (2004) The impact of pre-school on young children's cognitive attainments at entry to reception, *British Educational Research Journal*, 30(5): 691–707.

Sammons, P., Lewis, A., MacLure, M. *et al.* (1994) Teaching and learning processes, in A. Pollard (ed.) *Look Before You Leap? Research Evidence for the Curriculum at Key Stage Two*. London: Tufnell Press.

Schon, D. (1995) *The Reflective Practitioner*. Aldershot: Arena.

Schwienhorst, K. (1998) Co-constructing learning environments and learner identities – language learning in virtual reality. Proceedings of the ED-Media / ED Telecom, Freiburg.

Scottish Executive (SEED) (2004) *A Curriculum for Excellence*. The Curriculum Review Group. Edinburgh: Blackwells. www.scotland.gov.uk (accessed 10 March 2005).

Scottish Parliament (2001) *Official Report of Special Needs Inquiry*. http://www.scottish.Parliament.uk/official_report/session-01/sor0517–02.htm.

Selinger, M. (2001) The role of the teacher: teacherless classrooms? In M. Leask (ed.) *Issues in Teaching Using ICT*. London: RoutledgeFalmer.

Selwyn, N. and Fitz, J. (2001) The national grid for learning: a case study of new labour education policy-making, *Journal of Education Policy*, 16(2): 127–48.

Senge, P. (1990) *The Fifth Discipline: The Art and Practice of the Learning Organisation*. New York: Doubleday.

Shipman, M. (1984) *Education as Public Welfare*. London: Methuen.

Shorrocks-Taylor, D., Curry, J., Swinnerton, B. and Nelson, N. (2003) National Curriculum Maths tests in England at Key Stage 2: weights and measures? *The Oxford Review of Education*, 29(1): 51–66.

Shulman, L. S. (1986) Those who understand: knowledge growth in teaching, *Educational Researcher*, 15: 4–14.

Shulman, L. S. (1987) Knowledge and teaching: foundations of the new reform, *Harvard Educational Review*, 57(1): 1–22.

Silcock, P. J. (1999) *New Progressivism*. London: Falmer Press.

Silcock, P. (2002) Under construction or facing demolition? Contrasting views on English teacher professionalism from across a professional association, *Teacher Development*, 6: 137–55.

Silcock, P. J. and Duncan, D. (2001) Values acquisition and values education, *British Journal of Educational Studies*, 49(3): 242–59.

Silns, H. and Mulford, B. (2002) *Leadership and School Results. Second International Handbook of Educational Leadership and Administration*. Kluwer Press.

Simon, B. (1994) Some problems of pedagogy revisited, in B. Simon *The State and Educational Change: Essays in the History of Education and Pedagogy*. London: Lawrence & Wishart.

Siraj-Blatchford, I. (1999) Early childhood pedagogy, practice, principles and research, in P. Mortimore (ed.) *Understanding Pedagogy and its Impact on Learning*. London: Paul Chapman.

Siraj-Blatchford, I., Sylva, K., Muttock, S., Gilden, R. and Bell, D. (2002) *Researching Effective Pedagogy in the Early Years*, Research Report No 356. London: DfES.

Skemp, R. R. (1989) *Mathematics in the Primary School*. London: Routledge.

Skidmore, D. (2004) *Inclusion: The Dynamic of School Development*. Buckingham: Open University Press.

Skutnabb-Kangas, T. (1984) *Bilingualism or Not: The Education of Minorities*. Clevedon: Multilingual Matters.

Slater, J. and Dean, C. (2001) Proper jobs that need proper staff, *Times Educational Supplement*, 16 November.

Slavin, R. E. (1995) *Co-operative Learning*, 2nd edn. Massachusetts: Allyn & Bacon.

Slee, R. (2001) Inclusion in practice: does practice make perfect? *Educational Review*, 53(2): 113–23.

Smart, T. (2003) *Collins English Dictionary and Thesaurus*. Glasgow: HarperCollins.

Smeets, E. and Mooij, T. (2001) Pupil-centred learning, ICT and teacher behaviour: Observations in educational practice, *British Journal of Educational Technology*, 32(4): 403–17.

Smith, A. (1998) *Accelerated Learning in Practice: Brain-based Methods for Accelerating Motivation and Achievement*. Stafford: Network Educational Press.

Smith, F. and Hardman, F. (2001) Horse before the cart: developing an evidence-based approach to educational policy, in C. Cullingford and P. Oliver (eds) *The National Curriculum and its Effects*. Aldershot: Ashgate.

Smith, F., Hardman, F., Wall, K. and Mroz, M. (2004) Interactive whole class teaching in the National Literacy and Numeracy Strategies, *British Educational Research Journal*, 30(3): 395–411.

Smith, H. J., Higgins, S., Wall, K. and Miller, J. (2005) Interactive whiteboards: boon or bandwagon? A critical review of literature, *Journal of Computer Assisted Learning*, 21: 91–101.

Smith, P., Whitby, K. and Sharp, C. (2004) *The Employment and Deployment of Teaching Assistants*, LGA Research Report 5/04. Slough: NFER.

Smylie, M. A. (1995) New perspectives on teacher leadership, *The Elementary School Journal*, 96(1): 3–7.

Smyth, J., Dow, A., Hattam, R., Reid, A. and Shacklock, G. (2000) *Teachers' Work in a Globalising Economy*. London: Falmer Press.

Social Exclusion Unit (SEU) (1997) *Social Exclusion Unit: Purpose, Work, Priorities and Working Methods*. London: HMSO.

Social Exclusion Unit (SEU) (1998) *Truancy and School Exclusion*. London: HMSO.

Somekh, B. and Davies, R. (1991) Towards a pedagogy for information technology, *The Curriculum Journal*, 2(2): 153–70.

Southworth, G. (1995) *Talking Heads: Voices of Experience*. Cambridge: University of Cambridge Institute of Education.

Southworth, G. (1998) Change and continuity in the work of primary headteachers in England, *International Journal of Educational Research*, 29: 311–21.

Southworth, G. (2004) *Primary School Leadership in Context, Leading Small Medium and Large Sized Schools*, London: RoutledgeFalmer.

Spradley, J. (1979) *The Ethnographic Interview*. Fort Worth: Harcourt Brace Jovanovich.

Steedman, C. (undated) Impeccable governesses, rational dames and moral mothers. Mimeo, History Department, University of Warwick, Coventry.

Stewart, W. (2005) Heads fear end of budget increases, *Times Educational Supplement*, 7 January.

Street, B. (2003) The implications of the 'New Literacy Studies' for literacy education, in S. Goodman, T. Lillis, J. Maybin and N. Mercer (eds) *Language, Literacy and Education: A Reader*. Stoke-on-Trent: Trentham Books.

Stronach, I., Corbin, B., McNamara, O., Stark, S. and Warne, T. (2002) Towards an uncertain politics of professionalism: teacher and nurse identities in flux, *Journal of Education Policy*, 17(1): 109–38.

Tanner, H., Jones, S., Kennewell, S. and Beauchamp, G. (2005) Interactive whiteboards and pedagogies of whole class teaching, Paper presented at Mathematics Education Research Group of Australasia (MERGA – 28). Melbourne, Australia, July.

Tansley, A. E. and Craft, M. (1984) Mother tongue teaching and support: a Schools Council enquiry, *Journal of Multilingual and Multicultural Development*, 5(5): 366–84.

Tharp, R. and Gallimore, R. (1988) *Rousing Minds to Life*. New York: Cambridge University Press.

Thomas, G. and Loxley, A. (2001) *Deconstructing Special Education and Constructing Inclusion*. Buckingham: Open University Press.

Thomas, N. (1990) *Primary Education from Plowden to the 1990s*. Basingstoke: Falmer Press.

Thrupp, M. and Tomlinson, S. (2005) Introduction: education policy, social justice and 'complex hope', *British Educational Research Journal*, 31(5): 549–56.

Tilstone, C. (2003) Professional development for staff: steps towards developing policies, in C. Tilstone and R. Rose (eds) *Strategies to Promote Inclusive Practice*. London: RoutledgeFalmer.

Tomlinson, J. R. G. T. (1993) *The Control of Education*. London: Cassell.

Torrance, H. and Pryor, J. (1998) *Investigating Formative Assessment: Teaching, Learning and Assessment in the Classroom*. Buckingham: Open University Press.

Travers, K. J. and Westbury, I. (1989) *The IEA study of Mathematics I: Analysis of Mathematics Curricula*. Oxford: Pergamon.

Troman, G. (1996) The rise of the new professionals? The restructuring of primary teachers' work and professionalism, *British Journal of Sociology of Education*, 17(4): 473–87.

Troman, G. (2000) Teacher stress in the low-trust society, *British Journal of Sociology of Education*, 21: 331–53.

Troman, G. and Woods, P. (2001) *Primary Teachers' Stress*. London: RoutledgeFalmer.

Tunstall, P. and Gipps, C. (1996) Teacher feedback to young children: a typology, *British Educational Research Journal*, 2(4): 389–404.

Tymms, P. (2004) Are standards rising in English primary schools? *British Educational Research Journal*, 30(4): 477–94.

UNESCO (1994) *The Salamanca Statement and Framework for Action on Special Needs Education*. Paris: UNESCO.

Vincett, K., Cremin, H. and Thomas, G. (2005) *Teachers and Assistants Working Together*. Maidenhead: Open University Press.

Vulliamy, G. (1998) Teacher development in primary schools: some other lessons from Taiwan, *Teacher Development*, 2: 5–15.

Vulliamy, G. (2000) *New Labour and School Exclusions: Excluding Sociology or a Sociology of Exclusions?* Professorial Inaugural Lecture. York: Department of Educational Studies, University of York.

Vulliamy, G. (2004) The impact of globalisation on qualitative research in comparative and international education, *Compare*, 34(3): 261–84.

Vulliamy, G., Kimonen, E., Nevalainen, R. and Webb, R. (1997) Teacher identity and curriculum change: a comparative case-study analysis of small schools in England and Finland, *Comparative Education*, 33: 97–115.

Vulliamy, G. and Webb, R. (2000) Stemming the tide of rising school exclusions: problems and possibilities, *British Journal of Educational Studies*, 48(2): 119–33.

Vulliamy, G., Webb, R., Locke, T. and Hill, M. (2004) Primary pedagogy and teacher professionalism: a comparative analysis of England and New Zealand, *New Zealand Journal of Educational Studies*, 39(2): 255–74.

Vygotsky, L. (1962) *Thought and Language*. New York: Wiley.

Wallace, J. and Louden, W. (2003) What we don't understand about teaching for understanding: questions from science education, *Journal of Curriculum Studies*, 35(5): 545–66.

Wallace, M. and Huckman, L. (1999) *Senior Management Teams in Primary Schools, The Quest for Synergy*. London: Routledge.

WAMG (2004) Workforce Agreement Monitoring Group Letter. July.

Ward, H. (2004) Pressure still on primaries, *Times Educational Supplement*, 13 August.

Watkins, C. and Mortimore, P. (1999) Pedagogy: What do we know? In P. Mortimore (ed.) *Understanding Pedagogy and its Impact on Learning*. London: Paul Chapman Publishing.

Watson, D. (2001) Pedagogy before technology: Re-thinking the relationship between ICT and teaching, *Education and Information Technologies*, 6(4): 251–66.

Webb, R. (2005) Leading teaching and learning in the primary school: From 'educative leadership' to 'pedagogical leadership', *Educational Leadership, Management and Administration*, 33(1): 69–91.

Webb, R., Häkkinen, K., Hämäläinen, S. and Vulliamy, G. (1998) External inspection or school self-evaluation? A comparative analysis of policy and practice in primary schools in England and Finland, *British Educational Research Journal*, 24(5): 539–56.

Webb, R. and Vulliamy, G. (1996) *Roles and Responsibilities in the Primary School: Changing Demands, Changing Practices.* Buckingham: Open University Press.

Webb, R. and Vulliamy, G. (1999) Managing curriculum policy changes: a comparative analysis of primary schools in England and Finland, *Journal of Education Policy*, 14: 117–37.

Webb, R. and Vulliamy, G. (2001) Joining up the solutions: the rhetoric and practice of inter-agency co-operation, *Children and Society*, 15(4): 315–32.

Webb, R. and Vulliamy, G. (2006) *Coming Full Circle?* The impact of New Labour's education policies on primary school teachers' work. London: Association of Teachers and Lecturers.

Webb, R., Vulliamy, G., Hämäläinen, S. *et al.* (2004a) A comparative analysis of primary teacher professionalism in England and Finland, *Comparative Education*, 40: 83–107.

Webb, R., Vulliamy, G., Hämäläinen, S. *et al.* (2004b) Pressures, rewards and teacher retention: a comparative study of primary teaching in England and Finland, *Scandinavian Journal of Educational Research*, 48(2): 169–88.

Webb, R., Vulliamy, G., Sarja, A. and Hämäläinen, S. (forthcoming) Globalization and leadership and management: a comparative analysis of primary schools in England and Finland, *Research Papers in Education*.

Wegerif, R. and Scrimshaw, P. (1997) (eds) *Computers and Talk in the Primary Classroom.* Clevedon: Multilingual Matters Ltd.

Weiner, B. (1986) An Attributional Theory of Motivation and Emotion. New York: Springer-Verlag.

Welch, M., Richards, G., Okada, T., Richards, J. and Prescott, S. (1995) A consultation and paraprofessional pull-in system of service delivery: a report on student outcomes and teacher satisfaction, *Remedial and Special Education*, 16: 16–28.

Wenger, E. (1998) *Communities of Practice; Learning, Meaning and Identity.* Cambridge: Cambridge University Press.

White, J. (1982) The primary teacher as servant of the state, in C. Richards (ed.) *New Directions in Primary Education.* Lewes: Falmer.

Whitty, G. (2002) *Making Sense of Education Policy.* London: Paul Chapman.

Williams, D., Coles, L., Wilson, K., Richardson, A. and Tuson, J. (2000) Teachers and ICT: Current use and future needs, *British Journal of Educational Technology*, 31(4): 307–20.

Wilson, J. (2000) Doing justice to inclusion, *European Journal of Special Needs Education*, 15(3): 297–304.

Wilson, S. M., Shulman, L. S. and Richert, A. E. (1987) '150 Different Ways' of knowing: representations of knowledge in teaching, in J. Calderhead (ed.) *Exploring Teachers' Thinking*. London: Cassell.

Wilson, V., Schlaff, U. and Davidson, J. (2002) *More than 'An Extra Pair of Hands'? Evaluation of the Classroom Assistant Initiative*. Glasgow: Scottish Council for Research in Education.

Wood, D. (1988) *How Children Think and Learn*. Oxford: Blackwell.

Woodhead, C. (1998) Blood on the tracks: Lessons from the history of curriculum reform, Annual lecture, 24 January. London: Ofsted.

Woods, P. (1995) *Creative Teachers in Primary Schools*. Buckingham: Open University Press.

Woods, P. and Jeffrey, B. (2002) The reconstruction of primary teachers' identities, *British Journal of Sociology of Education*, 23(1): 89–106.

Woods, P., Jeffrey, B. and Troman, G. (2001) The impact of New Labour's educational policy on primary schools, in M. Fielding (ed.) *Taking Education Really Seriously: Four Years' Hard Labour*. London: RoutledgeFalmer.

Woods, P., Jeffrey, B., Troman, G. and Boyle, M. (1997) *Restructuring Schools, Reconstructing Teachers*, Buckingham: Open University Press.

Woods, P., Jeffrey, B., Troman, G. and Boyle, M. (1997) *Restructuring Schools, Reconstructing Teachers: Responding to Change in the Primary School*. Buckingham: Open University Press.

Woodward, W. (2001) Teachers demoted in class structure, *Times Educational Supplement*, 16 March.

Wragg, E. C., Haynes, G. S., Wragg, C. M. and Chamberlin, R. P. (2004) *Performance Pay for Teachers: The Experiences of Heads and Teachers*. London: RoutledgeFalmer.

Index

accountability, 3, 17, 20, 179–181
assessment
  for bilingual pupils, 135
  for learning, 3, 5–6, 53–54, 58
  performance data in schools, 36
  pupil and peer, 55, 56
  SATs, 5, 34–35, 36, 48, 79, 95, 176
  Teacher, 3, 48–53, 57–58, 101, 175

bilingualism, 129, 130–136
Bullock Report, 130–131, 136–137

classroom organization
  seating arrangements, 42, 184
continuing professional development, 7
Conservative government policy, 4, 9, 14, 17
curriculum
  balance, 2, 13, 24–25, 28–29, 29–30, 31,
    34, 44, 176
  creativity, 2, 14, 28, 43, 44, 175
  flexibility in, 38
  government prescription for, 10, 13, 17,
    20, 174
  National Curriculum, 1, 2, 4, 21–22, 25,
    62, 132, 150, 176
  organization, 41, 44, 99–101, 184

deputy heads, 163

Education Reform Act (1988), 9, 10, 18,
  23, 26, 37, 61, 149, 150, 162, 175, 184
English as an additional language (EAL),
  7, 128–138
extended schools, 14

ICT
  influence on pedagogy, 6, 45, 84–86,
    90–91, 97, 143
  interactive whiteboards, 6, 88–89
  interactivity, 85–86
  investment in resources in, 3, 11, 87
  National Grid for Learning, 11
  Virtual Teachers Centre, 11
  wireless mobility, 89–90
inclusion
  barriers to, 7, 107–111
  factors for successful, 106–107, 125–127
  New Labour policy on, 14–15, 104, 117,
    140
  professional development for, 111–114,
    138
  pupils' views of, 65–66
  teachers' views of, 108–109, 110
international tests league tables, 12, 23,
  25, 30, 31, 159, 178

KS1–KS2 transfer, 115–116
KS2–KS3 transfer, 92, 94–95, 116

leadership
  distributed, 8, 165–169, 171
  educative, 162
  headteacher, 162, 166–167, 170
  instructional, 8, 162
  pupil, 171–172
  transformational, 167
league tables, 5, 12, 35, 44, 176
lesson planning, 40

'many pathways' model of literacy
  learning, 136
marketisation, 11, 12, 107, 150

National Agreement on *Raising Standards
  and Tackling Workload*, 16, 181–182
National Literacy Strategy, 3, 5, 8, 10, 13,
  28, 30, 33, 36–43, 59, 72, 85, 86, 132,
  142–143, 176–179

National Numeracy Strategy, 3, 5, 8, 10, 13, 28, 30, 33, 36–43, 59, 72, 85, 86, 142, 176–179
New Labour policy
  approach to change, 9–10, 183
  contradictions in, xi, 2, 14, 15, 17, 44, 45, 105
  inclusion, 14–15, 104, 117, 140
  investment in education, 11
  rationale for, 10, 17
  social justice, 15, 17
  standards agenda, 2, 8, 11–14, 31, 34, 45, 110

OFSTED inspections, 8, 12, 37, 151
ORACLE project, 23, 31, 183

PACE project, 56, 71, 73, 79, 150, 169, 174, 175, 183, 184
parental involvement, 14–15, 137
pedagogy
  co-constructive, 6, 96–102
  critiques of, 26, 29
  government prescription for, 10, 13, 17, 28, 174
  ICT-influenced, 84–86, 90–91
  influences on, 81
  KS2, 92–94
  learner-relevant, 42
  match, 72, 76–77
  pupil-teacher partnership, 96–102, 137
  questioning, 42–43, 54–55
  SEN, 117–118
pedagogical content knowledge, 90–91, 178
performance management, 8, 16, 152, 180
performance-related pay, 16, 158–159
performativity culture, 2, 7, 12, 13, 15, 21, 26–29, 37, 44, 45–46, 79, 92, 95, 113, 162, 170, 179
personalized learning, 3, 7, 13, 29, 44, 92, 125, 140
Plowden Report, 17, 130
preparation, planning and pupil assessment (PPA), 181–182

Primary National Strategy, 2, 3, 5, 7, 13, 14, 29, 31, 32, 43–45, 72, 76, 78, 115, 125, 140, 141, 145, 170, 175
professional learning communities, 8, 113–114, 161, 169–172
pupils' perspectives
  curriculum, 3–4, 6, 66–69, 79
  inclusion, 65–66, 126–127
  learning, 73–80
  pedagogy, 67, 144
  relationships with peers, 6, 65
  relationships with teachers, 6, 62–64
  teaching assistants, 143–145

Ruskin College speech (James Callaghan), 5, 19

SEN
  behavioural, emotional and social development, 121–122
  cognition and learning difficulties, 120–121
  communication and interaction needs, 119–120
  confusion with bilingualism, 134–135
  pedagogy, 110–111, 117–118
  prevalence of, 116
  sensory and/or physical needs, 123–124
  teaching assistants for, 140
  teaching strategies for, 118–127

school effectiveness research, 12–13
school self-evaluation, 32
senior management teams, 163–164
Social Exclusion Unit, 14
Specialist Schools Trust, 13
subject coordinators, 164–165, 166–167
Swan Report, 131

target setting, 2, 5, 8, 11, 12, 16, 28, 34
teacher identity, 8, 45, 93, 149–151, 159–160, 176–177, 178, 183–184
teachers' perspectives
  accountability, 179–181
  assessment, 175–176
  curriculum, 175

General Teaching Council, 180–181
inclusion, 108–109, 110
in-service, 171
league tables, 5, 176
the Literacy and Numeracy Strategies, 3, 5, 36–43, 176–179
performance management, 180
Primary National Strategy, 43–45, 175
target setting, 34
    teacher assessment, 3
testing, 5, 34–35, 94–95, 176
threshold assessment, 8, 180
workforce remodelling, 145–146, 181–183
teacher professionalism
    educationalists' view of, 173–174, 176, 183

New Labour view of, 15–16, 29, 173, 183
relationship to pedagogy, 10, 17, 93, 173–174, 176–179
teachers' view of, 8, 174–184
teaching assistants, 7–8, 45, 139–148, 160, 181–182
teaching styles, 21, 27, 31, 184
threshold assessment, 8, 16, 152–159, 180
topic work *see* curriculum organization

visual, auditory and kinaesthetic learning (VAK), 44

whole class teaching, 5, 31, 39, 41, 45, 178
workforce remodelling, 15–16, 45, 139–148, 160, 181–183